Social Media
and the Good Life

Social Media and the Good Life

Do They Connect?

Mark Y. Herring

McFarland & Company, Inc., Publishers
Jefferson, North Carolina

LIBRARY OF CONGRESS CATALOGUING-IN-PUBLICATION DATA

Herring, Mark Y., 1952–
    Social media and the good life : do they connect? / Mark Y.
Herring.
        p.   cm.
    Includes bibliographical references and index.

    ISBN 978-0-7864-7936-8 (softcover : acid free paper) ∞
    ISBN 978-1-4766-2094-7 (ebook)

    1. Online social networks.   2. Social media.
    3. Information technology—Social aspects.   I. Title.

    HM742.H475 2015
    302.30285—dc23   2015017992

BRITISH LIBRARY CATALOGUING DATA ARE AVAILABLE

Cover image © 2015 Wavebreak Media/Thinkstock

Printed in the United States of America

*McFarland & Company, Inc., Publishers
    Box 611, Jefferson, North Carolina 28640
    www.mcfarlandpub.com*

For Lillard
1925–2014

"He loved his daughter better even than his pipe,
And, like a reasonable man and an excellent father,
Let her have her way in everything."
—Washington Irving, *The Legend of Sleepy Hollow*

Acknowledgments

I dedicate this book to my father-in-law, Lillard W. Lane, Jr., who passed away while it was being written. He never knew social media and would never have had time for it even if he had. I'm not sure he understood my work at the university or even why I would want to do what I do. But he enjoyed books, especially history. And though we were altogether opposites in just about every way, he tolerated me more than I deserved because I married his daughter. *Mors janua vitae.*

I have been helped by a number of people for this book, not least of which is my long-suffering wife. She read through this manuscript many times. In any other marriage this would be grounds for divorce. I have noted several other people in the notes, too, who have helped: Captain Jeffrey J. Krohn, ROTC, and Professor Jennifer Cease-Cook, Director, Winthrop Think College, both colleagues at Winthrop, where I work. The forbearance of my boss, Dr. Debra Boyd, provost (and for the last year, acting president), is apparently unlimited. The willingness of my staff to have me distracted more often than not when working on this book is a testament of their goodwill. Dot Barber, my executive administrative specialist, graciously arranged my schedule so that I could meet the demands of my "regular" job and this add-on. Erica Truesdale, a student worker in our office, checked all the online references for me once again before press time.

I am very grateful to Joe L. Boyd for his artwork; it has added immeasurably to the book.

I am greatly indebted to all these people. Their work and permissions are in no way an endorsement of any part of this book. As always, any mistakes are my own.

Table of Contents

Introduction

If the research is at all correct, a book about social media is superfluous. First, fewer than 15 percent of all Americans have opted out of the Internet, most of whom have good reasons, ranging from "it wastes too much time," to "simply too old to learn."[1] This leaves about 85 percent or so of the rest of us who are already online. When it comes to social media, the figures are even more strongly in favor of usage, though the overall acceptance is a little lower. As of 2013, over 85 percent of 18- to 29-year-olds used social media, over 75 percent of those between the ages of 30 and 49, over 55 percent of those between the ages of 50 and 64, and just under 50 percent of those 65 and over.[2] If the point of this book is to inform users about social media platforms, it's too late. Hardly anyone is ignorant of them, and nearly everyone is using them.

But that isn't the point of this book. This book has a twofold purpose. First, it reiterates the value of social media, *en passant*—in passing, because it is generally accepted that social media networks have been a great boon to the common good. We are often bombarded with stories, news items, and general cheerleading about how good social media platforms are for just about everything we do. Indeed, social media interaction is pointed to as the panacea for all modern ills that beset us in medicine, in socialization, in friendships, in business, in revolutions, in education, in crowdsourcing: in short, in every endeavor of human enterprise. Almost no one denies how social media have either created a new and better way to achieve our goals in a particular area or greatly improved upon a pre-social media function to the extent that we are aghast that we ever got along without them.

But this book also examines social media's dark doppelganger, that *alter idem* of social media that is the evil Mr. Edward Hyde to the more famous and presentable Dr. Henry Jekyll. The second point of this book is to alert users about some of the pitfalls of using what has become the single most preferred method of individual communication, even when those individuals are sitting face to face across from one another. Some of these pitfalls are legal matters, points where this preferred form of communication skirts beyond the color of law, spilling over into what is considered illegal, unethical, or both. Most of us posting to Facebook or tweeting some factoid never really think about these things. But it is in fact not only becoming a problem, but it is becoming an increasingly serious one that encompasses everything from mere "flame wars," in which two or more people have at it in an almost nonstop shouting contest, to harassing an individual to that victim's wits' end. In between these extremes are behaviors unacceptable enough that they should at least be called to attention as breaches of common courtesy.

When legal and ethical issues are not foremost, the issues are more down-to-earth, such as matters of principle. Social media networks exist off the backs of those who contribute to them, but none of the so-called contributors are paid, or at least only a very small fraction of them are. Facebook depends upon your contributions; Twitter, your tweets; Instagram, your pictures. If you are not posting, tweeting, or making pictures, these social media venues have little to offer. And yet, for all your labors, you are paid nothing for these, while the social media on which you post them earn tens of millions of dollars, or in the case of Facebook, billions of dollars, from your work. This is our "new normal," all right, but should it be? Intellectual property is a big deal, or rather it ought to be, to anyone who has any to sell. Social media networks, not to mention all of the Internet, say that information wants to be free, wants to be shared, and it should be free to everyone, free except to advertisers who pay to promote themselves. It is, if nothing else, an odd business plan. In another age, where all the workers were paid nothing and the "owners" made off like bandits, we called those owners robber barons. Today, we call them geniuses. Is this why Bill Gates suddenly feels guilty about making so much money?[3] Perhaps the problem isn't capitalism, but certain business ventures that prey upon the inherent narcissism in all of us.

A few matters of philosophy intrude throughout these pages. I raise questions about social media networks, their value, their balance of power, and where they are leading us. In the true form of a gasconading member of the clerisy, I do not presume to answer these questions, but only to raise them. Is this the social media we want and desire? Do these venues contribute to civil discourse or do just the opposite? For all the good this form of communication does in the world—and that is not denied—some bad remains. What are we going to do about that?

Finally, a couple of chapters deal with some of the deadlier aspects of social media, literally: tragic suicides, murder-for-hire, and simply murder. Some will fret that these are not social media problems. But the venues of social media have enabled all of these things, many of which would never have occurred without the existence of social media.

Throughout the book, laws that have made it through all the hoops emerge, especially the Communications Decency Act, or CDA. What is odd about the CDA is that as a law it failed miserably. But one portion of it, Section 230, provided what has become blanket immunity for anything that occurs on social media that is not the invention of the owners/operators of the site itself. I argue throughout the book that this particular blanket covers too much, making it possible for social media to be spared liability for any bad outcomes while reaping the benefits of only the good. The latitude granted social media via Section 230 appears greater than that granted any other entity. If the bad tends to outweigh the good mentioned here, it is only because we rarely hear much about the downsides of social media. Since we are embracing this means of communication, we should know what we are hugging so close to our hearts, shouldn't we?

Chapter One begins with a brief history of social media. Many of us may think the concept started about a decade ago, but the matter is a bit more complicated than that. The idea of social networking is much older, and while it may not have involved html or the Internet, it still involved people interacting with each other, albeit through a more limited network of a few hundred rather than today's few hundred million.

Chapter Two looks at various issues from the point of view of government. This not only encompasses how various local, state, and federal government agencies use social media platforms, but also how law enforcement, city agencies, and others employ them in their work. This chapter also looks at how social media have fomented more than one revolution but also quelled more than a few dozen. The power of social media often appears unlimited. This power can be used for good or its opposite. A chapter like this would not be complete without discussion of politicians and social media. Sadly, more than one politician has proved a veritable gold mine of bad behaviors, providing us examples of what not to do on social media. What makes this chapter and this topic so intriguing is that many of those responsible for the breaches are not novices to social media networks. They know only too well what they are and the power of their ubiquity. Yet they still make missteps, often in Brobdingnagian ways.

Chapter Three examines social media in the K–12 context. That young people are on social media comes, of course, as no surprise. That so many underage young people are on social media networks is also unsurprising, since there is no gatekeeper for them or for any of the Internet. This chapter also looks at various legal approaches to social media, including the famous or infamous, depending on one's predilections, the Communications and Decency Act (CDA), the Child Online Protection Act (COPA), the Children's Online Privacy Protection Act (COPPA), the Children's Internet Protection Act (CIPA), and finally, the Deleting Online Predators Act (DOPA). Even with this slew of lawful protection, nothing really got done as it was intended, and now the states must take up their own cudgels to wage war against predators who sedulously use social media to attack the unwary.

In Chapter Four, the kids have graduated from high school to college, so college students and social media are examined. One might think that moving from the young and inexperienced to those on the cusp of adulthood and beyond it would mean an improvement in all behaviors. Alas, we are dealing with humans, after all, and the behaviors, while certainly no worse, are not what we can call ameliorative. The question of whether social media help or hurt academic work is also taken up.

Chapter Five looks at the disabled and social media. The news is both good and bad. Social media networks started out as a boon to persons with disabilities, but they can end up doing more harm than good. On the one hand, they bring together people who could not otherwise be brought together. On the other hand, they expose persons with disabilities to even more abuse about their conditions from numerous, anonymous sources. Furthermore, surfing social media is not the easiest thing to manipulate, all the advanced technology notwithstanding.

Businesses and social media, in Chapter Six, began what appeared to be a torrid romance that would yield an abundance of lovely offspring. They were made for each other, and businesses could count on making millions by being on social media and interacting regularly with customers and would-be customers. The opportunities appeared endless, or so it seemed. Today they have ended up, not exactly in divorce, but certainly in indifference and a somewhat cooled ardor. Businesses are on social media, everywhere, of course. But those numerous and lovely offspring are missing. Whether or not social media do any business any good or whether they merely distract, whether social media cost more money than they save or deliver is anyone's guess, and it really depends on whom you ask. But everyone appears to think that any business *not* on social media is very much out of touch with the real world and may be even heading to that prehistoric dustbin.

One of the most damaging areas of social media platform is their exploitation of user privacy, the subject of Chapter Seven. Social media networks, if truth be told, really don't care much about users' privacy, hysterical protestations to the contrary notwithstanding. To lock down social media in the manner in which they should be to protect users' identities and privacy would be to defeat their usefulness in connecting total strangers to play Candy Crush.

Social media remind users frequently about how much they care about privacy, but it is a distraction to prevent users from realizing just how exposed they really are. Social media networks do this through "terms of service" (TOS) agreements, and this chapter examines these in some detail. But the bottom line is that TOS agreements are carefully worded legal-speak that provide protection to the social medium, not to you, the user of that service. Most of us take that chance regularly. The problem is, however, that privacy is important and that users are overexposed, in more ways than one. Once users are "out there" on social media, there is no getting back the lost privacy, and that lost privacy can be most debilitating if it falls into the wrong hands, ending up in trouble, angst, even murder, as this chapter reveals.

The loss of a given user's identity by theft I treat in Chapter Eight as a separate form of privacy loss. It occurs to about sixteen million people annually, and while that works out to only about two percent of all users, if you happen to be part of that small slice of social media life, your life is a living hell. About half of all social media users have been *targets* of identity theft, according to NextAdvisor, and we all know that we are only too eager to overshare about ourselves. Untangling an identity from theft is a long and arduous task, one that no one would want to sic on even our worst enemies. Sure, identity theft occurs in multifarious ways other than via social media. Thieves steal card registrations from locked vehicles and then find out where that victim lives, only to rob their mailboxes in order to obtain additional information. But social media networks have become the proverbial low-hanging fruit that makes that kind of identity theft easy pickings, so to speak. Why break into a car dressed in something to disguise your criminal intentions when you can do it from home, in your pajamas?

One of the last professional groups to get on social media, physicians, in Chapter Nine, are not as "connected" as other professionals might be, but they are getting there. While they may not be following you, we are certainly following them. On the one hand, connecting those with similar illnesses has proved an unqualified good. Those with similar illnesses can compare notes, treatments, physicians, and more. They get support, advice, and guidance through what can be very debilitating illnesses.

On the other hand, unfortunately, they can also get bad advice, poor support, and quacksalvers who bilk the desperate-for-a-cure of every dime they have. Physicians and physician groups are working together to make online medical advice safer and more effective, as well as to make drug protocols and interactions more explicit. All of these things will get better, of course, but any seekers of medical advice—and most of us are—must be more wary when online than we anticipate. Furthermore, our first point of contact about illnesses, Wikipedia, turns out to be the least reliable, not only in the opinion of medical experts, but even in the opinion of Wikipedia itself. The question of how to wean social media users away from Wikipedia to more reliable sources (such as WebMD) has been much more difficult than most observers thought.

Social media can be like a bad soap opera. Venues are filled with drama queens, scumbags, earnest people, religious fanatics, flat-earthers, and liberal revolutionaries. Most of the time these individuals are, like those actors in bad soap operas, merely stock characters who overact and over-dramatize events. But some of these folks can also turn to the dark side, so to speak. When they do, they appear to have nothing better to do than seek out those who are vulnerable and exploit their weaknesses. Cyber-bullying, Chapter Ten, treats the worst of those in this group.

Cyberbullying, or rather bullying, has now become something of a *cause célèbre*. This is both good and bad news: good because it has attracted attention to a problem that has existed since schoolchildren have congre-gated together; bad because it has made all the hoopla sound more like progress than it actually is. Furthermore, by identifying, as we have, every slight and every pique as the beginning of bullying, we have minimized bullying's more serious side. If everything is bullying, nothing is. Simply hopping on the bandwagon of the bullying crusade may not solve it for the 98-pound weakling who must face his or her bullies alone. The sudden rise of cyberbullying may be attributable in a small way to our very public campaign, essentially driving bullies underground to the web. Still, hope springs eternal, and perhaps dancers, rappers, celebrities, and smiley face stickers will help put an end to bullying after all.

Meanwhile, cyberbullying continues to rise, not just among school-children, though it certainly flourishes there, but also among adults, not only when they disagree, but especially when they divorce. It is hurtful and damaging and can also be fatal in a few cases, causing its victims to seek any respite, including suicide. The several cases reviewed here are the more public ones. And while they are few, thankfully, they in no way give a good picture of the hundreds of thousands of small intrusions that occur against victims on a regular basis.

Can social media get a conscience? It appears unlikely, but the ques-tion is raised anyway in Chapter Eleven, under the odd "Agenbite of Inwyt" rubric. The long-suffering of the users of social media is astonishing: appar-ently we'll put up with anything. But perhaps it's time to demand better from these ubiquitous entities that have taken over so much of our lives.

Do we have to put up with it? Not really. So why do we? When other service-oriented technologies have obtruded into our space, we have generally demanded that they adapt somewhat to social and civil norms. With social media, not so much. Some social media we have refused to tolerate (ask.fm is one treated in this chapter), but others that are *almost* as bad are simply considered part of what we must live with if we are to have the conveniences of social media.

This is a prevarication that allows social media to be dismissive of our privacy, dismissive of courteous behavior, and dismissive of common decency. Social medial platforms appeal to our innate narcissism, and therefore many of us are loath to require them to do better. But if they are to become anything more than a colossal time-waster, in order to become a genuine information clearinghouse, they will have to clean up their act a little bit. This chapter hints at what it will take to move it in that direction.

The header hashtags at the beginning of each chapter I have fashioned after those I have seen, but they are not verbatim. They are composites of tweets, posts and other social communications I have seen over the years.

ONE

#WhereDidItAllBegin?

A mere decade and half ago, social networking sites remained largely unknown to the general public. Those who knew about them possessed a certain amount of computer expertise and knew those sites in their rudimentary forms. So rapid has been the ascent of social networking sites into popular parlance that nine years ago, in 2006, *Time*'s book critic and technology editor, Lev Grossman, dubbed them—or rather their users—you—as the magazine's Person of the Year.[1]

In less than a decade, social media have become a vehicle for commerce, a melting pot of ideas, an unprecedented tool for collaboration, a source for medical opinions, and a worldwide community-building apparatus (#PresidentObamaCallYourOffice!). With telemetry-like features (relaying information in place and sending it for recording to another), social media can tag, locate, and relay what you are doing, where you are, and what you might like to see or do in a given location. Social media can track everything we do, whether at Target or while on Facebook. These networks are also subject to serious breaches of privacy by hackers. They can make us safer, predicting weather before we get there, alerting us about various traffic jams or accidents, and eventually predicting outbreaks of the flu or some other serious illnesses. They record tremendous amounts of data about us, but we also fill them full of data about ourselves. They are preparing for us what futurist Patrick Tucker calls our "naked future."[2]

Although social media sites can boast these very positive developments, they have also created a plethora of new legal issues by their presence, their makeup, their operations, and the manner in which they recruit their members. Social networking issues are unfolding in various ways and in nearly every area of human endeavor, but not all of those ways have been positive. We know that the online sites existing today will not be there tomorrow, and none of them may be around a decade hence. But they are here today, and they are changing the way we live our lives, in many ways for the better, but in some ways for the worse.

Before any social network could function, of course, there had to be the Internet, and for that we have, in large part, J.C.R. Licklider to thank.[3] It was not called the Internet then, but ARPANET. In 1969, Licklider invented the packet-switching technology that the Internet relies upon. It was not Licklider alone, of course, but a team of researchers working on the project funded by the Department of Defense. Licklider pitched his idea of an Intergalactic Computer Network, or "Galactic Network," to MIT in 1962.[4] Licklider discussed the social aspects of networking in a series of memos he wrote while at MIT. These served as the intellectual rallying point for what later evolved into today's Internet. At first, only four university institutions were connected via ARPANET. By 1974, over fifty different organizations and/or institutions were a part of this growing—and eventually global—network. While the Internet and the World Wide Web are not identical, though they often come off that way in various news stories, it is interesting to note that from the very beginning, the idea of a global (galactic) network that would have a social function was woven into its DNA.

Social Media: In Search of a Definition

So, what are social media? Are they anything on the Internet? Can emails be considered a form of social media? Is spam a nefarious form of social media? These are not easy questions to answer; there isn't one precise definition. More agreement exists on what social networking sites will and will not encompass. One ingredient cannot be gainsaid: the attraction of those with like social interests around a common theme is paramount to their creation, not to mention their success.

While a single definition may be not be agreed upon by all, we can define what this book means by it. The now defunct site Chatmine pegged social media as "a map of the relationships between individuals, ranging from casual acquaintance to close familial bonds. Virtual communities are built around affinity and similarity ... and taking place around ... 'virtual water-coolers,'"[5] and that definition is as good a beginning one as any. The ever-popular Wikipedia (and how can it be wrong if it's on the Internet?!) sees social networks as "[connected] by one or more specific type of interdependency, such as friendship, kinship, financial exchange, dislike, sexual relationships, or relations of beliefs, knowledge, or prestige,"[6] a very solid if a little pedestrian definition. The widely regarded *PC Magazine* defines social networks as "virtual hangouts" for members to communicate via chat, instant messaging, blogging, or videoconferencing, expanding the definition beyond mere texting.[7]

Two noted social media scholars have also taken a stab at defining social networking sites. Harvard scholar danah boyd [*sic*] (born Danah Michele Mattas), presumably the e.e. cummings of social media, and Nicole Ellison from Michigan State University define social networking sites as "web-based services that allow individuals to (1) construct a public or semi-public profile within a bounded system, (2) articulate a list of other users with whom they share a connection, and (3) view and traverse their list of connections and those made by others within the system. The nature and nomenclature of these connections may vary from site to site."[8] Ms. boyd has gone on to argue that "it's complicated," referring not just to the definition but also to what young people do on these sites.[9] Randi Zuckerberg (the sister of famous Mark, who invented one of the world's most recognized social networks, Facebook) finds social networks and our web-enmeshed lives around them complicated as well.[10] The offbeat online *Urban Dictionary* (http://www.urbandictionary.com/) defines social networking sites, seriously, as "a collection of websites that allow people to join to (1) socialize with people who have similar tastes," and tongue-in-cheek as, "(2) [vehicles to] allow [individuals] to stalk the girl next door." The attempt at witty repartee would be funnier if it weren't all too often true.

But simple definitions tell only half the story. Social networking sites can also be categorized into several types, and these types help augment narrowly focused definitions. Sites like Facebook and Twitter focus users on themselves. Sites such as Blackplanet, LinkedIn, or PatientsLikeMe attract users who share common interests, such as issues important to African Americans, business contacts, or those with serious illnesses. A site like Carspace attracts users who share similar auto hobbies. Finally, sites like Flickr, YouTube, Instagram, Pinterest, and Vimeo encourage users to share media: photos, videos, or audio clips. For the purposes of this book, social networking sites will refer to all sites that intend to focus and attract users to them by a common theme of interest or on a wide-ranging number of issues, subjects, or conventions and to connect them by any format available (text, photo, audio, video, etc.).

First Came Young Users, Then Everyone

Social networking sites rose meteorically among primarily young people at first. According to the Pew Internet & American Life Project, while blogging declined among the young (from 24 percent in 2007 to 15 percent in 2009), young people embraced social networking, especially via mobile phones, in huge numbers.[11] A staggering 73 percent of wired teens use social media, up from 55 percent in 2006. While over 70 percent of adults online use social media, 97 percent of young people between the ages of 18 and 29 use their smartphones to send and receive messages, and 88 percent use them to access social networking sites.[12] Researchers at the International Center for Media and the Public Agenda (ICMPA), located at the University of Maryland, revealed in a May 2010 study that young adults' love of social networking via their cellphones borders on addiction. Frankly, it appears they have crossed over the border to addiction and are well on the way to taking its capital! Tech-savvy senior citizens, according to Pew, are now social networking users. For some, like Clay Shirky, author of *Here Comes Everybody: The Power of Organizing Without Organizations*, social networking sites are the new Gutenberg. Suddenly, social networking sites are everywhere, covering every conceivable subject, attracting every age group, and occupying nearly every waking moment of most Americans' lives, young or old.

General Social Networking Use

Our use of social networking sites has only increased since their first appearance. In 2007, for example, Americans spent only about 10 percent of all their online time on social networks, or rather a social network, for it was mainly one: MySpace.[13] Today, that figure has risen more than five-fold, but the site of choice is certainly no longer MySpace or even Facebook, though the latter still dominates. Americans' social networking choices are dependent on who they are and even on their gender. Regardless, they are on social media, often to the exclusion of work, school, and even their significant others. Seventy-five percent of adults aged 30 and older accessing social networking sites have Facebook profiles, 36 percent have MySpace profiles, and 19 percent have LinkedIn profiles, the so-called "Facebook" for professionals.[14] For young adults (ages 18–29), the figures reflect a stronger preference for Facebook, at 71 percent to MySpace's 66 percent (but much of that is from overseas users). Neilson Online, a group that tracks users' online activities, reported in March 2009 that Americans now spend more time communicating on social networking sites than they do on email. Today, 47 percent of adults are using social networking sites, up from 37 percent in November 2008. But adults are fragmenting their use over a larger number of social networking sites: over 60 percent now have multiple profiles on many different social networking sites.[15]

Did We Ever Communicate Before Social Media?

To hear almost anyone talk about social networking sites, one would think we never communicated before there were smartphones. In fact, many social networking aficionados feel precisely this way. We never communicated, never really had a good conversation, and certainly never could get information from point A to point B the way we do today. Perhaps we can agree if we qualify this by saying that we could not do it quite as *ubiquitously* as we do today, but even that qualification will have its naysayers. It may be best to say that we have never done it quite as rapidly as we do today, or with so many people all at once.

Of course, we did communicate before social networking sites, both well and efficiently. For example, the ancient Romans had a very efficient means of getting important information out, something they called the "letter" (your grandparents will know what this is).[16] But even before the Romans, the Greeks published various texts meant to be read aloud and shared, some of which we still read today. Plato's *Dialogs,* for example, are still being read now, more than *2,000* years later, probably not what we'll do with archived tweets and "likes" even six weeks from now, the Library of Congress notwithstanding.[17] While the Greeks and Romans had an efficient method, the need to communicate and share didn't end with them. Martin Luther, readers will recall, had a very efficient method that did much to change the course of history, not only his but also our own.[18] It is possible to put forth a very credible argument that Luther's *Ninety-five Theses* is the first such social media message "posted" to a "wall"—in this case a literal one—that went viral for all time, all without benefit of the Internet, Facebook, Twitter, or any other social network.[19]

A very good case can be made that Johannes Gutenberg constructed the first foray into social media with his movable type.[20] In fact, many today claim the age of social networking began with Gutenberg and has now been improved upon. Social networking is the 21st century's movable type, or so many proponents claim. Perhaps. The point isn't that today is better than yesterday, or that yesterday's approach was better and more durable. It is rather that our history did not begin last week or even last year. We are social beings, we humans, and we have always had a penchant to talk with one another, no matter how asocial some of us may be individually. As a group, we love to communicate with people we know, and today with people we may never meet or know, and we love to talk about our favorite theme: us. One generation used a stylus, papyrus, or movable type. Today, we use 140 characters, and tomorrow, well, who knows? All epochs have communicated, of course, but the jury is still out on which epoch proved the most effective.

Social networking theory, if not any actual sites, did not begin last week, either. It has been around at least since the 1950s, although some would push it even farther back to the thirties, to the time of Kurt Lewin (1890–1947) and his work on the interaction of groups.[21] Lewin, a German-born social psychologist whose later work on groups and applied psychology brought him to America, is one of the early pioneers of social organization theory and applied psychology. Although Lewin's work predates social networking, his groundbreaking work explains how groups work, why people organize into groups, and the dynamics of group interaction. Lewin's work remains of interest to today's social networking theorists.

The English anthropologist J.A. Barnes first started using the term "social networking" in 1954 to describe patterns of group interaction in a small Norwegian town. Barnes limited his definition of groups to about 100 or so people, but he defined social networking in a way that remains valid today. Social networks, according to Barnes, are made up of "nodes" of individuals. These individuals are connected based on their likes and dislikes, shared or disparate interests, financial or intellectual interests, or even shared sexual affinities. Barnes's work restricted his networks to local communities, but today those communities are limited only by the World Wide Web, which is to say not at all. Communities on social networks can, of course, be as close as the person sitting in the cubicle next to you or 10,000 miles away on the other side of the globe. Barnes's "nodes" of individuals in his social networks numbered a maximum of 100, but today such groups are as likely to be five million as five.

Enter Sir Berners-Lee

The explosion of online social networking can in some ways be said to be the byproduct—although not necessarily the intent of—Sir Timothy Berners-Lee. Berners-Lee is a British-born engineer, computer scientist, and Massachusetts Institute of Technology (MIT) professor who is credited with inventing the World Wide Web and the language to make it speak, work for which he was later knighted. In 1992 Berners-Lee created both domain names (what we think of as URLs, uniform resource locators) and hypertext markup language (computer code used to create web pages and often abbreviated HTML). The two together allowed for the creation of websites and, eventually, social networking sites. What is fascinating is how Berners-Lee almost ended up as part of the dustbin of history.

Berners-Lee worked for CERN, the European Organization for Nuclear Research, as an independent contractor in the early 1980s. Berners-Lee noted how difficult it was to share information with fellow researchers quickly and efficiently. He suggested hypertext language as a way to do this and even created a system for doing so, one he called Enquire, a tool that was said to inspire the creation of the web. It was ignored by his superiors.

With Enquire, Berners-Lee envisioned a system in which computers everywhere would be linked with one another so that he could "program my computer to create a space [to link] ... [t]he bits of information in every computer ... [all over] the planet."[22] In other words, very much the way social networks function today. An individual in Singapore could post something for a person (in Berners-Lee's view, a scholar or researcher) in Peoria to view and respond to. And while perhaps not *every* computer everywhere is linked together as Berners-Lee envisioned it, the effect is very much the same. Indeed, Berners-Lee argued,

> The Web is more a social creation than a technical one. I designed it for a social effect—to help people work together—and *not as a technical toy*. The ultimate goal of the Web is to support and improve our web-like existence in the world. We clump into families, associations, and companies. We develop trust across the miles and distrust around the corner. What we believe, endorse, agree with, and depend on is representable and, increasingly, represented on the Web. We all have to ensure that the society we build with the Web is of the sort we intend.[23]

In many ways, social networks like Facebook and Twitter, at least in their social intent, if not in their execution, fulfill Berners-Lee's desire for the web. But Berners-Lee also questions the value of social networks and the web itself for its mere entertainment value and whether what we have created is not only what we want but also what we need. He is as worried about the downsides of social networking sites (e.g., stalking, sexual predators, and scams) as he is delighted about their obvious benefits (e.g., communication, shared interests, and exchange of information).[24]

The utility of social networks is confirmed and augmented by their web presence. But there are also some distinct differences, as Joshua Porter, social web writer, consultant, and interface designer, has pointed out. For example, people are social beings and tend to group around shared interests. The same is true of social networks in their virtual environment. People often interact with multiple groups and do so in social networking sites in manifold ways. They group themselves with family members, with relatives, or with those they have only known for just a short while; in online social networks, they may simply know that the individuals they are associating with share only one of their interests.

Six Degrees of Separation

One reason why social networking developed as quickly as it did may rest in a concept known as "six degrees of separation." Actor Kevin Bacon made the phrase popular in a movie by the same name, but the phrase goes back to a short story titled "Chains" by Hungarian writer Frigyes Karinthy.

American social psychologist Stanley Milgram proved the six degrees concept, but he called it our "small world" problem.[25] Milgram randomly selected people living in the Midwest to send a package to a stranger in Massachusetts. A sender knew the stranger's name, occupation and location, but not the address. Senders were told to choose friends they knew who might know that person and send them the package, instructing their friends to do the same—send it to a person they thought might know the stranger. It took only between five and seven intermediaries to get the package delivered!

While six degrees of separation may appear to be an academic exercise, it is not. The phrase (also referred to as the "human web") refers to the idea that each of us is only six steps away from any other person. As University of Notre Dame physicist and director of the Center of Complex Network Research Albert-László Barabási put it, "six billion nodes are separated only by six links from each other."[26] It is not entirely clear if it is this facility of possible connection that makes social networking so popular; it is clear that this is one key ingredient that makes social networking activity attractive to so many people. Clearly, if social networking sites managed no more than the stringing together of millions of people at random, it is unlikely that they would hold any enduring interest. But because we are "connected" socially with one another in ways we do not yet understand, social networking draws individuals in and holds them there. Once there, they are witnesses to their instant influence in a variety of ways. According to Barabási, social networks are not an ocean of random nodes and links. Rather, they are divided into continents, with villages and communities that overlap. Users can take up residence in one or many.

So Who Was First, Really?

The first social networking site is not agreed upon, but its form is. Prior to 2000, the only way individuals could communicate in a social networking form was through what were called "bulletin boards." While social networking sites per se had not yet been invented, a need arose to allow those who were "online" (in quotation marks because being online four decades ago was not like being online today) to exchange resources easily. Online bulletin boards provided that vehicle.

The first bulletin board was created by Ward Christensen in the late 1970s during what has now become a legendary Chicago snowstorm. With friend Randy Suess, Christensen created the Computerized Bulletin Board System (CBBS) that later went public in 1978.[27] Users logged in via a modem and a telephone line and left messages for others or chatted with whoever happened to be online. The "crowds" on bulletin boards in the beginning might be thought of as the cast of geeks from today's *Big Bang Theory*. The very slow speeds (110 and 300 baud modems) meant that users had to be patient and had to want to be online—rather desperately—in the first place. By the early 1980s, the speeds changed (to a whopping 1200 bit modems) and opened the door to many others.

But not so much the floodgates. Bulletin boards were more of a web forum with a dedicated administrator. The technology still proved cumbersome, relied on ASCII text, and required much more technological know-how than the average person knew or could easily acquire. The technologies also proved hopelessly unreliable, at least compared to today's online presence. Users today panic when Twitter is down for a few hours. BBS could go down for *weeks*. While bulletin boards still exist (some have for more than two decades), they are more a historical vestige than a commonly known entity.

Usenet, created only a few months later in 1979, did not have a central server but was distributed over many networks and servers. The creation of two Duke University graduate students, Tom Truscott and Jim Ellis, came about not as part of their graduate work, but in their "spare time," perhaps at least one reason places like Google, Apple, and Microsoft still provide "play" time for their employees and encourage the idea that it is okay to experiment (but not to fail too often). Users on Usenet could read and post messages for public viewing to various categories known as newsgroups. The early chat rooms used text-based messages only. Usenet was very much like social networking sites today but still required more technical expertise to master. Both moderated and non-moderated groups flourished on Usenet. Usenet still remains, largely owing to an April 2010 group that formed to save it financially.

Are BBS and/or Usenet groups the first social networking sites? Perhaps. But the debate is ongoing, sort of like an argument about whether the quill was the first fountain pen. After CBBS and Usenet, some scholars point to the 1997 short-lived site, SixDegrees, as the first true social networking site. Others are quick to debate that choice. It appears that the earliest social networking site offering most of the elements in common with the definitions set out above began in 1985 under the name The Whole Earth 'Lectronic Link, or the WELL for short.[28]

WELL launched virtual communities on a myriad of topics, dozens and dozens of them. Its "whole earth" name doubtless rings familiar to many readers over the age of 45. Co-creator Stewart Brand, a former Merry Prankster, was the founder of the *Whole Earth Catalog*. The hippy group Merry Pranksters were known for their protests and their organic farming.[29] They formed around author Ken Kesey of *One Flew Over the Cuckoo's Nest* fame. For a short time in the 2000s they existed only as a historical website at http://www.pranksterweb.org, but even that no longer comes up when googled.

WELL began as a bulletin board system and evolved as a dial-up, following closely the web's evolving access technology. WELL users proved a loyal and dedicated sort, and many pine so longingly for the site that it almost sounds as if they lost a loved one when they lost WELL. TheGlobe. com followed in 1994, along with Geocities. It began as an idea of two Cornell students, Todd Krizelman and Stephan Paternot. The initial Globe stock skyrocketed to a then record trading day, making millionaires of its founders, only to fall just as far later, impoverishing those same founders.[30]

Geocities began in 1994 as a small Internet startup connecting six thematic neighborhoods in California that grew to fourteen. Yahoo! later purchased the site, but Geocities failed, owing to lack of interest. Tripod launched itself as a social network for the college-aged, offering advice on how to live alone after college. It soon developed into a site that allowed users to post pictures and share messages. Sound familiar? In 1995, a website known as Classmates emerged seeking to connect old school chums with one another. Two years later, the aforementioned SixDegrees appeared, but after only two years fell on very hard times. Today it exists only as software with Youth Stream Media Networks, which bought it out in 2000. LiveJournal offered itself in 1999 as a way of connecting "friends" with one another. It continues to operate today, but on a much smaller scale than Classmates or any other social networking site that allows old friends and acquaintances to connect with each other.

Friendster, however, began a revolution that changed everything. Jonathan Abrams launched Friendster in 2002. Because Friendster offers many of the standard features on social networking today (texting, photo sharing, chatting, and the like), it is sometimes referred to as the "poster child" of the current social networking phenomenon. Friendster skyrocketed in popularity, its attraction being the idea that friends could meet virtually and share ideas, pictures, recipes, or just daily musings. Friendster quickly became the number one social network of choice, though MySpace first, and Facebook later, eclipsed it in users and popularity. Friendster still boasts 50 million users, the majority of whom reside in Asia. While Friendster refused a buyout from Google early on, six years later it agreed to a partnership—of sorts.

Abrams began Friendster in his basement and attracted the same investors who later backed Amazon, Yahoo and eBay. Friendster zoomed to first place among the other infant social networking sites only to come screaming down to rock bottom by the end of the first year. Most industry observers blame Abrams. Friendster is now studied in Harvard Business School as an example of how *not* to run a business. Abrams also founded HotLinks, a bookmarking community, and has worked at Nortel and Netscape. He is CEO of Nuzzel, a news aggregator, as well as the site Socializr, designed to allow friends to share events with other friends and invite friends to these events. But Socializr also fell on very hard times and was later bought out by Punchbowl in 2010.

After Friendster appeared, the deluge of social networking sites followed. First came a few dozen, then a few thousand. MySpace eclipsed Friendster in 2003, but it quickly developed a "skin" problem. Flickr, the photosharing site, emerged during the same year, as did the very early Harvard version of Facebook, known first as "Facemash" and then "thefacebook."[31] Almost everyone knows the history of Facebook, either having read Ben Mezrich's bestselling book, *Accidental Billionaires: The Founding of Facebook: A Tale of Sex, Money, Greed, and Betrayal,* or having seen the 2010 movie *The Social Network,* based on Mezrich's book. Whether the Winklevoss twins are right or not—that they and not Zuckerberg launched Facebook—isn't the issue.[32] Mark Zuckerberg's rise to fame via Facebook came at a great price to him and to his company. Of course, it also reaped billions in return. Whatever the story, the rise and fall and continuance of many Silicon Valley enterprises do not provide many role models of good behavior—civic, professional, or social. In fact, so bad has the behavior become (bullying, sexism, even physical abuse) that some are making a strong case for *dissuading* young people from wanting to work there.[33] The promise of millions, however, may be more persuasive.

Zuckerberg and Facebook are hardly alone in egregious behavior while creating a startup. The rise of Twitter has also been chronicled in a manner not unlike *I, Claudius.* Greed, betrayal, hatred, double-dealing, and visions of grandeur appear to be the main ingredients in the evolution of Twitter and other social networks.[34] It should not surprise when one considers the billions of dollars that circulate around these companies and how seemingly picayune decisions can turn a few thousand dollars into millions for one and not even a dime for another.

The next couple of years, 2004–2006, witnessed an explosion of copycat sites, some that went on to become as famous as Facebook, while others, like Google's Buzz, failed miserably.[35] YouTube, Bebo (now defunct as a social network), and Facebook (as it is known today) all emerged, not one of them entirely new, but all of them carefully improving a feature of social networking technology, from enabling the sharing of videos, photos, and audio clips to real-time chat features.[36] While most Americans are familiar with the name Facebook, many others are familiar to worldwide users: Cyworld, Tagged, Hi5, Bebo, Skyrock, and Nexopia are more familiar to users living in Canada, South America, Central America, Asia, and the Pacific Islands. Social networking sites are so prevalent on the web that it is almost impossible to think of an area, topic, or subject matter that might *not* be covered by one.

Slowing down the once rapid expansion was the so-called dot-com bubble burst that left many of the once fabulously wealthy suddenly and completely bankrupt. The burst created a mild economic recession but left a devastating hole in the confidence of Internet technology (IT) stock speculators. When IT investing resumed in the mid–2000s, the initial public offerings (IPOs) of those stocks initially no longer reached the stratosphere of valuations like theGlobe did early on or the purchase of Bebo by AOL of close to a billion dollars. But investors with money to burn have short memories, probably because they have to. By the end of the first decade of the 21st century, valuations and IPOs took off to the moon once more. Despite the rise and fall of so many different sites, they all served to carve out a niche for social networking as a web-based phenomenon. By the turn of the 21st century, these networks were the hottest available medium for communication, or, as *Time* had it, "a story about community and collaboration on a scale never before seen."[37]

Social networks rose rapidly during the latter half of the 2000s to today. Why the explosion of growth in social networking sites during these years especially? One answer is that social networking sites became regarded as destinations for individuals to share information mainly about themselves and so appealing strongly to the ego factor in all of us. Although there is no actual place in cyberspace, many users think of social networking sites as "places" to go to talk about themselves and their activities.

Another contributing factor to the rapid rise in popularity of social networking sites is the new and emerging technologies that make it possible for unsophisticated users of that technology not only to post a message, but also to post media of just about any format: sound clips, video streams, and still photos. Never before had this kind of technology been possible for anyone to exchange while online, save perhaps only among those with the most sophisticated technology and the highest levels of computer expertise.

The popular term for this change is the emergence of the web from its early 1.0 state to 2.0 and, as some have it today, to its 3.0 (though some dispute the terminology). Computer-savvy users will recognize the enumeration as typical of software upgrades or even computer game releases. Each number indicates increasing technical sophistication. Likewise, the web moved from its very early state of simply displaying information in a static manner to its current dynamism of multiple media display. Had the web and therefore social networking sites remained static, the vibrant nature of social networking might never have taken off.

Users today expect and even demand *interactive* content-sharing and exchange. Social networking users now communicate in real time in chat rooms, post messages for each other, share video clips, refer one another to content elsewhere, or create and upload content for one person or a thousand. What is more, technical sophistication is not required as it was in the early days of bulletin boards and Usenet. Most users master it quickly and easily with little or no formal training. A web 3.0 is being pushed by Berners-Lee, but opinion is divided on whether it is possible. But if successful, it would doubtless create yet another revolution in social media.

The Upside of Social Media

Why do we use social networks *in addition* to email or some other form of electronic communication? The emphasis on email is necessary because Facebook co-founder Dustin Moskovitz continues to warn us that email is dead.[38] Whether this is part true, part wishful thinking, or both, remains to be seen. In any event, social media networks appeal to us because we like talking about ourselves. No other topic warms us as much as expatiating about ourselves to another. As Andrew Keen, Internet entrepreneur and now social networking critic, puts it, social networks are "shrines for the cult of self-broadcasting … so that we can advertise ourselves: everything from our favorite books and movies, to photos from our summer vacations, to 'testimonials' prizing our more winsome qualities or recapping our latest drunken exploits."[39]

Surely there is more to social networking than mere ego involvement, some other thing that causes us to flock to it repeatedly? Unless we are a nation—make that a globe—of narcissists, then there must be something else. Social networking sites allow for many old friends to renew friendships—cyber-reunions, so to speak. They also connect strangers worldwide via their interests to one another in ways that make them feel an instant companionship or camaraderie. Furthermore, social networking allows for any personality type—either introverts or extroverts—to begin on an equal footing. Add all this together and the ingredients of a virtual, or cyberworld, social order emerge. Other forms of electronic communication do not allow for this. An email can be sent blindly, so to speak, and often without any expectation of reply. Because social networking sites link those of similar interests together, "formal" introductions are superseded by their shared interests. And replies, comments, and exchanges are, if not demanded, then surely expected.

Social networking sites attract, too, because the power to connect with others is a built-in human desire. Some contend social networking sites are powerful simply because crowds run effusively to new things, and so the newness of a thing resides in its ability to convince others to jump on the bandwagon. Novelty explains some of the initial attraction of social networking, but it cannot explain all of it. American business journalist and *New Yorker* magazine staffer James Surowiecki thinks crowds make social networking attractive. He also believes crowds make social networking powerful because genius resides in numbers. Surowiecki makes this point in his 2005 book *The Wisdom of Crowds*. Thus, individuals use social networking sites not only because novelty attracts, and not only because we like to talk about ourselves to others, but also because they give everyone access to the power of genius in numbers.

The Downsides of Social Networking

While social media networks give users a sense of identity, a sense of uniqueness, shared values with a group, and a sense of belonging, they also extract a price. Each positive value can also become a negative reason for reconsidering one's social networking membership. If those negatives become legally troublesome, the very nature of the web makes it difficult to find recourse in courts of justice because there is no place in cyberspace, and assignment of blame is very difficult. Blame can be assigned to an individual, perhaps, but sometimes the vehicle of blame—in this case social networking sites—is all that can be identified.

Because no one "oversees" the web, it is sometimes thought to be designed chaos. Likewise, social networking is sometimes thought to be determined messiness. But that messiness can be an intractable problem. In most court cases we have a prototype by which to judge matters as they are presented to us. But in the case of something entirely new, like social networks, the problem becomes more difficult. As American technologist David Weinberger put it in his best-selling 2007 book about social networking, *Everything Is Miscellaneous*,

> Sometimes we do have to draw sharp lines. A riding lawn mower, a motorized wheelchair, and a battery-powered skateboard may all be sort of vehicles and

sort of not, but the Department of Motor Vehicles has to make a yes-or-no determination when you drive up to the local office and ask to register it. We can stipulate a definition that will work at least pretty well, even though it's arbitrary and artificial. But that's not what experience looks like.... Lines come later ... [and] [w]here and how sharply they're drawn has everything to do with who is drawing them and why.[40]

Lines are, indeed, being drawn in social networks, but the lines are unclear and hopelessly irregular. Over the next few chapters, we'll examine both the regularities and irregularities of being connected via social media networks.

Two

#City#State#U.S.Government

"Avoid Main and State Streets. Water main break.
Intersection closed for the next four hours!"

All forms of government are now involved to some extent in social media, but it has not always been that way. The rush to embrace social media has been neither immediate nor universal among local, state and federal governments. This makes sense when one pauses to think about it. Governments at all levels deal in sensitive information, not just every now and then, but every week if not every day. Protecting information is not the aim of social media; widespread promulgation is, regardless of the sensitivity.

For example, according to James Grimmelmann, professor of law at New York Law School and affiliated with the Institute for Information Law and Policy, "Facebook is Exhibit A for the surprising ineffectiveness of technical controls, especially in light of its recent actions. It has severe privacy problems *and* admirably comprehensive privacy-protection architecture."[1] In other words, although Facebook attempts to manage security concerns well, it remains surprisingly ineffective at doing so. If the security measures of the largest social networking site in the world are ineffective, smaller social networking sites will not do any better. Privacy of social networking sites will be taken up in a later chapter, but for now it is an inarguable fact that anything posted to a social networking site should be thought of as having been posted, if not to a billboard, then surely to a postcard.

Still, governments at every level have something to share, whether it is just day-to-day public service announcements or something more important, like a broken water main in the example above. While the movement to social media began slowly among government agencies, it has increased dramatically in the last half-decade. Restrictions still occur, however.

Social Media and the Military[2]

The military arms of governments everywhere in the world restrict service personnel's access to social networking, at least to some extent. This has become more and more the case, especially in light of terrorist organizations and their use and/or monitoring of social media. In the U.S., troops can access sites, but there are guidelines and requirements.[3] The reason most often given is that social networking sites contain videos and other bandwidth-eating applications that slow down military networks. Even with all their precautions, military organizations slip up, too. F-Secure, a computer security company, reported in January 2010 that the British military had sent sensitive information over Facebook. Furthermore, the military argue that social networking sites are easily hacked and pose a threat to national security. Since the successful hacking by a then fifteen-year-old Canadian boy known as "Mafiaboy" into the private records of eBay, Amazon, and Yahoo in 2000, that threat is not easily dismissed.[4] The numerous accounts of successful hacking since then surely underscore the "low-hanging fruit" social media networks have become to hackers.

For troops in active service, however, the only Internet access they have is that provided by the military. For example, there is http://www.army.mil/media/socialmedia/, but the site acts as a clearinghouse for approved social media connections. Obviously, carting iPads and unrestricted cellphones into active combat would not only be cumbersome but also dangerous for everyone. But the acceptance of social media by the military for active duty personnel early on was an on-again, off-again love affair. The U.S. Marines banned access to MySpace and Facebook in 2008 and then added bans of Metacafe, Ifilm, StupidVideos (a YouTube-like network), FileCabi, BlackPlanet, Hi5, Pandora, and live365 soon thereafter. In 2009, Twitter was added to the list.[5] In the end, security and hacking concerns trumped all other issues as the rationale for blocking them. Following the Marines' ban of sites, however, the U.S. Army did an about-face and mandated access to Facebook on all U.S. bases. In 2010, the Department of Defense issued a policy that appeared to expand access to social media more widely, but it came with some caveats.[6] The change in social media access for U.S. military personnel was inevitable. But it still comes with many warnings, and the Department of Defense, through various handbooks and guides, does everything it can to help military families understand the dangers of completely unfettered access to military matters through social media. Each branch of the military has its own guides and its own regulations when it comes to social media.[7] But the relaxation of restrictions, especially with sites like Skype, has increased morale and drawn families closer together.

Security experts are, however, quite firm in their arguments opposing unfettered access.[8] According to Noah Shachtman of Wired.com, the names of some soldiers dying in Afghanistan have appeared on Facebook before being officially released. Furthermore, Erika Morphy, well known technology journalist and reporter on military activities, explained, "Every day, our networks are under attack from foreign invaders. Whoever thinks our enemies are out herding their camels is sadly mistaken. Our militant enemies have networks of very intelligent, trained operatives working night and day to hack into our networks."[9]

Columnist Todd Garvin argues the opposite side, however. Garvin believes men and women of the armed forces who put their own lives on the line daily must have easy access to their families via social networking sites.[10] Garvin contends that if bandwidth is a problem, as the military has at times argued, then the military should increase bandwidth; if security issues create headaches, the military should do the work necessary to fix them. Courts have not yet intervened on First Amendment grounds because the safety of military personnel takes precedence. But trying to restrict media designed to be unfettered in the first place is impossible, and social media access, both approved and not, remains front and center, so to speak, for military families.

Cybersquatting and Social Media

Yet another reason obtains why governments are slow to jump on the social media bandwagon. Every domain name-owning entity must keep an eye out for cybersquatting, but this is especially true for state and local governments. Cybersquatting takes place in one of two ways. When domain names are available, they can be purchased by anyone. Cybersquatters will buy many domain names they think will be popular with the sole intent of selling them later, often at extortionate prices. Cybersquatting also takes place when domain names are snatched up where previous owners forget to renew them, often with annoying or even embarrassing results. State and local governments have been victims of these hijinks—which often feel like hijacks—but so have businesses and even celebrities. Brand names are particularly vulnerable.[11] The cost for reclaiming them can run from a few hundred to several thousand dollars.

Some city governments are fighting with pornographers to get back their domain names. For example, in the early 2000s, the city of Baltimore, Maryland, lost www.baltimoremaryland.com to a pornographer who held it for ransom of $8,500. Cities eager to connect in the digital age found themselves connecting digitally all right, but to the wrong sites. Other sites that ran aground in the murky waters of the cyber cesspool include Detroit, Nashville, San Diego, and Seattle.[12]

While some city governments have been hijacked by porn sites, city governments are not immune to their own temptation to propagandize. Officials of Issaquah City in Washington State allegedly misdirected searchers from another city in Washington, Sammamish, to its own site.[13] This occurred when the two cities were locked in a battle over water quality and storm water runoff.

Cybersquatting is considered illegal, and attempts have been made to curtail it. But in the cyberworld of the ever free and unfettered Internet, such are the dreams of the naive or ill-informed. Cybersquatting makes it more difficult for government entities to connect with users. Unofficial Twitter accounts pop up; Facebook pages for the voice of local or state governments that are no more than the voice of the mischievous, or worse, miscreants, are now ubiquitous. But staying away from social media is also no solution. The same misguided individuals who hijack accounts or take on persona not their own will simply jump in and take on the entire personality for the sake of humor, mischief, misinformation, disinformation, or all of the above.

Government Employees and Social Media

Governments are also wary about employees being on social media sites. Three police officers were suspended from their jobs in Harrison, New York, after they made lewd, sexist, and racist remarks about the town's mayor and President Barack Obama on a Facebook account. Their expectation of privacy, a matter discussed in a later chapter, did not extend to social media. All too often, users of social networking sites forget that posting to a site is like posting information on a giant billboard in a heavily trafficked area. Only too late do they come to realize that their remarks, only minutes after writing them, circle the globe, literally, before they have time to give their tweet or post a second thought.

Governments are also very concerned about privacy, or rather the lack thereof, on social media. Some European officials have even threatened to quit social media unless the privacy matter is tightened, even if not resolved. But the appeal of social media for connecting governments to constituents—whether city, local, state, or federal—is often too tempting to ignore. In a survey of 463 local governments from across the U.S., researchers found a 70 percent overall use.[14] With the rapid decline and even disappearance of newspapers, and the annoyance factor many find in mass mailings, social media would appear to be the single best solution for governments, especially local and state ones, for connecting with individuals. In fact, Facebook now controls how millions get their daily news.[15] Why is this a bad thing? It doesn't have to be, but let's face it, giving any one entity all the access to the news one gets means you also get its biases.

While newspaper reporters have their own axes to grind behind their often thinly veiled ideologies, making between-the-lines reading mandatory, social media stories often seem false or too propagandizing. Further, while the price of social media in fund-strapped local and state governments is right (free, more or less), they also bring with them certain hidden and obvious costs: misinformation, failure to respond, flippant responses that turn into a social media meltdown, and more. Facebook and Twitter still predominate among governments, but YouTube is gathering steam among them as well. One problem with social media for governments is that, while the medium provides an easy way to affect a democratic presence, the same medium is also equally vulnerable to many missteps. Governments can take certain steps to avoid the larger public relations mess, but often these are no better than leaving themselves open to attack. Moderating their social media presences, or forbidding comments, is only an invitation to some to set up faux sites (if not cybersquatting ones) to counter the attempt to "curb" free speech. Governments will likely continue to use and abuse social media even at the risk of being abused by their own constituents.

The U.S. Government and Social Media

The United States government has been proactive in its use of social media. President Obama opened up the social media floodgates by strategic and targeted use in both of his campaigns, even complaining after his 2008 election that he could not use his BlackBerry as often as he wanted to. The GSA outlines appropriate and official use of social media sites by defining their use in various contexts.[16] The document contains commonsense applications, such as what is official and what is not and what should and should not be done. But it also contains useful advice on information collection, minimizing risk (both to the government and the employee), privacy matters, lobbying ethics, and the GSA's right to monitor and remove comments. None of this should surprise, but it does serve to outline just how carefully a government must tread when walking through the minefield of social media.

Politicians are, of course, using social media to augment their runs for government offices. Once elected, they use social networking to connect to voters or vent concerns. Obama's use of social media in 2008, alluded to above, drew the road map for successful use, both in connecting with voters and, more importantly for campaigns, in raising millions of dollars one, two and five dollars at a time. Yet not all users of social networking think that politics and social media go hand-in-glove. Just over one-third of social networking users employ their social media to keep up with politics.[17] Further, almost 85 percent of social networking users say they have posted little or nothing at all political to a social media site. Obviously, those users politically engaged already tend to view their political social networking as much more important than those who are not politically engaged. Democrats think social networking with respect to politics more important than Republicans do, but both parties, including Independents and splinter groups, recognize the importance of social media.

The cyber-savvy will look amused at guides to social networking use, such as the one GSA publishes, and even mock them, but the need for such guides continues to be undeniable, given how often social networking users slip up. Politicians, whether at the state, local, or municipal level, are famous for their social media blunders.

In Albuquerque, New Mexico, a politician attending a public hearing on raising the city's minimum wage posted an offensive remark about a woman who spoke in favor of it. Minutes later he was suspended from his position, and he had to issue an apology. In the same city, the school superintendent tweeted sexist remarks about the secretary-designate for the Public Education Department and nearly lost his job. To make matters worse, he was dumbfounded that his remarks could be seen by others outside his small circle of friends![18]

The list is endless, but none of them rival the disastrous social media blunder that the ironically-named Anthony Weiner committed. In a widely publicized story, Weiner tweeted pictures of himself in various stages of undress and sexual arousal during 2011, while still a junior congressman, to a 21-year-old Seattle, Washington, college student.[19] When confronted about these tweets, he equivocated (some say he lied), telling reporters he didn't know what pictures there were of him out on the Internet. He even went so far as to argue that his photo had been hacked, implying that perhaps someone had photoshopped him in those poses. The now familiar story not only didn't go away, mainly because it was true, but it also morphed into what came to be called Weinergate, cashing in on the congressman's most unfortunate surname. As the story grew, he backpedaled more. Eventually Weiner admitted to having had inappropriate conversations on various social media platforms and sending pictures that were not appropriate. He admitted to having exchanged these communications with as many as six women. Weinergate reached such a pitch that his own party called on him to resign. After more backpedalling, Weiner realized that he could not recover from his missteps and resigned from Congress.

A few years later, in 2013, he ran for mayor of New York City. For all intents and purposes, it appeared he had learned his lesson, and he even began by taking the sexting scandal head-on. He took questions on the matter, answered them straightforwardly, and managed to turn the discussions back to the political issues that were important to New Yorkers. They rewarded him, too, with early support, and he began a slow rise in the polls from the bottom of the candidate pile to near the top in a matter of months.

But then new charges of sexting emerged. Weiner denied them flatly, but screen captures and other online accounts began to show up, with one account under the hilarious name of "Carlos Danger." Eventually, three other women with whom Weiner had been sexting came forward. Although Weiner denied ever having a sexual relationship with any of the women, he had already lost all credibility with his previous equivocations and misleading statements. He stayed in the race until the bitter end, and the end was indeed bitter. He finished in fifth place in the Democratic primary with just under 5 percent of the vote, perhaps that 5 percent we are told are not on the Internet at all.

The Weiner story is unusual because it stretched over numerous years and involved many women and repeated offenses, while Weiner was married and even while his wife was pregnant with their first child. Weiner cannot be said to be ignorant of how social media works. Rather, his downfall was more likely the result that many in politics—and many outside it—fall victim to: hubris. He thought it did not matter, that he was entitled, and that as a politician, he could do what he pleased without recrimination. (Perhaps he even agreed with the deplorable Ashley Madison website: life is short; have an affair.) In any event, his is a story that serves to underscore the minefield that is social media for governments, politicians, and anyone holding or seeking public office of any kind.

Public officials especially must come to understand that social media platforms are very public places. If they intend to use them—and it is very unlikely that they can escape from using them—then they have to understand that they are unforgiving. Jokes, however seemingly innocent, can blow up into major scandals. Moreover, they can sink careers, derail important information, and turn the attention of constituents away from important issues to unimportant ones that occupy all the airspace available. Once a matter is on social networking sites, there is no retrieving it, despite what one hears about deleting profiles: someone will find a way to bring it back. And it will remain forever somewhere on the Internet. What's more, it will very likely have been captured by someone lying in wait to snag the unwary or careless politicians with whom he or she disagrees, or merely to expose them, for whatever reason. Using social media wisely and well requires attention to detail and careful thought. Even politicians or governments that outsource their social media presence are not immune and may, moreover, expose themselves to even greater risk. One cannot outsource one's persona to another and hope to be spared any embarrassment.

But let's be clear about this. Being hoisted on the social media petard is not always the result of stupidity or carelessness. The Weiner case is hyperbolic in its missteps. But even slight slip-ups can create major firestorms. Because it happens so often and to just about everyone, it may well be the nature of the medium itself. It simply lends itself to great use and widespread abuse. Perhaps because it has limitless possibilities for positive outreach, it also has an equally limitless downside. Governments and politicians who use social media platforms must use them with caution.

Just the Facts, Ma'am: Law Enforcement and Social Media

Social media platforms have also shown their value to law enforcement in numerous ways. In fact, they are fast becoming one of the most used resources to enforce the law. According to a 2013 survey of chiefs of police, 96 percent of police departments use social media venues in some way, with more than 80 percent of those departments saying they used them to solve crimes.[20] From the local police department to state bureaus to the FBI, law enforcement has used social media successfully in various iterations. But the adaptations of social media to law enforcement are not without risks. Unwise use or careless applications can result in harm to officers, weaken strong cases, and even expose these agencies to prosecution, both civil and criminal.[21] One obvious benefit of social media is to open up communication between law enforcement and the public. All too often, miscommunication marks, if not mars, the exchange between the general public and law enforcement at every level. Law enforcement can post pictures of suspects, items taken in robberies, or photos of missing persons to a wide general public with an eye to identifying or apprehending. Because social media networks have no expiration dates, pictures, identifying marks and/or clothing of criminals, and more can be posted of recent crimes and unsolved crimes from decades past in order to bring them to satisfying closure. By monitoring social media, police have also been able to thwart would-be crimes, the congregation of gangs, and even outright violence. Any time a crime can be averted or bloodshed prevented, it is a win-win calculus for everyone.

But the use of social media does not always have a happy ending. Police who have personal presence on social media can also open up themselves and their departments to exposure or worse. For example, by revealing too much about oneself, a police officer, judge, or attorney can put him or herself at risk, or even their families. A veteran police officer in Connecticut, for example, who taught D.A.R.E. classes, was fired last year for inappropriate social media contact with elementary school children.[22] But it can also take an even weirder turn. A police chief in Texas determined that demotion and termination of certain officers for inappropriate behavior, in this case, driving while intoxicated, were not enough. So he took to social media and made very public not only the firings but also the cause.[23]

Moreover, not everyone is happy with police using social media for apprehension. Law enforcement departments can now scan huge volumes of social media, looking for incriminating evidence. Many observers worry over the privacy issues that monitoring social media raises. But for now, anyway, the courts have ruled that users of social media, given their very public nature, cannot have a reasonable expectation of privacy. "People think that [social media postings] are private communications and that they can't be seen," said one state law enforcement member, "so they feel more free to discuss inside of an inbox as opposed to a post. Just when you think it's private, it generally isn't."[24] While the privacy concerns are legitimate (see Chapter Seven), even these are trumped by the apprehension of those seeking to do harm to others.

Social Media and Criminals

Just as law enforcement is using social media to its benefit, so also are those seeking to do wrong. The most obvious use of social media for criminal benefit is fraud and/or identity theft. Criminals often troll social media in order to find social security numbers, addresses, phone numbers, and so on. In some cases, they have even planned home invasions based on user identifications (geotagging) of where they are and how long they will be at certain locations, "cybercasing" the joint, so to speak. Pedophiles, a topic which will be treated in the next chapter, use social media to their advantage, too. The list is endless, including cyberstalking and cyberbullying, both of which are addressed in another chapter.

Let Freedom Ring: Nondemocratic Countries and Social Media

One of the many advantages of social networking is its ubiquitous nature. It *can be* anywhere. Whether or not it is, is another story. Bandwidth notwithstanding, governments all over the world have used social networking for their own ends. What was once thought to be the great leveler for all nations, making it putatively impossible for Cold War–type shenanigans to continue unabated, has turned out to be less liberating than was earlier thought. Eager and early adopters pointed to the rise of Facebook, Twitter, YouTube, and so on as the tools of the great and coming electronic democracy. And early on, it appeared that way. Revolutions could begin with a few tweets, or a posting here or there could rally thousands to the side of freedom and against tyranny, or so it seemed.

Like everything online, social networking is a double-edged sword. If I can tweet you about a rallying point against our oppressive government, you, as a government mole, can tweet my whereabouts and our rally location. And that is apparently what has happened. In 2013, the Turkish government launched a government-funded study to restrict social media.[25] Turkish officials claim the study is needed to fight cybercrime and other illegal activities. But the study came at a time when the country had been fighting dissidents for nearly three weeks.

Underdeveloped countries in the Middle East, Eastern Europe, and Africa routinely restrict social media access. When that doesn't work, they simply shut down the Internet. Under martial law, or rather under the guise of martial law, some countries will monitor some sites, shut down others, and restrict social media altogether.[26] China may be the worst offender, shutting down popular social media sites that hosted over 250 million members in order to curtail rumors of a coup in 2012.[27] Some will argue that democratic countries will do the same with social media during war-like conditions, and perhaps that is true. But in places like China, Russia, and Pakistan, shutdowns, blackouts, and the inability to access these sites (not to mention the surveilling that routinely occurs) make the social networking calculus far more dangerous for those members than it does for those in democratically run countries.

Some proponents of social media often tout its power to deliver news about governments quickly, and that is true. The fact that social media can often relay important information faster and to more people more quickly than conventional means is often seen as a positive that outweighs all negatives. This facility of social media platforms has also led some to tout them as a means to effect successful civil disobedience and even régime change. All of this may well be true, but these proponents must remember that what can be used for great good can also be used for great evil. So far anyway, while social media networks have been helpful in various protests and revolutions, they have been most success-ful in places where freedom is the mainstay of a given country's *raison d'être*.

Elsewhere, social media can just as easily be used to shut critics up. For example, Vietnam scours social media for those who oppose the Socialist Republic of Vietnam or who in any way would harm national security.[28] In 2013, Vietnam passed Decree 72, a circuitously written doc-ument that fines critics of the government up to 100 million dong, or about $5,000 U.S. dollars, for violations.[29] The same is true in many Mus-lim countries. Indeed, proponents of the Internet and social media are learning the hard way that this unparalleled freedom also provides those with evil intent unbridled power over them.[30]

It will come as no surprise that China, long a proponent of bridling any freedom of speech that is not "company policy," has now turned its attention to social media. Apart from shutting down dissident bloggers and harassing social networking moderators, China began in 2013 to tighten its grip on all of social media.[31] This has not proved as easy as the government hoped, so it has taken to restricting Google and Microsoft and their ability to do business in the country. Sadly, neither company has been as willing to stand up to the potential billions lost in traffic as those companies have been to criticize their own government. The desire for information in China is so great that Internet providers and the search giants could do much to bring that government, if not to its knees, then at least to a crouching position. Lamentably, both companies have restricted searches, blocked certain words, and, at best, winked at the gov-ernment and its censorious attitude. According to one observer, the Chi-nese government is schizophrenic as it "goes back and forth, testing the line, knowing they need press freedom and the information it provides, but worried about opening the door to the type of freedoms that could lead to the regime's downfall."[32] Reporters without Borders ranks China 173 out of 179 countries on its index of freedom of the press.[33] Even amid new initiatives, such as the 2010 establishment of a 24-hour news station, China maintains its stranglehold on any media that seek to report too much of the truth or too much unfiltered information. Social media are clearly within that grasp, and there are no signs that there will be any letup.

China is not alone, with similar restrictions in countries like North Korea, Syria, Iraq, Iran, and many other nondemocratic countries. Twitter is blocked or blacked out, photos removed or blocked, pages taken down, or the entire service itself is otherwise hamstringed. Clearly, inhabitants in all these countries, including China, are much better off having the option of limited social media than not having it at all. Yet when China, North Korea, Vietnam, Pakistan, Iran, and Eritrea block Facebook, Twitter, or YouTube, one begins to wonder just how helpful social media can be in liberating these oppressed peoples.[34] It is ironic to note that leaders in many of these countries use the very social media they ban! When governments can exercise tight control of even these media platforms once thought to be immune to any sort of censorship, the fragility of freedom, not to mention its preciousness, is all the more affirmed.

Restricting or banning of social media is not limited to nondemocratic states, as most anyone will be quick to point out. For example, democratic states like Australia, the United Kingdom, and New Zealand have been guilty of this over the past decade. But to compare, for example, the United States' restrictions on social media for its servicemen in order to keep them safe with the restrictions it places on social media to all the inhabitants of places like North Korea, Russia, or China is to compare apples with pineapples. For example, Apple restricted some social media in its U.S. stores because customers were using the devices to update their pages. Some social media sites have been restricted on military bases, as mentioned above, because they are considered high security risks. Likewise, some social media networks have been restricted or banned in school libraries and elementary or middle schools because pedophiles were using them to connect with adolescents.[35] Such banning, especially with respect to young children, not only seems fair but indisputably wise given the activity of child predators on social media. A government that would refuse to attempt to take some action in this regard to keep young children safe would appear simply irresponsible.

That is not the way many web-loving elutheromaniacs see it. For them, there should be no banning or restricting of any social media by any government for any reason. If men were angels, this approach would be imminently sensible. But we are not, and so we not only need governments, but we also need laws to keep us safe from those who would break them. Many point to the revelations of Edward Snowden as solid proof that our government is just as censorious as all the rest. But most fair-minded individuals make a distinction between governments that refuse to allow their citizens to criticize at all and those that monitor social media activity to keep their citizens safe. It cannot be gainsaid that the line is a very fine one between the two, but it is equally true that in our age of terrorists, monitoring is a must.

The use of social media by governments is, of course, very likely to continue. Proponents of social media platforms will continue to tout their undeniable benefits. But naysayers must be given their voice. For every benefit of social media to governments, there is also an equal and very powerful downside. Oppressive governments may be stymied for a season, but in the end, they will clamp down on social media, if not shut it down altogether. For every criminal apprehended via social media, there will be a crime perpetrated, facilitated entirely because social media exist. And for every politician who connects with a voter to his or her benefit, there will always be the Anthony Weiners reminding us just how troublesome the medium itself can be and just how stupid we humans are.

THREE

#K–12#SocialMedia# DangerousLiaison?

Social media and K–12 schools have had an on-again, off-again affair. On the one hand, social networking sites engage students' interests and, by doing so, hold out the promise of engaging students in real schoolwork, assuming it can be adapted to the social networking platform. The logic runs that if students are engaged in the process, they will be more likely to learn. But engaging them in the latest school gossip is not exactly the same thing as engaging them in long division. Still, social media *may* increase the reading abilities of some, *may* make some more gregarious than before, and *may* make some more willing to participate in a larger and less anonymous context. Participation in classroom discussions may also increase where it has been absent before. And we cannot rule out better dexterity and ratiocinative skills for those kids who are engaged in learning via gaming.

The very open and unrestricted nature of social media, however, also presents a plethora of problems. Students can say anything and usually do. They are unbridled in their contempt of fellow students they dislike, and bullying—a matter to be taken up in another chapter—is rampant among schoolchildren. The question often facing schools is how to navigate the turbulent waters of free speech and all the social media positives, while, at the same time, provide safe harbor for students from social media's downsides. It is not an easy task, and more than one principal has found the sailing anything but smooth.

Tinker *and Free Speech, K–12*

The question of free speech among the school-aged is hardly new. *Tinker v. Des Moines* (1969) is the *locus classicus* of free speech in K–12.

The story goes that on a dark, windy, and cold night in December in Des Moines, Iowa, a group of students met at the home of Chris Eckhardt to plan a public demonstration in favor of ending the war in Vietnam. The students decided to wear black armbands during the rest of the holiday season and hold a fast on December 16 and on New Year's Eve.

Following the meeting the next day, Mary Beth Tinker, a 13-year-old junior high school student, and Chris Eckhardt kicked off the protest by deciding (on their own or with adult coaching from the students' parents who were known war protestors?) to wear armbands to school to show their disapproval of the Vietnam War. The school board got wind of the plan and passed a ban prohibiting students from wearing armbands. When the students arrived at school the next day, they were asked to remove the armbands; they refused and were sent home. The next day, Mary Beth's brother, John, wore a black armband and was also suspended (eventually, a total of five students were suspended). Following the Christmas break, the students donned black clothing to replace the black armbands as part of their protest.

The case dragged on for four years and wound up at the Supreme Court. There it was decided in the students' favor, the court famously declaring that students do not "shed their constitutional rights to freedom of speech or expression at the schoolhouse gate."[1] The Court put a fine point on its argument:

> Under our Constitution, free speech is not a right that is given only to be so circumscribed it exists in principle, but not in fact. Freedom of expression would not truly exist if the right could be exercised only in an area that a benevolent government has provided as a safe haven for crackpots. The Constitution says that Congress (and the States) may not abridge the right to free speech. This provision means what it says. We properly read it to permit reasonable regulation of speech-connected activities in carefully restricted circumstances. But we do not confine the permissible exercise of First Amendment rights to a telephone booth or the four corners of a pamphlet, or to supervised and ordained discussion in a school classroom.[2]

Pivotal to the case from the Court's viewpoint was that the students wearing armbands did not disrupt the educational process; consequently, they could not be banned from wearing them. This same logic resonates, according to some social networking proponents, when schools attempt to restrict or otherwise block social media. These sites, they contend, are non-disruptive and educationally beneficial.

Social Media: Helpful? Harmful? Neutral?

But are social media networks really non-disruptive and educationally beneficial? Educationally beneficial is arguable. Some sites teach students to read, engage them in reading, help them learn to spell, or encourage better math skills. Edmodo, a classroom management site for teachers, provides them with opportunities to network, share ideas, collaborate, and provide information for parents about their children's progress.[3] English Companion is a social networking site that includes live forums for teachers, blogs, and discussion groups. Multimedia programs allow teachers to focus on certain grammar aspects that may need to improve in those students under their care.

Imbee.com, a social networking site designed for students 8-14, requires that parents submit a credit card to vouch for their children's identities. Parents are promised to be able to approve those contracts that students make, lessening the privacy concerns that parents rightly have (but see below). Social networking proponents argue that schools should encourage anything that improves better intellectual skills, however superficial they may be, not hindered or blocked. But these are social networking sites designed exclusively for educational purposes. It is unclear whether students, once engaged in them, will return to them without coercion. Such sites do not possess the appeal that Facebook has or that Twitter entices because they do not employ the ego involvement that most social media rely upon and even bait users with. Linking learning and entertainment typically rouses robust debate among educators. Learning and entertainment may be tied together temporarily, but the knot cannot be sustained since most advanced learning is its own reward and often involves grueling work. Sandbagging students with entertainment just to get them interested may not work, opponents argue, and even if it does, they contend, it may backfire when students no longer find the work entertaining.

But If Helpful, Why Not Exploit?

But others argue, shouldn't we take what we can get when it comes to engaging students in learning? If social networking sites do the trick, why not employ them, and why not employ all of them, whether or not they have any intrinsic teaching and/or explicit learning component? The very process, the argument goes, is an overall good because students' minds are engaged. The argument appears sound on the surface. Even on Facebook, students can learn to write and to express themselves, and learning will take place because they will be writing about a topic—usually themselves—that will hold their interest. Twitter will teach them economy of language. The collaboration on those sites will engage them with others to help move their learning along.

Such is the theory, but social media sites do not always bend so easily to theory. Because they are open and without restraints, social networking sites routinely violate obscenity and pornography laws, making them inappropriate for schools. Moreover, opponents continue, because sexual predators are known to frequent social networking sites and are looking to prey upon the unwary, the sites must be prohibited during school hours.

Social Media and Sexual Predators

Sexual predators and social media are not minor quibbles, given that young people are primary users of social networking sites. According to a 2006 study commissioned by Cox Communications and the National Center for Missing and Exploited Children, more than 60 percent of 10- to 17-year-olds have a profile posted to a social networking site, such as Facebook. More than 50 percent of them have posted pictures of themselves.[4] Social media are now one of the most preferred means of communication among teens. School officials believe access to social networking sites must be limited while at school, or it will interfere with students' pursuit of academics, not to mention expose them to dangerous encounters.

Additionally, many social networking sites, such as Facebook, Instagram, Tumblr, and others have pictures of underage drinking, drug use, nudity, and simulated or actual sexual intercourse, all activities parents would view as undesirable behaviors for teens to be viewing, especially while at school. School administrators, feeling pressure from parents, look for some legal means to restrict these sites without blocking them altogether, though blocking them has occurred and still occurs. School administrators looked to Congress for help, and Congress has not disappointed, though its success has been limited.

First Attempt: Communications Decency Act, 1996

The first such attempt was the Communications Decency Act of 1996 (CDA).[5] The CDA is part of a larger bill, Title V of the Telecommunications Act of 1996, and was a bipartisan proffering by James Exon, a Democrat from Nebraska, and Gordon Slate, a Republican from Washington state. The bill was the first attempt by Congress to update the Communications Act of 1934. Title V sought to regulate obscenity and pornography on the Internet, especially when it impacted children. Some detractors referred to the act a result of the Great Cyberporn Panic of 1995.[6] The CDA may not have come about exclusively because of a *Time* magazine article published that same year, but it was certainly influenced by it.[7] The magazine featured what has become an iconic image of a horrified child looking at a computer screen. The story was based on what many have discredited as a flawed study that found more than three-fourths of all Internet images to be pornographic. In a "cyber panic," Congress quickly followed up with the CDA, which sought to protect minors from indecent and obscene pictures over the Internet.

In treating the Internet as a "broadcasting" medium, obscenity and pornography laws were brought to bear in the same way they are to television and radio. The law struck out the words "telephone medium" and inserted the words "telecommunications facility." While many libertarians and First Amendment absolutists found the law obnoxious and unworkable, the effort was praiseworthy on its face. Clearly, the Internet is awash in pornography, but not to the extent that the *Time* article claimed. If we care about the quality of life, the CDA was an effort that should have been made. But it failed because of its overreach, its ineffectiveness, inherent loopholes, or all three.

The constitutionality of the CDA came under attack almost immediately. Ironically, the law was signed into effect by none other than President Bill Clinton, himself the perpetrator of acts that could not easily be recited verbatim in a family newspaper. The Supreme Court justices, all nine of them, struck down the indecency provisions in the CDA in *Reno v. ACLU*, 1997 (521 U.S. 844). The ACLU brought the action before the court under the guise of First Amendment violations of free speech. The justices sided with the ACLU and found the CDA in violation of the guarantee of freedom of speech, which putatively includes pornography and obscenity. Two of the nine justices agreed in part and disagreed in part.

Tucked away in the CDA was Section 230, what proponents of a wide-open Internet and a no-holds-barred view of the First Amendment saw as eternal protection of social media from any litigation. Ironically, the CDA sought to limit pornography and obscenity on the Internet, and that part of it failed miserably. But Section 230 survived, and because of it, the Internet has become either the bellwether of free expression or the protected cesspool of humankind's worse proclivities, depending on your viewpoint.

Could indecency and obscene materials be curbed over the Internet without also shutting it down? In order to clear up any confusion and to enact what the CDA failed to accomplish, Congress enacted the Child Online Protection Act, or COPA, in 1998.[8] The COPA sought to remedy any confusion by clearly stating that owners of social networking sites could not knowingly distribute pornographic and/or obscene materials over the World Wide Web. To do so meant certain significant fines outlined in the measure.

Child Online Protection Act or COPA (1998)

The COPA narrowed the reach of the CDA by restricting access by minors to harmful materials delivered over the Internet and imposed criminal or civil sanctions on those who knowingly distributed them. Although social networking sites' popularity had just begun in the late 1990s, most observers assumed the COPA applied to them because social networking sites relied upon the web for delivery. If those sites contained "harmful materials," then they could be restricted, or so the logic went.

Like the CDA, the constitutionality of the COPA came under scrutiny, this time in *Ashcroft v. ACLU* (2004), only one month before its enactment. While the Supreme Court did not think the COPA's reliance on "community standards" overly broad, it worried that the law might be too vague to apply consistently and therefore ruled that it could not be enforced. Several groups came forward to protest the COPA, including the American Library Association and the Erotic Authors Association. The Court reasoned that it would be better to protect the First Amendment against exposing the underage to pictures or writing that might otherwise mar them for life. Some observers even doubted if the COPA applied to social media since the sites were not named in the bill. After several other lawyerly tribulations, the COPA died, asphyxiated by the putative defenders of the First Amendment, among these the American Library Association. In the end, Congress failed to fashion an effective law to protect children while online, leaving children unprotected and leaving school officials in the lurch about what to do next with respect to social networking sites and underage children. The COPA sought to protect minors against harmful materials and failed, but what about protecting their identities? Could that be done?

Children's Online Privacy Protection Act, or COPPA, 1998

The COPPA tried to answer the question of protecting the identities of minors, and it was enacted October 21, 1998, but it did not take effect until 2000. The idea behind the COPPA was to protect the online information obtained by social networking sites and other sites that required some sort of signup of anyone thirteen years of age or younger. The COPPA provided a blueprint of what sites could and could not ask for and what they could and could not archive. It also set a trigger when those sites needed to seek verification from a parent or guardian. Congress empowered the Federal Trade Commission to enforce the COPPA. The COPPA allows the FTC to name a "safe harbor" proviso that, the logic went, would force social networking sites and other similar sites collecting personal information to self-regulate. While the COPA met with immediate and swift opposition from the usual suspects, the COPPA worked the other side of the street by limiting what data could be collected from minors, thus securing their privacy, or at least making an attempt to do so. The acts are often confused for one another, but they are separate and work in tandem, or so the prevailing wisdom went.[9]

The COPPA governs the collecting of data by any means. Sites that collect data directly or even through "cookies" are considered to be collecting data, and when children are involved, they must be protected. The COPPA also mandates that sites must display clearly understandable and visible notices to children (i.e., the notice cannot be hidden from view or hidden in legal jargon). The law also outlines "verifiable consent": if an underage child got on the site, before he or she gave out information, he or she would be forced to get a parent's or guardian's permission. Any sort of games or prizes offered could not be denied to children, even those children who had not signed up.

On the face of it, all appeared to be in order. But again, if men were angels, we wouldn't need government. Most sites put up a warning that if the "surfer" was not thirteen or older, he or she could not sign up. Of course, when you're on the Internet, no one knows you're a dog, and tens of thousands of underage children proceeded to sign up for MySpace, Facebook, Twitter, and a host of adult sites. Companies could make the effort, but most, if not all, took their chances. If caught, they would simply pay the fines. The COPPA might well make startups wary, but successful social networking sites appear not to give the COPPA a second thought. In other words, the law really has had very little impact and is easily bypassed. The attempt to protect children from the unwanted attention of predators is praiseworthy. But the execution, whether in the weakness of fines, the lack of oversight, the difficulty in policing, or all three, makes the COPPA merely another law on the books with very few teeth to take the bite out of those who traffic in criminal actions over the web.

If at First You Don't Succeed: Children's Internet Protection Act, 2000

Congressional opponents sought to conclude the matter with the Children's Internet Protection Act (CIPA, 2000). The new act focused on the so-called E-rate discounts (or service funds discounts) that come from taxes collected from telecommunications users. After applying for these federal funds, public schools and libraries use them to buy Internet access and computer equipment. The CIPA provision required public schools and libraries receiving these funds to use part of them to purchase a "technology protection measure" (i.e., filtering software) to block sites with pornographic images. The CIPA also included a time-sensitive element—18 months after enactment—for compliance with the law. One difference between the CIPA and the other bills proved its attention to detail. The CIPA outlined what it meant by "harmful materials." This included nudity, real or simulated sex acts, and so on. While the law did not block any social networking sites per se, it did block sites that trafficked in "harmful materials."

The law, compared to the others, appeared unassailable. Terms were defined, penalties spelled out, and sites put on notice regarding the kinds of materials that would subject them to the teeth of the law. The law even specified "filtering software" that would help block offending sites. On the surface, then, it appeared that the CIPA had closed all the loops.

Not exactly. The ink had hardly dried before groups began challenging the CIPA. In 2003, the professional organization of libraries (the American Library Association yet again) challenged the constitutionality of the CIPA in *United States v. American Library Association, Inc.*, in the U.S. District Court of the Eastern District of Pennsylvania. Like iron filings to a magnet, the ALA, in its absolutist view of the First Amendment, is drawn to cases that have even a hint of censorship. If it is true, as some opponents argue, that "Puritans" see pornography everywhere, it is equally true that the ALA cannot see it anywhere. The ALA challenged the CIPA on the grounds that the law requires libraries to block access to constitutionally protected information on the Internet. Because filtering software is not 100 percent effective, the ALA argued, it blocks protected information as well as harmful materials. Of course, those sites singled out for blocking intentionally were blocked in the aggregate, because the software blocks any site with the characteristics of harmful materials.

For example, filtering software might well block "Beautiful Bountiful Breasts" but also might block "Breast Cancer." So the ALA argued that the latter provided constitutionally protected information that could not be legally blocked. To block it violated First Amendment principles, the once conservative organization argued. But in truth, the ALA strained out a gnat to swallow the proverbial camel. In the same way that libraries routinely do not purchase items because of cost (think of it as "censorship" based on mere price alone without having even seen the content) so those constitutionally protected items are "blocked" from libraries, so also did filtering software block constitutionally protected materials by default, a default that could, however, be corrected. The argument is as ludicrous as it appears. Not long after its rollout, filtering software offered an on or off option. It did not take long before all filtering software allowed administrators to turn on sites that were constitutionally protected while leaving off sites that were not.

Further, the ALA argued, no filtering software is 100 percent effective. While technically true then and now, refinements in filtering software do make it more than substantially effective and far more effective than no filtering at all. In many ways, the ALA argument with respect to filtering was that since it's possible to prosecute the innocent, we should not prosecute anyone. Thankfully, the courts did not buy that argument.

This time the Supreme Court upheld the CIPA (and filtering the Internet, even for adults, was later upheld in a May 2010, 6–3 decision by the Washington Supreme Court).[10] Even so, the matter of social networking sites remained unresolved. Like Talmudic scholars, some argued that because social networking sites were not specially named, they were thereby exempt, much as they had been in the CDA and the COPA. At least two groups thought so. As late as 2008, the International Society for Technology and Education (ISTE) and Consortium for School Networking (CoSN) urged Congress to update the CIPA to include both social networking sites and chat rooms and what constitutes appropriate behavior on them.[11] By adding these, the groups argued, young people would be better served through education and not by filtering software alone.

The CIPA remains in effect today, however, and applies to any e-rated funded computers in schools and libraries. But are social networking sites covered? The debate continues, and no one knows for certain. Might the Deleting Online Predators Act (2006) be the right place to look for answers?

The Pis Aller: *Deleting Online Predators Act*

The Deleting Online Predators Act (2006) protected minors against "harmful materials" *and* specifically targeted social networking sites by naming them directly, clearing up any ambiguity in previous bills. Representative Mike Fitzpatrick (R–PA) brought the bill (H.R. 5319) before

Congress as an amendment to the Communications Act of 1934. The bill attempted to answer the question about social networking sites and chat rooms by singling them out specifically. Thus, schools receiving the benefits of E-Rate funds for computer hardware would have to protect minors from sexual predators while those minors used "commercial social networking sites" as well as "chat rooms" when their parents or guardians were absent.[12] In an effort to calm the naysayers about filtering software, the bill stipulates that filtering safeguards should be disabled when minors are under adult supervision or when the display of social networking sites is done for educational purposes.

In the face of severe criticism by Reps. Edward Markey (D–MA) and Bart Stupak (D–MI), the DOPA passed the House anyway (410–15; 7 did not cast votes), and it went on to the Senate, where it was referred to the Senate Commerce, Science and Transportation Committee. It languished there for the remainder of the year. The following year (2007), the bill, under the supervision of Senator Ted Stevens (R–AK) and Rep. Mark Kirk (R–IL), was referred to the House Committee on Energy and Commerce, where once again it died. That same year, state bills providing DOPA-type protection surfaced in Oklahoma, Illinois, Georgia, and North Carolina. The Illinois Social Networking Prohibition Act, for example, effectively does the same thing for Illinois that the federal bill would have mandated for the country. The DOPA died in committee, but school officials, having learned from their past mistakes of relying on Congress to act, took matters into their own hands.

Since Congress could not settle on a bill to the liking of the ACLU, the ALA, and other First Amendment absolutists, school officials did. Although most schools allow for broad Internet access, it is limited to academic content. And who can blame them? It is easier to tell parents that their son or daughter needs to look up material at home on their own computers about some topic, rather than explain to those parents why their fifth-grader is asking them about fellatio he saw while doing research on the web. In the end, however, all of this may be moot since the Court recently allowed commercial providers to restrict Internet access in what have been termed "net neutrality" cases.[13] (More about net neutrality appears in chapter eleven.)

State Legislatures to the Rescue?

Where school officials might deny access to chat rooms and social networking sites on the one hand, they are not at all bashful about using them freely to check up on students in their care who may be using them, even out of school. For example, schools in Massachusetts used social networking sites to catch and punish athletes for breaking team rules when pictures of these students drinking alcohol or taking drugs appeared in photos or videos on MySpace, YouTube, Facebook, or other social media.[14] Apart from the right to privacy this immediately raises, it also raises more serious legal issues. In a related case, a popular Tennessee basketball star, ready to make it big in college and subsequently in the pros, Taylor Cummings, found himself out of school for a Facebook posting.[15] Cummings, angry with his coaches, jumped onto Facebook one afternoon after school and blasted them in a foolish and grammar-delinquent manner: "I'ma kill em all. I'ma bust [expletive deleted] up from the inside like nobody's ever done before."

Cummings said he was joking, just letting off steam, and in a non-digital world, he might have been able to get away with it. But in a digital world couched in a zero-tolerance setting for violent expressions, Cummings's basketball career ended before it began.[16] Attorneys who work on civil rights and education cases said it raises legal questions because online materials can be tampered with (e.g., photoshopped). If schools punish students based upon social media evidence alone, the legal standing would be weak, given the ease with which the social networking sites can be manipulated.

As mentioned above, states have aided schools who want some legal means of controlling which social networks student may view while at school. About a dozen states now have laws that control access to social networking sites. School officials regularly restrict access to sites they believe contain materials harmful to children, are disruptive to the educational process, or interfere in some way with the education of those children (e.g., gaming sites). School officials believe they have this power *in loco parentis*, to act as parents or guardians when students' parents or guardians are not present.

Is the reaction of school officials to social networking sites correct, or is it more adult hysteria? Certainly some, like danah boyd, think it hysteria.[17] But not everyone is in agreement. Sites like Ask.fm, Kik, Snapchat or Poke may appear innocent enough until one pulls back the covers, so to speak.[18] Ask.fm is a site in which young people can pose questions about themselves and receive, typically, anonymous but horrific answers. The site is made up of those under 17, 42 percent of which make up some of the 120 million registered users worldwide and the more than 15 million in the United States. Ask.fm is a site created by two brothers from Latvia, Ilya and Mark Terebin, that allows users to ask any question they want anonymously in order to get the most honest answer possible.[19] According to recent news reports, Ask.fm has been a factor in at least 16 adolescent suicides since 2012. The site is a vehicle for the harassment, bullying, and the intrusions that occur on a wide and never-ending scale.[20]

The average age of those on Kik, a teen-friendly site, is 42, according to law enforcement. Sexting, based on a study done in the UK, has no easy answers, and the panic-laden stories in the media often get it wrong. But sexting does happen, and often to young girls (as opposed to older politicians). Finding a way out of a relationship that begins with sexting is not easy, and as many as 15 to 40 percent of teens may be involved in some form of it.[21] And sexting is not always a predatory male exploiting an underage female. Teens are often their own worst enemies. A Canadian teen, sixteen at the time of the offense, sent naked pictures of her boyfriend's ex-girlfriend with the idea of intimidating and humiliating her. The court convicted her of trafficking in child pornography, but the verdict will be challenged.[22]

Earlier, mention was made of Imbee, a site specifically designed for young people ages 8 to 14. The site held great promise, and Education Week, a respected education information site, covered its rollout in 2006.[23] But things did not go as planned. In 2008, only two years after its rollout, Imbee settled a $130,000 fine from the FTC for violation of the COPPA (see above). After promoting the site as a safe haven, "free secure, social networking and blogging destination" claiming to ask for parents' credit cards before allowing students to sign on, it allowed more than 10,000 children to create accounts with only their first and last names, dates of birth, personal e-mails, parents' emails, gender, usernames, and passwords before ever alerting the parents. These children could create blogs, post pictures, and connect with others. While parents were sent emails asking them to confirm the signups, if the parents did not respond, their children's registrations still remained active.[24]

The story is illustrative. Imbee.com surely meant no harm, but it did not abide by its original promise. Even companies claiming to provide a safe haven on a social networking site may, in their zeal, overstep the bounds of responsibility. This makes it only more difficult for school administrators to simply allow free and unfettered access to social networking sites for young people over whom they must act *in loco parentis*. Two sites that are COPPA-compliant, however, are KidzVuz and Bibliona-sium.[25]

Let the Sun Shine In, and the Floodgates Open?

The number of Facebook users alone now exceeds 1.2 billion active users monthly. The number astonishes by its Brobdingnagian size. With no certain way to tell who these users are or what their intent is, opening up schools to this vast number (containing as it surely does numerous pedophiles), leaves school officials little choice if they are to remain responsible.[26] It would be unfair to expect school administrators to police students' use of social networking sites in order to prevent any mishaps. It isn't how many pedophiles lurk on these sites, but the risk that one child could be the victim of any one of them.

Consider, for example, the two Tucson men arrested in February and June of 2014. Roy Combs was arrested for luring minors on a social networking site for the purposes of sexual activity.[27] Combs went to meet what he thought was a juvenile with whom he had been communicating online and to whom he had made it clear their meeting was for sexual congress. He was arrested by U.S. Marshals. Later that same year, the Tucson Police Department arrested Steven L. Cathcart, 33, for trying to lure a young female for the purposes of sex, but it turned out he was online with a police agent. During his interrogation, he admitted to having sexual contact with a minor on several other occasions in 2011.[28] Finally, there is Jeremy Brendan, a 23-year-old man in Santa Barbara, California, who used social networking sites to "trick and extort" more than a dozen young girls and boys into sending him naked pictures and videos of themselves. Brendan would solicit the pictures after finding the young teens on Facebook sites of music stars popular with teens. In one case, he got explicit pictures from one young girl (after luring them in, he would often threaten the young teens with telling their parents) and then posted them to her own Facebook page.[29]

These three quite randomly found stories point to the problem facing school administrators when it comes to debates about an open web, or open access, and why the web can never be truly open in K–12 schools. Predators are on social networking sites and looking for the unwary minor, a young girl in most cases who does not feel good about herself, does not have anyone in her life to encourage her, or perhaps does and is simply going through one of those stages of adolescence so typical of teens. Once they have found a victim, these predators strike, and if they are successful, lives may be lost or ruined forever. Most web proponents will downplay such stories, will argue that there are simply not that many and, oh, by the way, the police are using social networking to catch many of them, so it is a non-issue. But this, the paucity argument, only works if it is not your child or if you are not involved.

Social Media That Harms or Encourages Harmful Behavior

Pedophiles lurking on social networking sites or teens sexting one another are only two of the many problems that school administrators must be wary of. Administrators must also be wary of sites that perhaps encourage or do not discourage negative or unhealthy behavior. So called "pro-ana" or "thinspiration" sites that promote anorexia give tips, provide support, and encourage those already suffering from poor self-esteem with practices that can only be described as harmful in the extreme. Young women especially are drawn into these sites that offer advice, such as avoiding all white foods, drinking glasses of water incessantly and especially before meals, cutting food into many small bites, and "snacking" on ice.[30] Self-injury sites, or "cutting" sites, provide information that proves dangerous to young people who see self-injury as a way of relieving emotion pain.

If we are willing to look long enough, we can find that social networking influences teens in good and bad ways, leading to more sex, less sex, more boozing, less boozing. This is another way of saying that the relationship with teens is not easy to tease out with everything else going on in their lives, and the influence of anything, including social media, often depends upon the individual teen. On the other hand, social media undoubtedly present to some teens harmful ideas and constructs they would not have stumbled upon without it.

Given how social media are constructed to reel in the maximum exposure for minimum privacy, social networking sites are not going to find many principals willing to open up the floodgates and hope for the best. Perhaps technology will enable more web freedom in the future, but that future is not foreseeable.

Teachers and Social Media

Teachers connecting to students on social media also pose a problem. Some teachers' unions have even gone to court over the use of social media. When Missouri passed a law in 2011 limiting the use of social networking for teachers and students, the Missouri teachers' union went to court.[31] In New Hampshire in April 2014, a substitute, told to unfriend the 200 Facebook friends who were also current students, refused. The school system said they would not use her as a substitute again.[32] The knee-jerk reaction is to scream for First Amendment rights and to cry out for justice. But things are never as simplistic as we make them. In the New Hampshire case, a 29-year-old teacher at the same school had just been arrested for sexually assaulting a 14-year-old girl he communicated with through text messages. How can administrators run the risk?

But even blocking sites is no solution for schools. An email message sent from a school system near me reminded teachers that when they use universal hashtags on Twitter as a way of following conversations on certain topics, they are also inviting others to follow *all* the conversations about that topic, including those that are lewd and inappropriate. While school administrators cannot shut down access to Twitter or the Internet, they have to be strict in outlining what can and cannot be done in order to protect the school system and, most of all, the young children.[33]

Is there any hope of expanding social networks in schools officially?[34] Never say never. But given the wide-open approach to social networks, their lack of privacy, their inability to control what is said and by whom, and widespread abuse by pedophiles, bullies, and others that make its use guarded, to say the least, broad unrestricted expansion of it as an official tool in K–12 schools appears unlikely. Even with strict social media use guides, or guides for parents to use with school-age children issued by school districts, social media use without strict boundaries appears less and less a possibility. Too much can go wrong, and too much can go wrong even accounting for all its possible positive benefits (and there are many). School administrators have enough to worry about without adding to their woes with an unfettered Internet and no-holds barred social media expansion.

This is not to imply that schools will not increase the use of technology tools like iPads. But one wonders about this use in an age where dollars are scarce and resources more scarce still. Many superintendents jump on iPads as if they are the solution for every child's lack of progress. After a school district shells out tens of thousands of dollars, they discover these iPads are not used much by teachers because they must be locked down for security purposes. The use the iPads do get is limited to gaming, and not much used by teens (unless to hack the firewalls or resell them at a profit).[35] It may be possible at some future date to control social networking sites in limited environments, making their use in the educational process freer and without today's current drawbacks. But until that time comes, schools will continue their approach in a wary and conservative manner. Social media as they are currently configured leave schools with little choice but to limit their access.

FOUR

#We'reAllAdultsNow# CollegeRulz#StudyingSucks!

"Can someone post the answers to the Art History quiz, like ASAP!"

Reasonable people will accept that *some* precautions are necessary with social networks when children are involved, so long as those children remain in elementary, middle, or even high school. With the possible exception of the American Civil Liberties Union or the American Library Association, rational people understand that young people with still developing minds and unsettled hormones need strong guidance while making their way in the world, especially in a cyberworld full of possible missteps. School administrators have to exercise their role when parents are *in absentia.*

This is not the case when those children become legal adults, and that's the age of most of the young people we find in college. Colleges and universities have embraced social networking in a variety of ways, not just by making access available to those who have matriculated, but also via their admissions and news reporting features. Rare is the college or university that does not have dozens of Facebook pages associated with its athletic programs, clubs, organizations, and even various disciplines. For the most part, colleges and universities have used social media effectively and well.

Professors and Social Media

Even professors are slowly beginning to ease into social media as if easing into a cold pool, one toe at a time. For at least the first decade of social networking, many professors resisted the urge. Some were so dead-set against it they banned it in the classroom or penalized those caught posting to a social network while in class. But as the popularity grew, even professors came to understand that, like publish or perish, they had better post or tweet, or their careers might perish.

According to a 2013 Babson Pearson report, still less than half of all professors (41 percent) are using social media in the classroom. But that is up from almost 34 percent the previous year. According to the 2013 *Annual Survey of Social Media Use by Higher Education,* almost 60 percent of faculty agree that mobile technologies and the interactive nature of social media do offer the potential for a better learning environment. But 60 percent isn't a ringing endorsement. If that sounds a bit contradictory, it's not. Almost the same percentage of faculty, 56 percent, agree that social networking and mobile technologies are *more* distracting than they are helpful to student work. About 80 percent of faculty believe that mobile technologies have increased student-faculty communication, for better or for worse, some would add. Twitter has the least amount of classroom use, less than 20 percent, while blogs the most, coming in at almost 30 percent in 2013. Podcasts are a close second in use, with LinkedIn and Facebook at about the same as they were in 2012, just under 20 percent.

Faculty are most concerned about the integrity of online submissions and secondly about privacy. They rightly fear for the privacy of their students, but even more, they fear for the privacy of the classroom itself. In their view, those not registered for the class should not be allowed to participate and should not even be able to view classroom discussions. All of these issues are being worked on to some degree by social networking sites, but as they do not offer much value-added result to social media, they are likely not to be a high priority for any individual site. For example, online submissions could be verified with some sort of voice recognition technology or even a fingerprinting service. If online educational companies have either of these in the works, they are not yet discussing it in public. For companies like Turnitin (an online submission site for papers) and Blackboard (an online, interactive site for online and hybrid courses) one would think these would be high on the agenda, but so far there is little conversation about it.[1]

Faculty are, however, using social media personally and professionally. Where the usage drops is in actual teaching. About 75 percent of faculty use social media personally, but of those same faculty, just over 40 percent use it in the classroom or connect it in some way with their teaching. This trend is likely to change dramatically as younger faculty are hired. Already there are a number of faculty who use social media extensively, both professionally and in teaching. Some have even made the top fifty social media savvy list.[2] Such lists change frequently, and the criteria by which they are measured are hard to ascertain. Perhaps the best take-away is that many professors are not only making social media important in classroom teaching, but also using the platforms in very exciting and innovative ways. What would make such lists far more helpful would be some assessment of their success: what their students are actually learning and how that compares with traditional methods.

Social Media in the Classroom

In the college where I work, several faculty are doing just that. A course that one might not think would lend itself well to social media—chemistry—has had strong successes in student learning outcomes, as well as remaining popular to students. While social media are only one part of this outreach, the sum of the parts taken together makes for a robust online learning experience. In our college of education, students are not only exposed to new technologies, but they are using them and discovering both the merits and defects, the power and the limitations of these technologies. Granted, I do work here, but even comparing us with other, much larger institutions, we appear to be making some very novel in-roads to social media in the classroom.

My own experience had less than celestial results, however. In 2009, I taught a class required of all students, our human experience course. The class is designed around readings that are meant to challenge students to think and read critically, as well as to write persuasively. Soon after the Kindle DX appeared on the market, I purchased twenty of them for the students I taught and encouraged them to use them exclusively. While the technology was still maturing and web access proved difficult at best, I still urged them to use that technology as exclusively as possible. I also required them to contribute to a blog, and I posted short-answer questions via Twitter for them to respond to. I used the blog and the Twitter responses to help assess student participation, but I also drew from comments and tweets that extended classroom discussions. My thought was that even students less willing to contribute in class might find the less public and near-anonymous nature of tweeting more to their liking. While all tweets were visible to all who participated (access was by password), the class was small, eventually ending up with about eighteen participants. I hoped, too, that for the less extroverted, social media might provide a vehicle for getting these students "talking" and possibly extend their interest in the classroom. They could get their feet wet online, I reasoned, and then swim out with confidence in the larger classroom pool.

By the second week, students, most of them, were petitioning me to be able to buy the printed textbook. I made them wait one more week to be sure they were at least giving it the old college try. Facebook postings were astonishing only in their paucity of words and shallowness. I had hoped the page would allow for freewheeling discussion, but it did not, no matter how provocative I tried to be. Twitter responses, because they were shorter, remained at least more visible but only until the fourth week. By the fifth week, only two foreign students were communicating that way regularly. Offering extra credit to join either of the online conversations did nothing to increase the number of student participants. Ironically, the two most active students were two students from France. They also turned out to be two of the three most engaged students in the class.

Obviously with a research set of one, not much can be extrapolated, but some generalizations are possible. Clearly 2009 proved premature for the technology. My own ineptitude had something to do with the lack of success of all but two students. Still, granting my own ineptitude (which I do), students in 2009 simply were not interested in learning via a medium they typically play on or entertain themselves with. Yes, social networking is engaging and it does engage students mentally, but does it engage them beyond the rather short attention span of novelty? It is a subject that we will return to at the end of this chapter.

Does Social Media Hurt or Help Grades?

It should come as no surprise that there are claims that show college students who are deeply engaged with social media have lower grades. It should also not surprise that claims are being made that students who use them can actually get better grades. And finally, there are studies that show that there is *no* correlation between the use of social media and grades at all.[3] Too many of these claims are mere correlations and nothing definitely has been shown, and perhaps this cannot be shown. Some common sense, however, must intrude here.

Students who spend hours a day on social media with mainly friends may well see a decline in their grades, much like watching too much television, going out too much, or, in short, simply not studying enough, a key ingredient in the failure of many students. But the problem with social media, and with it mobile technologies, means that colleges and universities must, in order to get the attention of the students they serve, connect with them through the media in which they have put much of their energies.

It is an understatement to say that research regarding social media and grades is unclear and that it may not hold true for frequent cell phone use. College students in specific and young people in general use mobile technologies to stay in touch with family, friends, significant others, and, of course, social media. A Kent State University study showed that this constant texting, updating, and calling leads to heightened levels of anxiety, unhappiness, and lower grades.[4] The research involved more than 500 university students. Daily cell phone usage was recorded and clinical measures of anxiety assessed. The students also allowed researchers access to their university records for their GPAs. The 500 students were equally distributed across all classes—freshmen, sophomores, juniors, and seniors. The study showed strong correlations with high anxiety, frequent cell phone usage, and lower GPAs. More study is required, of course, but these tentative results do provide some insight into college students' cell phone usage. Teasing out the difference with social technologies, accessed through cell phones and grades, is harder and perhaps one reason why their connection to grades is less clear.

It is safe to argue that social media and college students are going to be connected, if not at the hip, then at the ear for the foreseeable future. There are many advantages to this connectivity, too.[5] Social networks allow college students to connect not only with their friends but also with their parents, a point that baffles many of us who were in college in the late sixties and early seventies. This hyper-connectivity *can* lead to expanded collaboration. A college student struggling with calculus can easily find another student, perhaps one not even attending the same university, who can lend a hand. Likewise with any other subject. Social media networks also involve learning outside the classroom, and in that less than stressful place, students may be able to grasp what the traditional classroom setting does not allow.

Social media networks may also help students become more innovative, more willing to try something outside their comfort zones, especially when they are connecting with those who have done this successfully. For the very shy and retiring student, they can open up a new world and provide him or her with the necessary social footing to come out of his or her shell.

But clearly, social media platforms have their drawbacks even in the university setting. Because they are ubiquitous with the advent of mobile technologies, they provide an escape that may interfere with everything else. We have all read stories of young people walking into signs or even falling into uncovered manholes.[6] And, saddest of all, we have even read stories of those engaged with social media getting critically hurt, even fatally, texting while driving.

Shirley Turkle and Robert Putnam have both written eloquently and wisely on the power of social networking, and Internet use in general, to make us less social.[7] There can be no denying this. We tend to like the idea that we can "shoot" a text to friends more easily than we can call or see them in person. And while it is true, it is only easier because personal engagement requires all of our faculties and not just one of them. While social media may make the shy more extroverted, it may well be making the extroverted more introverted. Too much of even a good thing can be bad for us in the long run. We may all have thousands of Facebook friends but not one real friend on whom we can call when we are facing very difficult times. Yes, there are many stories of individuals who have repaired to social media as they struggled with severe illnesses. But there are an equal number of stories of those who, because they felt so alone in the midst of so many "friends," ended up in deep depression and also with suicidal thoughts.

Because college students use social media so exclusively, some claim informal use has degraded their already weak communication skills.[8] Their formal writing in papers, some claim, now includes inappropriate abbreviations and poor spelling, or simply truncated spelling, again inappropriate for formal papers. At my own college, colleagues complain routinely how often their students email or text them with "netiquette" that can only be described as disrespectful effrontery. More than one colleague has complained that students begin messages with "Hey Dude!" whether they are addressing a male or female professor.

Scorched Tweet Policy

Perhaps worse than this is the contribution social media communication has made to the degradation of civil discourse. It does not take long for an email communication or tweet to unleash an avalanche of discourteous and uncivil replies. Is this solely because it is so easy to reply on social media without thinking through what is being said? Perhaps. But it happens often enough to make social media a drawback. It can begin between a professor and a student, between two students, or after a decision has been made by a department, administrator, or the university president.[9] Because of the hyper-connectivity of social media (some might call it hyper-democratization), some college students are bewildered why decisions made at one level are not first run by them. Pretty soon there are complaints that escalate into piques and more. Before long, what precipitated the conversation is long forgotten, but feelings are hurt, individuals have been insulted, and the repair work, which must begin, commences under the worst possible conditions for success.

Although we will treat this issue in a separate chapter, it should be pointed out here, too, that social media expose college students to unwanted intrusions. Moreover, according to a study conducted by an Australian researcher, students expect to have social media privacy but also have the university step in when other students become aggressive or uncivil on social media.[10] In a sense, they want it both ways, something that universities are hard-pressed to give. Universities can do everything possible to teach responsible social media use, but inevitably there will be students who will ignore that teaching. If universities are not vigilant, they could find themselves on the wrong side of a serious legal problem.

Your Posts Are Our Data

Take, for example, Facebook's recent foray into a study of users' behaviors.[11] Without asking those users, Facebook tinkered with about 700,000 users' news feeds as part of a psychological experiment conducted in 2012. What should have come as no surprise is that Facebook, notorious for saying it's sorry for violating users' privacy, manipulated those users without their permission. That anyone should be surprised by this is the bigger shock than that Facebook used users' data to its own advantage. The study that provides the "shocking" finding that happier users post happier feeds, sadder users, sad ones, and that these messages can result in "emotional contagion" blew into a firestorm.

The fireworks had little to do with the findings and more to do with the fact that the study was conducted by academic researchers (at Cornell and the University of California-San Francisco) but without the standard "informed consent" of those being tested, either by Cornell's ethics board or Facebook's nonexistent "implied" user consent. Facebook has issued its standard Saturday Night Live "Emily Litella" apology: "never mind."[12] The trouble is not that such studies are being done, of course, but that they are being done in such a way to make certain no future one can be conducted without hovering under a miasma of suspicion and intrusion.

Colleges and universities are somewhat complicit in these sorts of things because they make social media accessible to students, and regardless of the myriad handouts on social media responsibility, nothing will cover this multitude of sins once they are committed. Is there a solution that allows free and unfettered access on the Information Superhighway without the attendant potholes of looming disaster? Some think so, provided there are clear guidelines on what can be done, what is prohibited, and requiring students to sign off on those guidelines.[13] So, in other words, not really.

Cyber-Snooping Made Easy

One reason there is not any easy solution is because colleges and universities are using social networking sites for a variety of reasons themselves. For example, colleges and universities use social media to check up on their scholarship students. Admissions officers routinely check the public social networking sites of high school seniors who apply for scholarships and other awards.[14] Once cyber-snooping begins, it may never end.

Meanwhile, college-bound students may think their applications and recommendations are the only content for deliberations by college and university admissions' officers, but that is hardly the case. Students are now screened for their worthiness not only for what they placed in their application files, what their recommendations say, and what is contained in the application essays, but also for what they posted to Facebook or *allowed* their friends to post on their news feeds. Moreover, what others post about them on their Argus-eyed information gatherer—"hey dude, you were really wasted last night"—provides lamentable reviewing data for the screening process.

Colleges and universities use Facebook and other social media pages to vet potential scholarship candidates, according to Jeff Olson of Kaplan Test Prep and Admissions.[15] A 2008 Kaplan Test Prep and Admission's study reveals nearly 40 percent of checked sites had a negative impact on admissions evaluations. By 2012, the Kaplan survey of admissions had not changed much; the net just widened: 26 percent of admission counselors checked Facebook pages, and 27 percent Googled applicants. The applicant online image made a huge difference, and in 35 percent of the looked-up cases, the difference was negative, up from only 12 percent in 2011.[16] While there is a slight trend away from these sorts of "background checks," they still occur. Given that colleges and universities are having to account more and more for what their employees *and* their students are doing online, it's a safe bet that the cyber-snooping may well increase in coming years.

Is this fair? From a legal standpoint, it is. Information found on social media is considered "public knowledge," and these pages act like billboards taken out in every city when a would-be student applies for college. Whether or not it is ethical is another matter, but then those seeking favorable outcomes to things as important as scholarships should not be so quick to wash their dirty laundry—common though it may be—in public. What trips up today's college-bound student is her belief that these pages are "who she is" and should be disclosed for all the world to see *and to accept*. Right or wrong, the world is not quite there yet, and that belief has sunk more than one student who began as scholarship material but ended up with nothing.

As mentioned earlier, once on campus, of course, the screening doesn't end. Some universities now routinely use social networking sites as "surveillance" for solving crimes, running down leads, and otherwise checking up on the rowdy behaviors of some students.[17] After a night of heavy drinking in 2006, a student at the University of Illinois at Urbana-Champaign was urinating in a bush when police spotted him. He ran off, but his friend, whom he left behind, was questioned by police. The friend denied any knowledge of the act and even knowing the student in question. After officers checked their Facebook pages, they found both parties and their connection to one another, even down to the time of the incident. Both students were ticketed. The officers claimed the information was on a public site and so open for public viewing. Indeed, much of it had been posted by the students themselves.

"Killer" Tweets: No Laughing Matter

Sites are also being used to determine whether a degree should even be granted. The United States District Court for the Eastern District of Pennsylvania handed down an illustrative decision on December 3, 2008.[18] Teacher-in-training Stacy Snyder posted to her MySpace page pictures of a party where she had obviously consumed too much alcohol. Further, she posted negative comments about her supervisor. When administrators discovered the page, they denied her degree. Snyder sued. The court held that that the university had every right not to award the degree. Snyder had been fully warned about using her personal webpage in any manner regarding her student teaching. Because Snyder violated all stated prohibitions by the university, the court upheld the university's decision.[19] Amanda Tatro faced a similar problem when she posted to her Facebook page a timeline of her angry breakup with her boyfriend. The story is told in full in chapter ten.

Dr. Dryasdust Pontificates Poorly

Students are not the only ones getting into trouble on social media. Professors often find themselves in the same leaking social media boat. These same professors often make similar mistakes as their students. Almost no professor gives any credence to www.ratemyprofessors.com, unless those ratings are stellar. Students repair to this and other similar sites, and occasionally they will rate a professor highly, often, however, for the wrong things, as for example giving them "hot chili" ratings, referring to their sex appeal. This can be insulting, but all too often, students go to these sites and vent their spleens, either for a grade, for a boring class, or for revenge. Professors would do well to ignore them. Sometimes they do not and will post videos ranting back at the ranter.[20] This brings to mind the wisdom of Proverbs 26:4: Do not answer a fool according to his folly.

But professional blindness doesn't end there, unfortunately. In 2013, tenured University of Kansas professor of journalism David W. Guth responded on his Twitter account to the Navy Yard shootings, "#NavyYardShooting The blood is on the hands of the #NRA. Next time let it be YOUR sons and daughters. Shame on you. May God damn you."[21] Politicians called for his firing, but eventually his suspension was lifted. The Kansas Board of Regents, however, responded later with a new social media policy that allows the public universities and colleges to fire tenured and untenured employees for "improper use" of social media. Critics see this as a "chilling" effect on First Amendment rights, but proponents see it as regulating the speech of employees, something every other company has the right to do.[22]

The problem is never so black and white as it may seem. Public universities rely heavily on donations from the public. When behavior by employees threatens those funds, universities have a choice to risk everything for one professor, or to protect them all by regulating what can be said when those professors speak *ex cathedra*. Professors often have a hard time understanding that their public personas are almost impossible to disentangle from their employment. Furthermore, most professors, without that employment, would likely be ignored. But it does create a tension between the rights of professors to express their opinions, and the right of the university to be able to conduct business successfully. The controversial research of some professors has always stressed this tension when professors choose to conduct research that some in the general public will find offensive, as, for example, the study of pornography, or the study of the employment of sex workers. But the ubiquity of social media allows controversial statements to get a very wide public airing, instantaneously drawing unwanted attention to the university. The tension is made all the more strained because university professors as a group remain much to the left ideologically of the general public. Resolving the leftward tilt of professors and the ubiquity of social media will be a problem for colleges and universities for some time to come.

The case of Steven Salaita is a prime example. Salaita is a professor who took to Twitter to argue his case against Israel.[23] His book, *Israel's*

Dead Soul, is highly controversial, but so are a lot of books by academics. In this case, Salaita's tweets about Israel (and even earlier about the NRA) became increasingly outrageous and pointed. Some likened them to what a white supremacist would say about blacks. His appointment to the University of Illinois at Urbana-Champaign seemed a sure bet. But his tweets came back to tweak him, and the appointment was denied. The hue and cry on both sides of this debate have been loud and anguished, and this is not the place to argue one side or the other. The case is illustrative on two counts. First, public intellectuals have a right to say whatever they please in social media. Second, so also do institutions have a right to accept or reject what those public intellectuals choose to say. Many in academe, however, accept the first premise but reject the latter. In the age of social media, that is no longer possible given social media's reach, even to the most remote corners of the globe.

While a visiting NYU professor on leave from the University of New Mexico, Geoffrey F. Miller, an associate professor of evolutionary psychology, took to Twitter to express his opinion about obese people. "Dear obese PhD applicants: if you didn't have the willpower to stop eating carbs, you won't have the willpower to do a dissertation. #truth."[24] The comment was deleted quickly, but only after a torrent of criticisms followed. Why the professor felt compelled to let the world know his views on this subject remains a mystery. After the firestorm settled slightly, he added, "My sincere apologies to all for that idiotic, impulsive and badly judged tweet. It does not reflect my true views, values or standards." Interestingly, no one claimed First Amendment rights for his indefensible comment. More recently, incoming Boston University professor Saida Grundy's tweets about white men, race and slavery may well end her career before it begins.

Retweeting Isn't Acceptance, or Tenure

If professors misunderstand the nature of cyberspace and its instant publication, they also misunderstand its relative effectiveness. Twitter buzz about academic papers is only that: momentary buzz. It does not mean that citations to that paper will follow.[25] A study conducted on scientific papers concluded that the most cited by social media do not translate into top academic papers by way of citations. There is, in other words, little correlation between social media and academic success as measured by academics, at least as far as papers in science go. Researcher Stefanie Haustein of the University of Montreal writes, "Twitter citations do not reflect traditional research impact."[26] But the research was conducted in 2011, and already early results in more recent years do have some impact.

It isn't clear whether "Twitter buzz" will surpass alternative metrics (altmetrics) that measure more than just social media (they include downloads and inclusion in online databases), but for now, altmetrics provide a better gauge.

This is important for academics who often use such information for tenure and promotion. In fact, some professors are known to cite even Rate My Professors for tenure and promotion because these provide a so-called "third party" verification, as well as a more genuine assessment than evaluations that are generally given the last day of class by a professor or her proxy. Some students believe these evaluations may be monitored or may otherwise come back to haunt them, and so the evaluations may lean more to the positive side of the ledger. In any event, the altmetric evaluations appear better for now since the other kinds of evaluations are subject to inherent biases.

Social Media Enhances or Distracts?

This may well be why many professors see social networking sites as distractions, especially one like Twitter, where the limitations are so severe as to beg error.[27] According to researchers who have examined the data, "[S]tudents who use their mobile phones during class lectures tend to write down less information, recall less information, and perform worse on multiple-choice tests than those students who abstain from using their mobile phones during class."[28] The evidence that any individual social networking sites help or hinder academic performance is cloudy. What isn't murky, however, is that the use of them *during* class is a clear distraction, both to the student using them and to those around him or her. Unfortunately there does not appear to be any one best way of dealing with these. Best practices for dealing with accessing mobile technologies while in class range from restricting them altogether to allowing them for certain kinds of classroom experiences. None of these approaches work well because today's students are so wedded to their handheld connections that separating them from these devices even for a few minutes often is a game not worth the candle. All of this appears as so much common sense. We know that no matter how many of us think we can multitask, very few of us really can.[29] We end up doing each of those tasks less well than we would if we concentrated on each of them individually.

Some professors have even resorted to posing as students in online environments just to start discussion, to cyber-spy on students to see whether or not they are doing their own work, or to help move the class along.[30] This has raised some serious ethical questions. If this took place in another context, it might be seen as "sandbagging the client," but in the online context it merely raises hackles in some, ethical questions for others.

But in point of fact, each of these cases for students and faculty poses mild to serious legal issues. One issue raised through this chapter (and to be treated later) is privacy. Student and faculty privacy is put at risk when social media are involved. Merely gaining access to social media exposes one's identity in significant ways. Furthermore, once there, the exposure to other matters is hardly anything to be dismissive about. It can be as mild as stupid rants by others, or as significant as libelous statements, pornography, and more. As we have seen above, neither students nor faculty are immune to these possibilities. We do not now know what the exposure is for an institution, beyond embarrassment, when a faculty member repairs to Twitter or Facebook to rant about a policy or simply to speak his or her mind, but in a less guarded way than he might if doing it in person or more formally. Attorneys are still trying to ferret out whether the use of social media by campus police is legal, not to mention ethical; and no one knows for certain what level of admissions activity on social media is ethical as a tool for determining scholarships. The legal questions loom large.

Cybertheft and Cyber-Cheating

Of less legal concern, but of a significant ethical concern, is how much online cyber-cheating among students continues. In one 2011 study, almost 62 percent of students admitted to cyber-cheating, or using the Internet to get higher grades. Cyber-cheating by definition involves any form of cheating that can take place using the Internet, including submitting paper-mill papers for class. But some of this cheating involves social media and sharing answers, even while taking tests.[31] For many students, it simply isn't cheating when "everyone else is doing it" and not doing it means your grade suffers. While this argument has always been the one that many wrongdoers repair to first, in the case of something as ubiquitous as the Internet, and as easy to access, it may have at least a small toe in the door of this debate.

Like everything else on the web, it has its excesses. Roy Sun, a student at Purdue, appeared to be making straight A's. The only trouble was he never went to class. Instead, he was hacking into professors' gradebooks and changing his grades. It landed him in an Indiana courtroom, where he received a three-month jail sentence.[32] But Sun is part of an ever-growing number of students who would rather hack than study.

While faculty worry about students and academic cyber-cheating of any kind, professors are falling victim to it as well. Most of it occurs in the form of plagiarism—presidents "adopting" entire addresses from others, faculty falsifying research, and professors "borrowing" without attribution from what they think are arcane resources. University faculty and administrators are not only the victims of cybertheft of lines or works or phrases from blogs, tweets, and other social media pages, but they also appear to be the perpetrators.

If faculty are posing as students, some students are posing as faculty. A former adjunct at Central Michigan University is suing a student for parodying him on Twitter.[33] The two have squared off, the faculty member complaining that the parody cost him jobs and accounts, the student arguing that the fake Twitter account was just in good fun and did not really harm the adjunct. The case is now in the hands of lawyers.

At the beginning of this chapter, the claim was made that we could agree that young people might have to be protected from social media. As it turns out, so-called adults also have trouble using it successfully if they are not very circumspect each and every time they log on. Sticks and stones may break bones, but words, especially limited to 140 characters, can sink careers before they begin, or even if they are established, get you expelled, land you in court, or leave you wiping egg from your face on a regular basis.

FIVE

#PersonswithDisabilities

"Most of the time, it's the only way I meet other people."

Of all the groups and/or issues treated in this book, none prove as damaging or as embarrassing for some free-thinking social media creators as the differently abled. As a group, the differently abled have been ignored, passed over, or otherwise forgotten when it comes to social media. The variety of social networking sites abounds for persons with disabilities; one minor difficulty remains: accessing them. Without advocates like Ability.net in the UK and advocacy groups in the U.S., there might not be any social media access at all for persons with disabilities. As it is, persons with disabilities must fight for their rights, even though the World Wide Web Consortium (W3C) sought from the beginning to make the World Wide Web accessible for all. Even with that support, with the Americans with Disabilities Act (ADA), and with Section 508 (originally the Federal Electronic and Information Technology Accessibility and Compliance Act that became the new Section 508 of the Rehabilitation Act of 1973), convenient and reliable access to social media remains more than a minor challenge. In some cases it proves downright daunting.

To the credit of social media and their creators, the need to make these sites more accessible to the differently abled has not fallen on deaf ears. And it's a good thing. According to the world report on disabilities from WHO/World Bank, estimates of the handicapped now top more than one billion worldwide, or about 15 percent of the 7 billion now residing on the planet.[1] Between 2 and 4 percent are severely disabled. Not surprisingly, many of these individuals (about 20 percent) are living in developing countries, which makes access not only to services, but also to social media, an ongoing challenge. Providing access to the Internet in general and social media in specific must become a higher priority than it currently is. From the beginning of the World Wide Web, it always has been a goal. Sir Berners-Lee, creator of HTML code that made it possible, wrote:

> As we move towards a highly connected world, it is critical that the Web be usable by anyone, regardless of individual capabilities and disabilities.... The W3C is committed to removing accessibility barriers for all people with disabilities—including the deaf, blind, physically challenged, and cognitively or visually impaired. We plan to work aggressively with government, industry, and community leaders to establish and attain accessibility standards.[2]

It isn't just Berners-Lee, either. It is helpful to recall that the person who launched the idea of a World Wide Web, Vannevar Bush, author of "As We May Think," was Roosevelt's Director of the Office of Scientific Research and Development.[3] Bush mentions "a machine called a Voder" that had been showcased at "a recent World's Fair." Bush recalled that the girl "stroked its keys and it emitted recognizable speech. No human vocal chords entered into the procedure at any point[.]" It cannot be said, of course, that Bush advocated speech-recognition for persons with disabilities that long ago. But he did see its benefits if only for increased efficiency (and possibly for libraries), thus putting it on record for future development.

Common Standards Still Bedevil Social Media

While approved standards have not been made in every case, most social networking sites are more accessible to persons with disabilities than they were only ten years ago. Furthermore, by the time this book reaches publication, more improvements will have been made. Still, more work needs to be done, and we cannot allow our efforts in this regard to lag. While social networking sites can be made more easily accessible with additional tools and by removing certain barriers, they cannot avoid all the potential pitfalls, such as bullying, making light of a person's inability to manage online, or the inherent learning disabilities that may become magnified in an online environment.[4]

Many social networking sites do not exhibit all, or even most, of the elements of universal design.[5] The Center for Universal Design identified seven attributes emblematic of universal design, or a design that would be open to everyone regardless of his or her ability. The site must be equitable by being useful to a large number of people with varying ability and disability; it must be flexible enough to be used in a variety of ways; it must be easy to understand without regard to the users' knowledge, ability or background; it must convey information that is not predicated on the users' sensory ability; it must have a tolerance for error; it must have a low requirement for physical effort; and it must allow for user navigation regardless of his or her own posture, mobility, or confinement. While social networking sites meet part or some of these requirements, it is clear that they are a long way from meeting all. As more and more content comes from users, the ability of sites to meet these high standards has diminished over time.

The Web Accessibility Initiative (WAI) of W3C has done much to make universal design standard in websites. But these are *voluntary* guidelines, conceding the difficulty of making them mandatory and then having to come up with an effective policing mechanism that is nearly impossible. This has not been the case, however, with physical environments that are now part of building codes. While legal standards, such as Section 508 of the Rehabilitation Act and the ADA, oversee the United States government websites and their contractors' compliance, nothing urges commercial websites to comply in a similar manner.[6] California adopted these standards wholesale in 2003, as other states adopted parts of it and parts of the guidelines from the World Wide Web Consortium's (W3C) Web Accessibility Initiative (WAI).[7] In fact, most commercial websites do not. The same can be said for most of social networking sites, as many of them are commercial ventures with advertising platforms. But even with these laws, the decade of growth during the 1990s and early 2000s made it exceedingly difficult for websites to keep up with the goal of universal accessibility. This does not excuse those sites but offers one possible explanation. While these laws and similar ones in the UK, Australia, and other countries remain critical to accessibility for all, the laws must be enforced, and loopholes must be closed. The history has been one of two steps forward, one step back. Rather, let's, as Léonie Watson says in a recent Vimeo, "design like we give a damn!"[8]

Early Accessibility Cases

When America Online (AOL) opened its operations in the early 1980s, it had a captive audience. As it grew and its audience grew with it, it provided access to millions ... of visually able members. Persons with disabilities did not have access, however, to any of its offerings, including many of its bulletin boards open to members. Although discussions began early on with AOL about making its access more impairment-friendly, it was not until the National Federation for the Blind (NFB) brought legal action in 1999 under the ADA that AOL took notice. The NFB dropped the case in 2000, but only after AOL began making changes that made the site more blind-friendly.[9]

When Target settled with the California branch of the National Federation for the Blind in 2006 in a similar case, other websites took notice. Target's website, Target.com, proved inaccessible for persons with visual impairments, claimed the California NFB. Using the ADA as the legal trump card, the California Unruh Civil Rights Act and the California Impaired Persons Act, the California NFB sought civil action. The case ended when Target agreed to an undisclosed settlement and a timetable to make its site more accessible to persons with disabilities.[10]

Such cases are not easy to bring nor easy to win any agreement upon. The Target case did not leave a precedent since it was settled before it went to court. Furthermore, prior case law with respect to business and the ADA refers to physical spaces. Trying to establish a clear precedent in cyberspace—or no space at all—has proved very difficult, though the Kindle case (cited below) did provide a foothold. When Access Now tried to use the ADA against Southwest Airlines for its inaccessible website four years earlier (2002), the judge in the case would not allow a broader definition of accessibility beyond bricks and mortar. "To expand the ADA to cover 'virtual' spaces," he wrote, "would be to create new rights without well-defined standards."[11] Even when the case has a somewhat successful ending, some disability groups want to know why compliance comes only when certain social networking sites are challenged.

Hidden Obstacles

AbilityNet, a national computing and disability charity in the United Kingdom mentioned earlier, has been at the forefront of helping to revolutionize social networking sites and getting them to understand how they fail persons with disabilities when they ignore their concerns. Ability.net was one of the first sites to bring attention to the fact that the five most popular social networking sites at that time (Facebook, MySpace, YouTube, Yahoo, and Bebo) were in violation of the Disability Discrimination Act of 1999 by effectively "locking out" persons with disabilities (in effect, denying them access), the majority of whom were unable physically even to register in order to participate in online communities.[12]

For example, differently abled users can face difficulties typing in responses, making themselves understood verbally, or being able to read the words in a captcha-box, those annoying boxes used to distinguish whether the user is a machine or a human. But it isn't just captcha-boxes either, but dropdown menus, text size and the ability to adjust it, or how it must be adjusted, the layout of the site (most are designed with the visually able in mind) and certain specific preferences that can be set, or not. What appears to the abled as commonplace and easy become major roadblocks for those with mild to severe disabilities. For example, sites with speech tools or background music should be on different tracks, or the assistive technology might not work. Although such obstacles are becoming less frequent on many sites, they still appear, especially in comments portions of many sites, making participation by persons with disabilities very difficult, even when possible. Those suffering from a wide range of disabilities have trouble seeing, reading, or responding to captcha-box requests and so are denied access. Their impairment could be as commonplace as being legally blind (more than 20 million are classified as such nationwide), suffering from a stroke, or as severe as having cerebral palsy, in which both speech and motor skills are compromised and either typing or verbally responding is difficult.[13] In all cases, maneuvering around a social media site can be exceedingly problematic.

Taking Their Business Elsewhere

So problematic has this become in fact that some of the differently abled may have moved from early sites like MySpace to Facebook because the former was so slow in making its site more friendly to persons with disabilities. That isn't to say that Facebook has made all the necessary changes it needs to make. Indeed, it didn't make them without prompting from those who found the site hard to use. With now more than a billion users worldwide, one would think that high on the list for Facebook would be its accessibility for all its users. Facebook CEO Mark Zuckerberg has made it clear that he does, indeed, want this. As recently as July 2014, Zuckerberg was calling for an Internet as accessible as dialing 911.[14] It is a worthy goal, and the billionaire is putting his money where his pen is by targeting poverty, especially in places like Africa. Zuckerberg argued that just as anyone can dial 911 without a phone plan, they should have access to the Internet without having to buy a smartphone with a data plan. But in his editorial for *The Wall Street Journal* he makes no mention of the differently abled who live not only in Africa but also doubtless just around the corner from him, or of any plans to help them find social networking more accessible. Wishing that the Internet "is accessible to all" does not make it so. As he concludes his piece, "Connecting the world is within our reach, and if we work together, we can make this happen."

Social Media a Godsend for Persons with Disabilities

This less than best of all possible social networking worlds is surprising since, for individuals with disabilities, social networks can be a godsend. Research indicates that those suffering from a disability of any type tend to cope far better if involved in a social circle, virtual or otherwise. Paul Carter of Disability Now, himself a quadriplegic, contends that "In many ways, social-networking sites can be a boon for persons with disabilities because they remove some of the barriers faced by those who want to socialize and network."[15] But he is quick to point out that trying to gain access to these sites is anything but easy. The so-called Web 2.0 has helped to eliminate early difficulties, but it has not removed them all. Web designers have not kept it simple, and for many of the differently abled, this poses more than a minor obstacle. Even with speech-activated surfing, getting around a high-feature page will be slow going. If the individual happens to suffer from disabilities that compromise both her physical ability to move a mouse and her verbal ability to be understood, then speech-activated sites will also become barriers.

The legal issues surrounding these sites remain clear. Both the ADA and section 508 of the Federal Rehabilitation Act guarantee access, or so it would seem. The Rehabilitation Act specifically applies itself to U.S. government websites and their access for everyone, regardless of ability. While Section 508 applies only to U.S. government sites and not, for example, to state and local ones, it still is not working consistently for all U.S. government social media sites. Individual websites hosting government information appear to be careful about making them accessible to all. But once these sites launch off into Facebook, Twitter, or other social media sites, the ball is often dropped and persons with disabilities left behind.[16] This is most often the case for the individuals with visual disabilities, those with impaired hearing, or those who suffer from multiple handicaps. Some of these sites contend that there is no real government information on social media sites. That may well be true, but there is discussion on these sites, and often in those discussions users can uncover valuable information. If, however, that valuable information is linked to a non-government site, persons with disabilities may still be locked out.

Young People with Disabilities and Social Media

Young people and social media go hand-in-hand, of course, but what if that young person does not, for example, possess working hands? Social media sites are not necessarily blocked if there is a supportive group available to them, such as parents, teachers, and other friends who can teach them the skills they need, help them to navigate the sites, and make them aware of the help that is available.[17] This group is not as likely to use Internet access or social media as routinely as young people without disabilities are. Imagine for a moment that you are 14 years old and suffer from a terminal illness, or that you live in an isolated area and must get about in a wheelchair. Without the assistance of others, you might not be able to gain access to social media. For young people suffering from terminal illnesses, access to social media connects them to others with similar or the same impairment, and such sites offer encouragement, social connection, and even friendships.

Help is available through software like writing software (WYNN), screen readers (JAWS), scanning and OCR software (such as Dragon), screen magnifiers with ZoomText, and the like. But the key is whether or not a person with a disability is aware of these helps, and whether he or she has access to them. Further, the aiding software must be compatible with the assistive technology needed for the physical disability in question.[18]

Social networking sites will help lessen isolation, allowing persons with disabilities to connect with others who share the same or similar disability, enable them to vent or even to discuss possible treatments and/or reactions to treatments that both parties may be undergoing. Just having another person to listen and respond can mean the difference between severe depression and the ability to cope. But if the illnesses or additional handicaps obtrude, those young people have no other recourse but to hope for intervention by others. Sites such as Patientslikeme.com allow patients—and their caregivers—much needed support and reinforcement. Sites for those working with multiple or single handicapped children provide the same kind of support and freedom from alienating effects these diseases have on their victims and their caregivers. Yet having the sites is only half the battle. Those suffering from these disabilities need to be able to find refuge in these sites as well. All too often, however, it requires extraordinary action, especially for private or even so-called "taboo" topics.

Sex, Social Media and Persons with Disabilities

One would think that with so much sex on the Internet, the pairing up of this topic with persons with disabilities would be an easy matter. But sex is not a topic often discussed in connection with persons with disabilities. When *they* need help or want to discuss a matter but not with family, which is often impossible, the Internet would seemingly provide the perfect intermediary. Not, however, if to get to the needed sites, one must engage, at worst, a family member or, at best, a stranger. Using the Internet for the sex education of anyone, however, can be more than a passing matter of concern. Access to the unfettered web's sex content is fraught with difficulties, given the volume of pornography versus the number of helpful, informative sites. When it comes to young people with disabilities (e.g., intellectual disabilities), useful sexual information can not only be difficult to locate but also problematic even when found on the Internet. Often that information is not comprehensible to a teen who suffers from mental impairments. The matter becomes even more troubling because teens with disabilities are likely not to have an adult in whom they can confide and who will be a helpful guide.[19] While there are groups who will assist individuals with disabilities in connection with this topic, those persons with disabilities must know about those groups and know how to get in touch with them. In other words, it is getting better, but more work remains to be done.

Even once the differently abled are on social networking sites, the experience can be a mixed blessing. In one study, a young woman with an intellectual impairment lent her password out to a friend who later used it to send inappropriate messages to the differently abled young woman's friends. Once she regained control, she became a victim of cyberbullying by women she knew who posted things about her on her Facebook page that she did not want others to know. Later, a man she knew "friended" her, only to eventually begin sending her messages of a sexual nature. The young woman responded inappropriately, which only heightened the nature of the relationship in a direction she did not want it to go. She did not know how to undo it, but also didn't want her parents to know. In another case, a woman with a mild intellectual impairment and autistic traits had trouble understanding what the word "friend" meant in the Facebook context. When parties were posted on Facebook, she thought they were intended for her and she went to them, often to parties where she had never met anyone but through Facebook. This placed her in vulnerable situations.[20] Some reading these stories might think that caregivers are to blame, not social media. But that is decidedly not the case when businesses are tasked with building ramps, accommodating tables, and installing handicapped bathrooms, all at significant costs to those businesses. We should expect social media to make similar accommodations, especially when the costs for doing so are insignificant in comparison to the problems and legal issues that may unfold later.

Social Media, Persons with Disabilities, Schools and Universities

These accommodations will be all the more important, especially in higher education, as more and more universities and colleges move toward online or hybrid education.[21] "Digital inclusion," as some researchers have referred to it, will become all the more important.[22] One would think that, given the legal accommodations required by the federal government with respect to public higher education, this would be one area that does not need much comment. In large part that is true, but as in most things, the devil is in the details. Those of us in higher education often assume, wrongly, that college-aged young people are technologically savvy. They are, but only in those technologies with which they are familiar. That familiarity does not always transfer, either, and so more work and training are required. Persons with disabilities are no different from the rest of us when it comes to transferring technological skills to new surroundings. We cannot assume that because they are familiar with certain assistive technologies, they are familiar with all of them and need no training. This is particularly true because all students will rate their familiarity with technology as high.[23]

With students with disabilities, it is important to remember that because of their impairment, studying often takes longer. Throwing in a technology they must first learn to use makes that task even longer, not to mention harder. Colleges and universities must make a determined effort not only to think through what social media will require of students with disabilities, but also how difficult it will be and whether necessary accommodations will only make students with disabilities appear more stigmatized because of those accommodations. My own experience with these assistive technologies is limited in a university of only 6,000 students, but I have witnessed firsthand how certain accommodations are not always appreciated by the abled student, some of whom snark about why special devices and technologies are set aside "for only two or three students."

As we saw in the previous chapter, college and university students are very connected. Furthermore, professors are demanding more and more that students respond on Facebook, keep a blog, use Twitter accounts, or otherwise engage via social media. Unless these courses are made accessible to all, those with certain disabilities will not be able to enroll in them. While some colleges and universities get around this by offering some sections online and some sections in a traditional classroom setting, it isn't clear whether this is a permanent legal solution or merely a stopgap measure. Students without disabilities can choose. This solution forces those with disabilities to have the choices made for them.

More Legal Challenges

In our enlightened age regarding the differently abled, it is somewhat astonishing that a popular tool like social networking overlooks this important constituency. Readers are doubtless familiar with the American Foundation for the Blind's legal challenge to Amazon's Kindle.[24] When Kindles began appearing in colleges and universities for course use, the AFB challenged that use because the differently abled could not easily use them. It is surprising that some similar action from AFB has not been pursued against social media. In any event, a number of social networking sites for the differently abled emerged out of necessity. Most of these were developed by those suffering from disabilities themselves who knew how to create the necessary accommodations. The courts have not yet taken up the matter, but that cannot be ruled out. Social networking sites have done much to improve access for persons with disabilities but still have more to do before accommodating them completely.

Clearly those with disabilities want to get connected, and social networks provide a significant means for allowing them to do just that. Research indicates that social media must develop and augment their offerings for persons with disabilities. Indeed, even their continued progress and/or significant coping is reliant upon the individual having a social network to fall back on. But when those individuals are confined by space and physical limitations, social networking sites provide another way to accomplish this important task.

Among those with traumatic brain injuries (TBI), isolation and loneliness are not only problematic but can also become chronic, prolonging their psychological adjustment to the injury.[25] As their injury endures, they see less and less of friends and spend more and more time in solitary pastimes, such as watching television or listening to music. But these conditions are not related exclusively to those with TBI but to any individuals suffering from injuries or diseases that make it impossible for them to be around other people regularly or without significant intervention of others. While it is true that many persons with disabilities are using social media, many more cannot or do not have enough familiarity to use these sites. Some of these individuals cannot because of the inherent barriers to gaining access as mentioned above.

Vocal Recognition, Text-to-Software, Captioning

In order to do this on a wider and more inclusive scale, however, vocal-recognition and text-to-speech software for persons with disabilities will have to be more readily available. Google Glass might have helped in this regard for those whose eyesight is not also impaired but it is now defunct. YouTube would appear to be a natural site for the differently abled, provided they have the proper viewing tools. By 2006, captioning was available on many videos. But in 2009, after Google had purchased the company, captioning became automatic. Ken Harrenstein, a Google software engineer who is himself deaf and uses sign language to communicate, announced the good news of automatic video captioning:

> Since the original launch (2006) of captions in our products, we've been happy to see the growth in the number of captioned videos on our services, which now number in the hundreds of thousands. This suggests that more and more people are becoming aware of how useful captions can be…. However, like everything YouTube does, captions face a tremendous challenge of scale. Every minute 20 hours of video are uploaded. How can we expect every video owner to spend the time and effort necessary to add captions to their videos? Even with all the captioning support already available on YouTube, the majority of user-generated video content is still inaccessible to people like me.[26]

And therein lies the problem. YouTube, like all of the Internet, relies heavily on user-generated content. Social media are, by and large, user-generated content exclusively, apart from ads and possibly news feeds from various other sources. How captioning can be perfected for all these sites and made to work seamlessly is hard to comprehend. Furthermore, things like ambient sound make it inexact and the quality faulty, if not incomprehensible. In another place, Harrenstein acknowledges all this but compares it to closed captioning on television in the early days, and he points to its growing perfection over the years. The hope is that as technology develops and innovation continues, a mechanism will be available that will help reduce the massive number of videos and other disability-unfriendly content residing on sites and will make them more readily available. On the other hand, television had a limited number of content-generators and a kind of quality control that sent shows and movies through a pipeline that was heavily regulated—all components missing on the World Wide Web. Have we sacrificed equality and accessibility for the web's inherently fierce independence and lack of controls?

Social Media for All or for Only the Most Able?

Some will argue we're well into the so-called Web 2.0, or a web that is highly interactive and intuitive. But this isn't always the case when it comes to persons with disabilities. When lawsuits or court cases are not the norm, hacks of some kind are necessary to turn "market ready" sites into disability-friendly ones. Given the "Silicon Valley" awareness (I use the term as synecdoche) of the accessibility of sites for the differently abled, it is hard to envision technology going forward without adjustments. How far forward will technology advance before it decides to go back and make the necessary changes for persons with disabilities? And when will it only go forward when all can advance?

Those once singled-out groups for oppression and determined marginalization, such as women and minorities and those of nontraditional sexual orientations, are now finding themselves more and more in the so-called mainstream.[27] But persons with disabilities are often not thought of at all unless attention is riveted upon them in a stark fashion, typically through legal sledgehammers.

This does not discount either the number of sites that are available to persons with disabilities or the value to them to text and communicate on a level playing field. Moreover, the value of sites such as Second Life that circumvent physical appearance and allow everyone to be whoever they wish to be cannot be gainsaid. But the promise of technology, especially as it touches upon social networking, must be made less a velleity and more of a common reality. It's easy to make promises as we see each year around election time by all politicians; it's far more difficult to turn those promises into solid and permanent change.

Are Legal Challenges the Only Solution?

How does this happen? Some with far more expertise than I have suggested that new laws, or an augmentation of current ones, such as the ADA or the Rehabilitation Act of 1973, will be necessary.[28] But new laws on the books to replace old ones is a favored approach in politics that strikes me as a way of "doing something" that robs us of the energy and will to make old laws work. Much like the current immigration controversy today that calls for new laws and more money to throw at a problem that has already had many laws and millions of dollars hurled its way, there is no guarantee that it will work. Indeed, has it ever, or has it acted as a political nepenthean to allow us to forget the matter at hand and go on to the next problem? The political hoopla fixes little but gives us the impression we have done something.

Perhaps a new way would be to enforce the laws we now have, to bring laws to bear on (if not take down) sites that are not living up to universal accessibility. Is it possible that one successful and significant lawsuit would be enough to cause others to fall in line, and far more valuable than a half-dozen new laws that merely repeat what we already have?

It is easy to dismiss persons with disabilities as powerless and "but a few" that cost so much to accommodate, but such thinking is only done by those who are free to do as they please and only repeat the tired example of blaming the victim. New technologies, such as those that allow patients without limbs to "think" their prosthetics to move, or, even more miraculous, to cause another to move, may hold some promise. Technologies that track eye movements and predict their patterns may also prove helpful in this regard. What we cannot do is lose momentum as Web 2.0 (and 3.0 and 4.0, etc.) takes off, promising creators more and more lucrative benefits, yet bypass the millions—no, the billion—who now suffer from some form of disability. If it is market share that web developers seek, why not that market share that numbers just over a billion?

It is not just the millions of social networking sites that are on the web today that matter. It's all of technology as it moves forward. Will sites like Facebook and Twitter be a part of the future ten years from now when very successful sites like MySpace and Orkut have already gone the way of forgotten cyberspace? It is not very likely, but it is likely to be *something*, some form of technology not even thought of today that will replace some, most, or all of them. Will those of us who are abled sit idly by, waiting for the next "it" and forgetting our neighbors—for that is who they are—who cannot even now make a cup of coffee without difficulty, or retrieve their own mail without great planning?

Social media have come a long way, indeed. When I was an undergraduate, now more than forty years ago, one of my work-study assignments included reading to blind twin brothers. The brothers were different in ability, and I spent more time with one than I did with the other. But for both of them, finding readers proved essential since much of the class material was not available in Braille and assistive technologies were nonexistent. The point of this chapter has not been to dismiss the progress we have made for those in similar situations today. Certainly young people today have many assistive technologies available to them, far more than were present for those twin brothers.

I hope it has been helpful to remind readers that we are not "there" yet, especially with social networking sites, and that we cannot assume that because we are so far removed from "Braille days" that we need not think of those who are differently abled because surely there is "something" for them. It may well be true that there is, but this "something" is not available to all, does not work in every technological context, and even when it does, may work only haphazardly. I am reminded of a humorous anecdote that I will share as illustrative but by no means parallel.

My wife and I were traveling in Vienna one summer and took a tour that included all German speakers, save for us. The tour guide was exceptional and quite personable. But when he stopped at the first point of interest in the church we were touring, he spoke for about three minutes in German. His audience laughed, smiled at each other, and even gave verbal consensus to what he said. My wife and I were eager to hear what came next. He began, "Now, in English. Old bones." He moved on to the next station. And so it went for the next ten or twelve stops —uproarious laughter following a disquisition in German, then one or two words in English.

My wife and I have joked about this since it happened. But it strikes me that this is often, yet on a much grander scale, what persons with disabilities must daily endure when it comes to social media and other technologies. We are accommodating them all right, but with only one or two words "in English." Some hope resides in the new standards, WCAG 2.0, that cover, as seen from its title, the Web 2.0, as it were.[29] WCAG 2.0 has a helpful mnemonic to apply to websites: POUR. POUR stands for perceivable, operable (navigable), understandable (operation of the user interface), and robust (can be interpreted by a wide variety of assistive technologies). The only question now is whether these standards will be enough, or if more cases will have to slog their way through the courts. Still, I worry that we will simply leave it as "old bones" for those who struggle with impairment.

Let us hope as we move forward in our brave new world, we do not leave behind those for whom social media mean so much.

Six

#BossNearby

On the face of it, businesses and social media would appear to be a match made in heaven. Whether we are referring to restaurants, law firms, banks, retail outlets, universities, libraries, or even hospitals and their physicians—all of them seek to connect with their clientele in as complete a way as possible. What better way to do that than social media? Depending on the business, some want to make new clients, some want to communicate with them, and some want to get a service in front of their customers. On the other side of the coin, these clients seek to find out about businesses, to look for new places to take their business, to find a physician, or to look for a new place to eat. This seemingly is a perfect match of the message with the medium. And most of the time, it is. Social media provide consumers of whatever the product with a means of finding out about that product. Nothing could be better, right?

Social Media and Work: Not Always the Best Match

Usually. Yet sometimes social media and businesses mix about as well as oil and water. Much of that uncertain mix has to do with the nature of social media, communication of a no-holds barred approach, and the nature of those businesses to put only the best foot forward; hide the club foot, so to speak. Social media want to be open, free, and unencumbered. Businesses want to present their positive charms only, never their dirty laundry. When the two come together, the open and prying nature of social media can clash with the private, hidden nature of how businesses conduct their public personas. On the one hand, employers cannot hide from social media, and on the other, employees will not hide *anything* from social media, even when they should. When the two get together, it does not always turn out well for the business, and it sometimes does not turn out well for the employee. The music just does not end on a harmonious note.

The potential off-key songs begin right from the start. Let us say you are an unemployed female and looking for work. What could be better than to hop onto the Internet and begin ferreting out the possibilities? Not much. Hardly anyone uses print newspapers anymore. Everyone begins with the Internet by searching business websites. So, you begin a search and find what appears to be a perfect match of employer needs and your skills. You input your resume and perhaps even make contact by email with the firm. Soon you get a call and an interview is set. The interview goes well, or so it seems. Then, suddenly, what began well ends badly. For reasons you cannot fathom, the line goes dead. No one returns your calls, emails go unanswered, and your tweets fall on deaf ears. What happened?

Tweets Happen

Facebook, Twitter, Google: in short, what happened might well be social media. What most likely happened is that the business did precisely what you did: they Googled you as you had them, or Google-stalked you, as one phrase has it.[1] Regardless of whatever else you may hear, employers still check social networking to screen the hires. Many states now have laws regarding how businesses can use social media in the recruitment process and prohibit them from asking for passwords, or similar privacy invasion questions.[2] Twenty-eight states have legislation pending or introduced regarding how social media can be used in the employment recruitment process. In 2014, Louisiana, Oklahoma, Tennessee, and Wisconsin enacted laws governing how much information employers can ask regarding social media sites.[3] A law on the federal level will eventually be forthcoming. But how long that will be is anyone's guess. When H.R. 537, the Social Networking Online Protection Act, was introduced into the House of Representatives on February 6, 2013, the prognosis that it would be enacted was slim to none.[4] The act would prohibit employers from asking potential employees for social media passwords and usernames, whether candidates were applying in the private sector or at a school or a university. House and Senate Democrats introduced companion bills, collectively called the Password Protection Act of 2012. This bill would have prohibited current and future employers from coercing employees into providing access to their private accounts and/or punishing them for not providing same. The bill died in committee.

Better Safe Than Sorry

So, while waiting on Congress, forewarned is forearmed. Having a law on the books does not mean it will be enforced. In the case of social media and employer violations, how it will be enforced remains a mystery. While more and more young people find social networking sites a good place to find out about jobs, or about the working climate of a given corporate culture, employers are using social networking sites to find out about employees, before and after hiring.[5]

For Millennials (18–34 years old, though the term is disputed), there is no one social network. They use Facebook, Twitter, Tumblr, Instagram, Pinterest, LinkedIn, and Snapchat, according to comScore, but not one of them to the exclusion of the others.[6] This may be good news to those trying to build social networks—if you build one, Millennials are likely to come—but it also means there is a downside. They use many of them and, as a consequence, leave themselves open to employers finding out more than they may want them to know. The courts continue to be ambivalent on this matter, deciding in one term that it is unlawful for employers to try to secure access to private accounts under false pretenses; in another, deciding that this very public information voluntarily supplied is fair game.[7]

Employers Check Social Media

Fewer than half of all employers surveyed in 2009 indicated they check social networking sites before hiring a new employee.[8] That dropped again a few years afterward, but has since risen to over 75 percent, according to the Society for Human Resource Management.[9] Sites most commonly checked are Facebook, LinkedIn, and Twitter, to name but three. Employers use these sites to recruit individuals, but they also use the sites to follow up on potential candidates later. While it is not exactly ethical, employers do it because it provides information that would not otherwise be available to them. Employers can safeguard against discrimination if they scour social networking sites on all potential employees and have a checklist of "unacceptability." Doing so skirts legal lines, but those seeking work would do well to understand that what they do on social media that is not work-related may well scuttle their careers. Many potential employers believe that whatever is publicly available is fair game.[10]

The best advice may be what some have come to learn the hard way: think twice before posting. Social media users want all their information at their fingertips, and yet all that personal information may well fall under the TMI (too much information) heading. Social media users are warned about this repeatedly, but it becomes critically important when that user is looking for work or hoping to hold on to a job.[11] Oversharing can make looking for work or maintaining a job a nightmare. Regardless of the efforts one might make to keep the information private, it will not be for long. Again, consider the recent brouhaha over the exposure, so to speak, of several celebrities' nude and/or compromising pictures from the cloud.[12]

About half of all employers have found material on social media that caused them not to hire candidates.[13] This number is up from 43 percent in 2013 and 34 percent in 2012. The number of ways social media platforms scuttle careers or potential careers is both obvious and not. Candidates have lost out on jobs because their social media names sounded unprofessional or they posted inappropriate pictures or photographs. Some have excoriated previous employers, while others posted texts and other messages with poor grammar, bad syntax, or poor communication skills in general. Young people find it astonishing that anyone would care what they wrote on this very ephemeral media. They use social media in nonprofessional contexts to communicate quickly and easily. They cannot imagine someone paying attention to subject/verb agreement errors or consistent misspellings. But employers not only check before hiring to glean information they think they need, they are also very wary of hiring anyone who has bad-mouthed former employers on social media, according to Career Builder in the UK.[14] The top reasons for not hiring, based on what employers found on social media, are drinking and drug habits, bad-mouthing previous employers, provocative or inappropriate photographs, poor communication skills, criminal behavior, or discriminatory comments (race, religion, gender, and so on). The good news is that if the opposite of these is present—good communication, background related to resume, well-rounded, positive online image—employers were more likely to hire.

As a group, Millennials indicate they have lied about their qualifications, posting material that inflates their resumes or even contradicts them. An astonishing number, just over 40 percent, post something about excessive use of drugs or binge-drinking. Finally, some Millennials post political views that are extreme, or they post racially prejudicial material. Again, they are surprised anyone pays attention and cannot fathom that these posts could ever prove a detriment to their employment.

It Isn't Just Young People

A surprising number of individuals post something about a bad breakup or about a past divorce or ongoing divorce proceeding. Others will post inappropriate materials about a relationship; let us say, euphemistically, that they overshare about that relationship's more private matters. For example, one individual posted information about his wife's shooting him in the head, or his subsequent lawsuit. Another posted information about his dental exam results, and yet another posted his successful entry into a demonic cult.[15] Some readers will laugh in derision about the stupidity of these candidates, but the distance from these extremes to the more common postings—sexcapades, drunken sprees, inappropriate pictures—is very small. Individuals delude themselves if they believe that their social media presence is not something employers will check. It would be somewhat understandable if the number of social networking users who did not think employers bothered to view their pages were only older social media members, those in their forties and fifties, but, alas, it is not. All too often the so-called tech- savvy are the ones who are most likely to be the biggest offenders of oversharing. The solution is not so much to make the social media presence private, although that surely helps. It is to make one's social media presence, wherever it is, professional. Even separating professional presence from a private one does not generally work as well as we might hope. Social media users should remember that the idea behind social networking sites, like Facebook, Twitter, and LinkedIn, is not privacy but publicity, and as much as can be made public, will.

Asking About the Taboo Without Asking

Questions that interviewers know are off-limits may now be checked via social media, and the checking may not be what the potential hiree wants known. What social media users—the descriptive phrase has a certain but appropriate addictive ring to it—fail to remember is that no one forces them to post stupid drunken pictures on Facebook, not even the devil, and yet they do it, routinely. Moreover, they also forget that what is posted may never be removed, or in the adapted words of the Omar Khayyam for our hyperconnected world, the updating news feed addict posts on, nor all his piety and wit can lure it back to cancel half a line, and none of his ctl-alt-delete can un-post a word of it.

Employers are also watching those already hired, thus monitoring the overall costs of employees using social networking while "on the clock."

Legal observers argue this practice goes too far because it violates employees' and potential hirees' privacy. But does it? Employers argue that there can be no expectation of privacy (freedom from unwanted intrusion) when information is posted to a public social networking site that anyone can see. So far, court decisions tend to favor employers. Knowing that a boss is likely "following you" or reading tweets really has to make a difference in an employee's online behavior. Sadly, it often does not. Savvy employees refer those with whom they work to a site like LinkedIn. But again, nothing online is ever really private, even when you make it so. Employees need to remember that what may be humorous outside work is not exactly funny to those who authorize the paychecks. Compromising pictures and salacious stories (or even personal histories) will not play well, either in the job market or afterwards.

This is particularly true of the NSFW sites, or "not suitable for work" sites. While this most often refers to pornography (both hard- and soft-core), it can refer to gambling sites, gaming sites, or sites with depictions of gruesome violence. Employees appear to think they have an unalienable right to game while at work. Employers, conversely, have no right to "spy." Whether it is right to spy or not, employers are watching in many cases, and surfing to the wrong sites can impact an employee's evaluation or even result in his termination. Worse, employees sometimes post information about the company, its products, or even its mistakes. Unless a company is doing something illegal, disclosing this information is likely to put the employee on the wrong side of both employer and the law.

Employers' Rights Versus Employees' Wrongs

Employers must protect themselves and their products. Disclosing confidential information on social networks is only asking for trouble. Often, employees are clueless about what this means. They post information about trade secrets, make references to minutes in a meeting, even disclose what took place in a meeting if only to highlight a humorous anecdote, and all too often with an eye to making the "boss" look bad. Heaven forbid someone disclose something about a business rolling out a new product, or completing its work for an IPO. And yet, it happens, is happening. It can easily be something as silly as using a patented trademark logo but forgetting that such use is protected.[16] It does not even have to be something written or tweeted. It could be as innocuous as videotaping something at work thought to be "hilarious" and posting it to a social media site, only to discover too late that what was visible on the walls in the background was a one-of-a-kind logo copyright protected by the company, never mind using time at work to goof off while recording the video. Or, it could be that some enterprising employee decides it is high time the company come clean on its corporate social responsibility, and so discloses that company's failing in this regard. In all these cases, one thing remains constant: social media is not the place for this to occur.

Doing Business in the Hi-Tech Age: Is Social Media Worth It?

Clearly, social media sites have changed the way we do business. Whether they have changed the way we do it because they are fundamentally important tools or because they are simply a new bandwagon everyone has jumped on is a matter of debate. For example, when it comes to Black Friday sales, social media sites like Twitter and Facebook have almost no impact.[17] And yet companies not on social media—assuming there are still one or two—face ridicule and insult if their low-tech selves are decried. Social media are, obviously, a good way to get business exposure. But is the exposure a game worth the candle when you add social media employee (from the CEO to the doorman) blunders? No one knows for sure.

What we do know, however, is that businesses see an uptick of online ordering, especially around the holidays. Whether this is driven by social media or by convenience is anyone's guess. About one-third of marketers worldwide are seeing a return on investment, according to ExactTarget.[18] About half the respondents think that they will *eventually* get a return, but most, more than 75 percent, still think it is ineffective. Marketers see some gains when they are able to curate content that interests potential customers over a variety of social media. But those who think social media marketing is worthless are wrong, or rather they are doing it in the wrong way.[19] The trouble is, not many businesses are able to figure out what the right way is when all the merits are weighed against all the defects.

Books like the *Social Media Bible* tend to reinforce the idea that businesses must be on social media or be left out.[20] The point is not that businesses should be there, but that both employers and employees need to know that there are inherent dangers that can threaten both the survival of the company and the employment of individuals. When one adds up all the opportunities for disaster—blogs, emails, tweets, postings to any number of social media, photos, videos, and so on—it becomes increasingly clear that there must be social media conduct guidelines governing what is expected of employees. Those guideless need to be clear and explicit. Neither appears to be the case in most businesses.

Courts, Social Media and Businesses

With respect to hired employees, the courts can be ambiguous. A New Jersey federal court case unfolded in 2009 involving two restaurant (Houston's) employees using a non-work computer and an invitation-only discussion on a MySpace site.[21] Employee Brian Pietrylo created a group on MySpace and titled it "Spec-Tator." He defined the purpose of the site to "vent about any BS we deal with at work without any outside eyes spying on us." The MySpace group was classified as private and could only be accessed by invitation. Pietrylo then sent out the clarion call to his co-workers: "Let the s*it-talking begin." And so it did, with workers, especially Doreen Marino speaking negatively about their work supervisors, venting their spleen about work, the way they were treated, and the other customary litany of complaints that employees have against their employers. But then the discussion moved away from work complaints to sexual remarks about Houston's management and its customers, jokes about quality service or lack thereof, and references to violence and illegal drug use.

One of the Houston's greeters, Karen St. Jean, showed the site to a Houston's manager while dining in his home. He asked for the password and she gave it to him, later testifying that she feared for her job if she refused. That manager and another supervisor began to look around the site. The social media site, the managers determined, violated the four core values of Houston's restaurants: professionalism, positive mental attitude, aim to please, and teamwork. Pietrylo and Marino were subsequently fired.

The case went to court, and the jury decided against the restaurant under the Stored Communications Act (SCA), as well as an invasion of privacy. Houston's argued it did not violate privacy or the SCA since the password was freely given. Although both employees found jobs quickly thereafter, the court ordered Houston's to pay back wages. The case is intriguing because other similar cases have gone in exactly the opposite direction. But it does serve to underscore the importance of employers treading very carefully when asking for passwords and access to social media sites from which they are deliberately blocked.

In an unrelated case, three police officers were suspended from their jobs in Harrison, New York, after they made lewd, sexist, and racist remarks about the town's mayor and President Barack Obama on a Facebook account. In both cases, accessing information on public sites does not appear to exceed an individual's expectation of privacy.

Undoing a Legal Victory

No other case better highlights this problem, though in a roundabout way, than that of the recent case of *Patrick Snay v. Gulliver Schools, Inc. and School Management Systems, Inc.* Snay was the headmaster of Gulliver Schools. When the school system did not renew Snay's contract, he sued on the basis of age discrimination. After a long court battle, Snay and the school system came to an agreement. Gulliver Schools would pay Snay $10,000 in back pay, $80,000 to Snay as a 1099, and $60,000 to Snay's attorneys. But the agreement was reached on terms of strict confidentiality. Neither Snay nor his wife could violate the confidentiality, and if they did, portions of the agreement were null and void.

Enter social media. The Snays' college-aged daughter took to Facebook only a few days following the trial. She wrote: "Mama and Papa Snay won the case against Gulliver. Gulliver is now officially paying for my vacation to Europe this summer. SUCK IT." It seemed like a good idea at the time and certainly beat the usual summer fare of pictures of food or love's travails. Judge Lopez of the Florida Circuit Court for Miami-Dade County found that revealing the details of his settlement with Gulliver to his daughter did not constitute a breach of the confidentially agreement.

So far, so good. But on appeal, the Florida Court of Appeals reversed the decision of Judge Lopez, holding that the nondisclosure agreement had been violated. Moreover, the judge in this case, Judge Wells, found that the subsequent promulgation of the settlement by Snay's daughter's to her 1,200 Facebook friends, not a few of whom were among graduates or current students of Gulliver, heightened the violation. Judge Wells rescinded the $80,000 settlement, perhaps the most expensive Facebook post by a college student to date.[22]

What makes this case so interesting is that it does involve employee-employer social media missteps that were neither the misstep of either the employee or the employer, and yet, both are implicated. It serves to point out to social media users that any post at any time in any context relating to any sort of job situation may result in blowback, and that blowback can be serious, in this case a vacation to Europe that, well, really sucked after all.

More Employee Social Media Missteps

In another case, the deputy chief Rex Duke of Clayton State University Police Department, who had worked there for eight years, posted to his *personal* Facebook feed a picture of the Confederate flag and the words, "It's time for a second revolution." The comment came not long after President Barack Obama had been reelected to a second term in 2012. Clayton State University demoted the chief and reduced Duke's pay. Not long after the demotion and pay decrease, Duke resigned. He took the matter to court, claiming freedom of speech retaliation against his employer. Duke ostensibly looked at the matter as a personal comment on his personal page that did not have anything to do with the Clayton State University Police Department, posted no doubt on his own time and not on university or police-owned equipment.

The United States District Court for the Northern District of Georgia did not see it that way and dismissed his case. Judge Story of the District Court argued that the former chief's remarks impeded the ability of the police department to do its job, raised concerns over prejudicial behavior or intent on the part of the employee, and cast the department in a bad light. The department's ability to effectively carry out its duties in a non-biased manner overshadowed an individual's desire to speak his mind.

Again, here is a case in which social media behavior figures largely into the equation. On the face of it, it would seem that an individual has the right to speak his or her mind. It is, moreover, highly likely that in an age before social media, this misprision would have gone unnoticed, or noticed by so few as not to rise to the level of punitive employment measures. But the ubiquity and immediacy of social media figure into both the Snay and Duke cases, making what might have been "done in a corner" before social media now play out on the world stage of tweets and news feed posts.

Understanding Social Media's Reach

This process of "cybervetting" both before and after hiring continues to raise legal issues. But employees post such information voluntarily, for the most part. With respect to potential hires, Todd Malicoat, an Internet consultant and founder of the blog stuntdubl.com, makes clear the new environment: "The average job hunter doesn't realize that their potential employer is going to run their name in quotes through a search engine and keep digging until they find dirt. Like it or not, Google results are your new resume." Malicoat goes on to point out that most of the "dirt" is coming from ill-advised Facebook and other social media profiles that, once on the web, are hard to get off. Even after being hired, the monitoring does not end as profiles created during one's twenties can come back to haunt five years later. The courts have not ruled on the legality of this practice, but the expectation of privacy does not appear to be violated since the information is placed on a site meant for public viewing. What businesses are not always careful about is whether the information they are gleaning from social media is accurate. The appeal to employers is obvious: this is free and revealing information in the form of "low hanging fruit." But what happens when that low-hanging fruit is poisoned?

In the case of *Gaskell v. University of Kentucky*, C. Martin Gaskell was the frontrunner for the position to lead an observatory at the University of Kentucky. His credentials were impeccable, his research consisting of more than 100 articles, many of which had appeared in prestigious journals in his field. He had lectured all over the world. From a purely academic point of view, he had to be one of the leading candidates, if not the first choice. Then someone Googled him, as it were.[23]

What followed varies from story to story, but it appeared that Gaskell had a robust evangelical faith and that set off alarms at the University of Kentucky. Some academics at the university shot off emails disparaging the professor to others, including students. Some claimed that his statements made him a creationist and so ineligible for any scientific post. Gaskell disavowed the creationist claim but did not dispute his robust faith, as evident by his "Google trail," his personal website, and other social media. Gaskell later sued the university and won a settlement of $125,000.

As might be imagined, critics on both sides have chimed in. The case, whatever its merits, do provide a glimpse of the minefield that is social media when it comes to employers and employees. In *Yath v. Fairview Clinics*, an overeager employee decided to reveal too much about a treated patient. *Yath* was filed in June 2009 in the Minnesota Court of Appeals. The story is that a clinic worker at Fairview created a MySpace page. On her social media page she revealed that the plaintiff had a sexually transmitted disease, had recently cheated on her husband, and was addicted to plastic surgery.[24] The site was only up for 24 hours, and the courts determined that it may have been seen by as few as six people. Still, the court held for the plaintiff. In this case, the court did not regard the number of views as much as it did the slanderous information that the clinic worker made public, information that was only available through her place of employment. It would appear obvious that revealing such information would not be legally (and certainly not ethically) appropriate. And yet such cases as these, while not abundant, continue to occur. Private information becomes instantly public and may be known far and wide. The trouble resides in the fact that once it is sent, posted, or otherwise made available on social media, it cannot be retrieved.

In a dreadful 2014 movie with no basis in technological reality, *Sex Tape*, starring Jason Sigel and Cameron Diaz, a couple trying to get their love life back on track, makes a sex tape that "accidentally" gets uploaded to YouTube. The movie spends much of its time with the couple trying to prevent its widespread promulgation. *Sex Tape* is a "comedy," apparently because it is funny to watch a couple try to prevent a "private" event from becoming "front page news" so to speak, as they attempt to hide it from employers, parents, friends, and school organizations. But for anyone who has gone through an embarrassing social media moment—even something as "minor" as sending an email meant for one person that goes to an entire group, the resulting chaos, and in some cases, dismissal and legal action, is anything but funny.

The First Amendment, Social Media and Employees

First Amendment access issues continue to roil within the employer-employee context based on the presumed "right" of employees to access social networking sites while at work. Courts have yet to determine these boundaries. The continuum on which social media policies are stretched is as strict as no access or as lenient as free access to do whatever the employee wants to do. Yet limits remain with respect to appropriate speech and confidentiality, even extending to on and off duty, especially if it relates to one's employment.[25] To say businesses are finding themselves caught in a quandary is an understatement. If they allow social networks in the workplace, how do they monitor them to be sure work is being done instead of mere play? Furthermore, do companies have the right to monitor their employees' online activities? The two-pronged question is not an easy one to answer.

It should be clear to most employers that social media access is not a minor thing. Employers must know that employees are going to access social media. Employers should also know that this access results in a loss of productivity, a cost in sales, and a cost in morale, assuming the social media policy isn't handled well.

Teasing out this information is not easy. Since most businesses are using social media sites to attract new business, then how can businesses block access to those sites? Besides, companies that tried it have found that employees can usually discover workarounds, workarounds that cost more in lost work productivity to untangle. Other employees opt for the easy solution of simply bringing their own devices (iPads, smart-phones, iPods) to work. Then there is the disagreement about whether or not social media use is really lost work time. On the one hand, Marshall Kirkpatrick of Read, Write Web reports on an Australian study that use of social networks increases worker productivity by nine percent.[26] In 2007, Jacob Silverman of How Stuff Works reports on a study that the frivolous workplace use of social networking costs businesses $260 million annually in lost revenues.[27] When social networking surfing is not losing businesses money, it exposes their networks to malware, spyware, and other unwanted software or web intrusions.[28] Of course, emails also raise the risk of malware and spyware. But social networking has all but replaced email as the preferred means of communication. Social networking activity now exposes company networks to greater potential exposure than email to these problems. In a 2008 survey of 100 large employers in the New York City metropolitan area, 38 percent blocked access to social networking sites outright, while 56 percent acknowledged monitoring sites to see if work was being done or if employees were using work time for personal gain, a practice as we have seen, that may not be legal.[29] No court cases have emerged to address these concerns as no employee has sued for the right to access social networking sites while at work, but it is likely only a matter of time. Security experts at Safe and Savvy (http://safeandsavvy.f-secure.com) argue that businesses must post social networking rules before hiring an employee, make sure social networking conduct is clear from the first day of employment, and require employees to follow that protocol carefully. Meanwhile, accessing public sites meant for public viewing and posting information on them appears to close the door on an individual's right to privacy.

But isn't this just a small problem today? According to Basex, a business research firm, the cost of workplace interruptions and abuse and misuse of social media, the so-called social media frolic by employees, today costs businesses about $650 billion annually, as opposed to $250 million only six years ago.[30] The figure may seem preposterous to some, but Nielsen/Incite's Social Media Report for 2012 showed employees frittering away 74 billion minutes or 20 percent of their work time on social media sites. So, while companies are making billions on social media, they are also losing billions in work productivity. Taming this use is not easy, either. We are all social beings, even if we want to socialize alone, and social media sites satisfy those seemingly contradictory desires. For businesses, it is damned if you do and damned if you don't, or so it would seem.

Workplace Social Media Involvement: Get It in Writing

Some employee prohibited social media activity has been hinted at already. This includes language that may be damaging to the company or derogatory statements about individuals with whom one works. Any language that is profane, vulgar, or obscene is also prohibited, as well as any pictures that would have the same effect. All of these things appear to be "common sense," but the sense displayed on social media is anything but common or extraordinary. The only recourse an employer has is to delineate what is expected of employees in a social media policy. To make sure employees get that policy on their first day of work, employers must make sure employees sign something—a form, an email—that indicates they have read and understood what is expected.

If written agreements are present and legal battles ensue at a later date, the courts typically side with employers. Where the matter becomes less clear is when that occurs during off-hours, but even these (e.g., the Snay and Duke cases) tend to lean toward the employer. Given this state of affairs, social media should make every employee Christmas party more sober and more tame than they may have been before the advent of social networking sites. Dancing drunk on the office table with a lampshade on your head may be hilarious to all present, especially if alcohol has been consumed in large quantities, but this does not sit well with employers when embarrassing photos show up with the employer's logo in the background on someone's Facebook page.

Employer Social Media Policies: Train Early and Often

What makes a good social media policy? Some elements have been hinted at already. The need for a sound social media policy should be obvious by now. HMV is a British entertainment retailer. When the company had to lay off 200 employees, a bad situation grew into a worse one.[31] One of the 200 laid-off employees was left in charge of the corporate Twitter account. Soon he was tweeting, "Mass execution of loyal employees who love the brand. We're tweeting live from HR where we're all being fired." In twenty minutes, the site's traffic jumped 20 percent—not exactly the increase in publicity an employer would want. But this kind of company chagrin can be avoided with a little thought and a good bit of common sense, beginning with the it-goes-without-saying point that you do not leave fired employees in charge of your web presence.

Employers who are ahead of the social media "game" inform employees of the social media policy as soon as an employee is hired. Waiting even a week to get new employees trained on the social media presence may be too late.[32] The training needs to be something employees will view as substantial, not just five points on a half-sheet of paper. The less serious an employee takes the training, the more likely he or she will violate the policy. The training should become a part of the corporate culture, too. It's what the company does, how it proceeds, and it is very important—as important as benefits—and so it should have that kind of cachet with employees.

As has been mentioned before, social media polices must be clear and specific: do this, do not do that. Employees should also know that when they are on social media, they speak for the company, whether they want to or not. Linking this or that piece of news, or this or that new feature should have enough information in the tweet, post, or blog to let readers/followers know that they are speaking for the company. Tag lines or introductory phases do this sufficiently. Employees should also be rewarded for publicizing the company in a good way.

There should also be ongoing improvement, as well as follow-up training. It will do little good to have one or two social media training sessions with no subsequent follow-up. An approach that gives the impression of "one and done" tells employees this is not important and does not really matter in the larger scheme of things. Finally, there really must be both prohibited behaviors and punitive measures. Nothing will scuttle a social media policy faster than the impression that yes, this is important, but there is no *dies irae*, as it were, no day of doom if violated. It is astonishing how many colleges and universities—especially with respect to faculty—have this approach. X or Y is prohibited or required, but when nothing is done when it is violated, or nothing done when the deadline is passed, employees get the message loud and clear: it really does not matter, or it doesn't matter with respect to this class of employees. Of course, faculty are going to play the "academic freedom" card whenever they can, but if policies are clear, and violators punished, then social media policy, even in a university setting, can be successful and will reap many rewards.

Social Media Bragging

One piece of advice that could help both sides of the aisle—employers and employees—is to hold off on the bragging. Instagram is particularly bad about this on both sides, with pictures from businesses tantalizing those who cannot get there or afford to be there. But employees will do the same, with pictures from Paris, Mexico, Madrid, and Cancun, showing off pictures of glad-you're-not-here-but-I-know-you-wish-you-were. It is what some have come to call Instagram-envy. "For many urban creative professionals, it is not unusual to scroll through one's Instagram feed and feel suffocated by fabulousness," wrote one reporter.[33] Those posting all these pictures are really only trying to inspire us, or so they say. Others think it is "unadulterated voyeurism."[34]

The constant bragging, whether personal, professional or propagandizing, is part and parcel of social media. There does not appear to be a way to end it. As mentioned in an earlier chapter, what makes social media so enticing to many is that it helps us focus on our favorite topic: us. But the constant me-ism that the social media help us to inflict on others also helps to make us less human. None of us, even the most socially awkward, would ever dream of going to lunch with friends only to spend the entire time talking about ourselves, what we have done, where we are going, or with whom we were having dinner. And yet this is what social media has become for many: an endless conversation about ourselves and our successes. Business can be no different, bragging about only one thing endlessly. But endless bragging wears thin, no matter who is doing it, and eventually it becomes noise that cannot be heard, or if heard, then always avoided. Is there an antidote for this endless bragging? Some say no.[35] But a good place to begin would be in social media training.

Can employees and employers reach a truce on social media, one that benefits both without harming the other? Probably not. We are all just too much into ourselves not to disclose everything, and no business can hide all of its secrets all the time. But with the right training and with the right understanding of social media defects and their merits, we might be able to reach a point where the good and the bad factor each other out.

SEVEN

#Privacy#GetOverIt

"Hey dude. This is so funny. My boss got so drunk, she hit on me.
But don't mention this to anyone, okay? I mean she was blasted and
really coming on to me. I can't tell you what happened next!"

The above post is fictitious. But such personal information gets aired daily, whether on Facebook, Twitter, Instagram, or some other social network. Our fictitious poster posts information that he considers "private" and even adds, just to be sure, "Don't mention this to anyone." But he may as well be posting it to a billboard in Times Square because within minutes of his posting, it is everywhere. His next post may be something on the order of, "Damn, dude, her husband said he'd blow my brains out if he found me. How did he know? Hope he's kidding!" The sad fact of the matter is that almost everything we do on social media—no, make that *everything* we do on social media—is public knowledge.

No other issue rankles us like the idea that someone is spying on us. Just witness the hue and cry over the revelations of one, Edward Snowden.[1] Mr. Snowden revealed what most of us already knew: that the NSA and other spy-type operations were basically monitoring the world in order to keep us safe from those who wished to kill or otherwise harm us. He also revealed what many of us suspected: a good deal of that activity has nothing to do with surveillance that might protect us, but it is the kind of surveillance that would embarrass most of us—racy pictures, checking up on old paramours, and so on. Some did not take offense at the idea of being watched if it meant keeping us safe. Better to read about Mr. Snowden and the ensuing hysteria than about dozens of downed planes, derailed trains, burning buildings, and tens of thousands dead because no one was paying any attention to what the mean-spirited plotted over social media and elsewhere. Some of us, however, found the very idea that the NSA and other agencies were watching their own countrymen to be offensive, surely illegal, and downright outrageous.

Social Media as Your Personal Spy

And yet, despite it all, dozens of social media sites watch what we do, record how we do it, offer us suggestions on what to buy, expose our likes and dislikes to the world, and even test their hypotheses about us, and no one raises much of a peep.[2] Well, okay, we were prompted to peep, but only after we realized about one million of us had been used as guinea pigs.[3] But so far, it has not mattered to the social network in terms of loss of members. On the other hand, if government so much as peers at anything we do online, we fall into hysterics, to the extent that we did when Mr. Snowden came forward with his revelations. The point is, we seem not to care when social media platforms bypass our privacy and hyperventilate when government does so even if to protect us. Perhaps it's naive to think that the government might be a bit more circumspect about your privacy than Mark Zuckerberg.

Because personal profiles contain private information—information about religion, sexual orientation, causes or special interests, places of interest, even how a person looks or distinguishing features that person has—that information, when it becomes public, can be all too identifying. Information of this type is typically information the law strictly forbids being asked in non-social networking situations, like employers asking about marital status, sexual orientation, or religion.[4] Placing information online about likes and dislikes more than indicates personal preferences. It can allow predators to "snare" unsuspecting victims by offering those preferences as enticement for things that do not really exist in order to get the unwary to reveal yet more about themselves. And, of course, it does not have to be a malicious predator or a pedophile, either. Spammers also use these sites, as do telemarketers, to acquire the same information in order to reel in prospective buyers. Even some e-readers are taking a look at what we read and using that information to their betterment.[5]

We all sense this. A majority of Americans feel they have lost control over their personal information, not only at places like Target, Home Depot and the U.S. Post Office, but also on social media.[6] Over 80 percent say they do not feel safe on a social network like Facebook or in trusting their personal information to a large company. But these sorts of surveys are now old hat. Americans have worried about privacy lost since the early 2000s. They are not, however, worried enough to do much else than wring their hands over it. But should they do more when it comes to social media?

Social networks are successful because they offer widespread participation, but at the same time, they open their users up to unnecessarily dangerous exposure. Registrants often take it for granted that security on social networking sites is tight, that their profiles are hidden away, and that any information they provide will not be made public unless they agree to it. They forget that security breaches are commonplace on social networking sites, and even in multiple so-called failsafe locations. For example, big banks, social security numbers, the White House, the Department of Defense, businesses, and university records have all been frequent and successful targets of hackers. Social networking sites are like the proverbial low-hanging fruit for hackers: easy information they can use to do serious damage. Social networking sites provide hackers with an easy, vulnerable wealth of private information. Snapchat, once considered a safe place to share private photos, now turns out to be as public as all the rest, and as easily hackable.[7]

Private Information as Public Revenue

According to Peter Mika, a Yahoo computer researcher and blogger on social networking topics, lack of privacy has even created "an urgent need to clarify the legal and ethical boundaries of carrying out social science research on the Web. The [exposure of personal information] serves as a reminder of the possible collision between the public interest on [one] side and the law and the markets as regulators on the other side."[8] So far, however, there is only talk about the lack of privacy and the need to tighten it. Meanwhile, those in charge of social networking sites provide a veneer of privacy only to come back later to tell us that our privacy has been violated. Instead, they talk more about how information wants to be free and how users control their information and with whom they wish to share it.[9] In other words, it's our fault if our privacy gets compromised. We now know that the velleity of privacy and its reality on social media are two different things. While social networking poobahs will talk about their concern and how much they care about your privacy, in point of fact, privacy is the bane of these networks.

Creating a profile filled with personal information is not the only problem, either. If it is easy for users to create one, it is also easy for someone to "fake" a profile and fashion it in a manner meant to attract individuals only to defraud them in some way. Once logged into a social network, "connections" or "friendships" are quickly made. In a short while a relationship evolves to the extent that the unwary comfortably reveal more information about themselves than they would in a face-to-face social connection of equal duration. Although it did not last long, Unvarnished, a social media site that is the antithesis of LinkedIn, allowed individuals to wail on each other professionally. It had the great potential to destroy careers with rumor, innuendo, and verisimilitude.[10] Because social media sites tend to make narcissists of us all, that same narcissism can become the bane of our public and private lives.[11]

When users of social networking sites post to a social network, the lines between the personal and the public are quickly blurred, and this clouds the privacy question. Social networking scholar danah boyd sums it up this way: "What it means to be public or private is quickly changing before our eyes and we lack the language, social norms, and structures to handle it."[12] But this implies that it is not the fault of social media, only the fault of the "language" and "social norms" to stay caught up, a kind of blaming the victim. This change occurs because when users create profiles, the information asked can border on the discriminatory, but social networking sites claim it is important in order to match users up with one another, for whatever the reasons (likes, dislikes, dating, shared interests, etc.), and besides, users can keep it private. But the nature of the information—race, religion, sexual orientation, education, marital status—is not allowed to be asked by law under most other circumstances. Further, the nature of social networking posts is such that anyone can post anything on a social networking site. At times, users' posts may sound discriminatory, harassing, annoying, off-color, off-putting, entirely out of bounds, and, oh yes, occasionally informative. Flippancy aside, when all the baby pictures, cat photos (also an area of privacy invasion, but more on that later), food pictures, and envy-status updates are excluded, not much is left on social networking. But when content exceeds the bounds of proprietary, who is at fault, the individual or the social network, and who is at fault for invading privacy to make it so?

Social Networking Is Murder

In a bizarre Craigslist case, but hardly the first of its kind, an Iowa woman was sentenced to more than seven years in prison for using a help-wanted ad on the social media site.[13] U.S. District Judge Linda Reade gave the seven-year term to 23-year-old Meagan Schmidt of Dubuque. Schmidt pled guilty in November 2013 for soliciting, via Craigslist help-wanted ads, someone to kill her father. She offered $10,000. She told one man who responded to the ad that he had better use a gun to kill her father "as he is a bigger man," and anything less than a bullet might prove the killer's own undoing. The man she attempted to hire alerted police to her

Being on social media means you have no privacy (drawing by Joe L. Boyd).

ad. The police later did an undercover operation, exposing the woman's attempted murder-for-hire.

Hiring out murder isn't the only way social media can be deadly. In drug-ridden parts of Mexico, locals have used social media to warn others where trouble may lurk and how to avoid it. Tamaulipas is one such place where a courageous woman who went under the name "Felina" warned her neighbors repeatedly. Local news had been silenced by the cartel, so social media proved the only way. But "Felina" proved too good at her tweets, and the cartel used social media to warn her to step back. She did not, and one week after her warning, she was murdered, shot in the face.[14] It has not stopped others from taking up her cause, to be sure, but it has understandably cast a pall over an area already shrouded in the dark night of drug cartels.

Not all Craigslist murder-for-hires have a happy ending, either. Elytte Barbour, a 22-year-old man, plotted with his wife to lure a man to his death. Forty-two-year-old Troy LaFerrara proved the unfortunate victim. Barbour and his newly wedded wife, Miranda, just "wanted to kill someone together," so they advertised Miranda as a 19-year-old who offered delightful conversation and companionship. LaFerrara arranged to meet her and instead met his death, as he was picked up by the couple and stabbed to death in the newlyweds' Honda CRV. The plan had been for Miranda to say the code words, "Did you see the stars tonight?" and her husband Elytte would jump from the backseat and choke LaFerrara with a cord. Miranda claimed she gave LaFerrara an out by telling him she was only sixteen. According to her, had he left, he would have remained alive. Instead he said he still wanted to have sex with her, proving in her mind that he deserved to die. When Elytte did not react to the code words, Miranda took a knife out of the door pocket and stabbed LaFerrara in the chest 20 times. Miranda later admitted to 22 other murders as part of a satanic cult in Alaska. Prosecutors are seeking the death penalty for LaFerrara's murder. Police are not sure if the other 22 murders occurred, but they are investigating them to be certain.[15] The Barbours are responsible for their own actions, but is Craigslist immune to any prosecution for providing the vehicle through which this crime could be committed easily? It would appear so, and the reason is explained below.

CDA Section 238 to the Rescue Once More

Even before social networking sites made it possible for the widespread publication of any and all musings of any individual, the courts tried to answer the content question. They tackled the issue of what was allowed and what not by attempting to make clear who was responsible for content and under what conditions. On October 29, 1991, in the United States District Court for the Southern District of New York, the court heard *Cubby, Inc. v. Compuserve, Inc.*, in which Robert Blanchard filed for libel, business defamation, and unfair competition owing to comments in a newsletter CompuServe "published" on its forums, long before social networking sites ever existed. CompuServe did not, however, supply its own content but contracted with Cameron Communications for it. Did this make a difference to the court? Yes, because CompuServe did not have editorial rights on the newsletter that became the subject of the case. *Cubby* did not address social networking sites *per se* because the case occurred before social networking sites existed. But *Cubby* still guides the courts with respect to social networking sites because they act in a similar manner by not editing third-party content. Users' posts are their own fault, but they are also the lifeblood of social networking sites. We all work for Facebook now, and we are all responsible for the content that Facebook gets for free.

In a similar case, the New York Supreme Court sent out a confusing signal only four years later, in a 1995 decision in *Stratton Oakmont, Inc. v. Prodigy Services Co.* The court found that online service providers *could* be found liable for the speech of its users in certain cases. In October 1994, an anonymous user of Prodigy's Money Talk bulletin board created a post claiming that Stratton Oakmont, Inc., a New York securities investment banking firm, committed fraud when it made initial public stock offerings of Solomon-Page, Ltd. The anonymous poster also made disparaging comments about Stratton-Oakmont's president, Daniel Roush. Stratton-Oakmont sued Prodigy for, among other things, defamation. The court agreed. So what changed in the few months between *Cubby* and *Prodigy*?

Not much. The court held that Prodigy exercised editorial control over the messages on its board by posting content guidelines for users, enforcing those guidelines with board leaders, and utilizing filtering-type software to remove offensive language. Prodigy established editorial control and had content-ownership and therefore liability. In a very real sense the court punished Prodigy for *attempting* to control its content. The message sent to future social networking sites was unmistakable: do not try to control content in any manner. And so they have not.

Outing Yourself When You Didn't Mean To

While users often reveal much about themselves willingly in profiles, the court intervenes when social networking sites ask for what the court considers forbidden information. *Fair Housing Council of San Fernando Valley v. Roommates.com, LLC* (2007) attempted to settle, legally, the difference between a social networking site asking for the information and the user freely supplying it. Again, the distinction follows along the same lines as the decisions in *Cubby* and *Prodigy*. When social networking sites ask for it in a certain way, it is considered out of bounds; when users supply it willingly, it is not.

Roommates.com is a roommate finder and search service. Users signed up and answered questions about their likes and dislikes, including questions about race, religion, sexual orientation, and so on. Roommates. com held that such questions had to be asked in order to match up individuals with one another. Two Fair Housing groups charged Roommates. com with a violation of the Fair Housing Act (FHA). The FHA strictly forbids asking questions about race, religion, or sexual orientation.

The district court found that Roommates qualified for immunity under CDA Section 230. The Ninth Circuit reversed the decision and remanded (sent back to the lower court) the case. The Ninth found that websites create content (and so are liable) by having members answer questions in profiles. By filtering those profiles based on answers to the questions from drop-down menus, information is "channeled" into certain categories. The panel held Roommates in violation of the Fair Housing Act regarding discrimination. The filtering point divided the court and proved controversial, especially as it went against conventional thinking widely held until then that social networking sites were immune to liability.

Social Media Immunity: Channeling Versus Asking

As mentioned in another chapter, section 230 of the Communication Decency Act (Title V of the Telecommunications Act of 1996) offers protection from liability for providers and users of an interactive service publishing third-party content. In that clause, no provider of an interactive service is treated as the publisher and/or speaker of third-party information, or information provided by others. In other words, these interactive providers are channels for the information, not the creators or publishers. The courts determined in *Roommates* that it was not a passive participant in the gathering information, or in its use of that content. Those who view CDA section 230 as ironclad, however, argue that the application of the "channeling test" may expose social networking sites to future legal action. Those who see Section 230 with exceptions do not. Roommates.com did file an "en banc" appeal (asking for all of the court to hear the case, not just a panel), but the Ninth Circuit ruled against it.[16]

The difference in cases is often difficult to see. In *Zeran v. America Online* (1997), Kenneth Zeran claimed to be a victim of a slanderous Internet hoax. An unknown poster held that Zeran offered tasteless t-shirts for sale following the tragic Alfred P. Murrah Building bombing in Oklahoma City, Oklahoma, by Timothy McVeigh. The poster included Zeran's telephone number, from which he ran a home business. Zeran was inundated with emails, phone calls, and death threats. AOL removed the post and deleted the anonymous account. Zeran sued AOL, but the U.S. District Court for the Eastern Division of Virginia in Alexandria dismissed the complaint. Following an appeal by Zeran, the Fourth Circuit Court of Appeals affirmed the lower court's decision. The Supreme Court, from which Zeran sought redress, denied his Petition for writ of certiorari. So, what was the difference? In Roommates, the material was sought out and used by the interactive site; in Zeran, AOL was a pass-through, a channel for the information that Section 230 covered with its immunity.

Revenge Porn and Social Media Immunity

The frustration with this immunity is never more clear than in the case of what is now being referred to as "revenge porn." Revenge porn occurs when explicit pictures show up online that have been taken either without permission, posted without permission, or both. Often these occur on social media sites following a relationship that has soured, with Facebook pages or tweets that were once romantic turning devilishly hellish. Young women are most often victimized, having agreed to certain arrangements in the spring of a relationship, only to have it come back to haunt them in its winter.[17]

Why would they agree to do things that are so ill-advised and capture it in photos no less? These stories are tragic, and the privacy intrusions harsh. Whether one should or should not have agreed in the first place is immaterial. None of us should have to live with the consequences of a very bad decision, however ill-advised, to haunt us for the rest of our lives, and have that decision splashed all over the Internet for the world to see. Conjugal pictures or worse show up and are linked back to the individuals, including their locations. Sometimes these pictures are hacked, but often they are pictures that are shared freely during the relationship at its most intimate and halcyon heights. Even when culprits are caught and jail time follows, the pictures remain on the web, and in some cases, in hundreds of places. While some effort is being made to counter this trend, Section 230 makes it more difficult to do.[18]

A glimmer of hope remains, however. As this book goes to press, news comes from the United Kingdom that those posting revenge porn could face up two years in prison under the new Criminal Justice and Courts Bill that specifically addresses this despicable practice.[19] Not only is posting the pictures illegal, but so is the physical distribution of them. The law, according to authorities, was changed so that victims would know the law sides with them and to send a message to those so inclined to seek revenge in this way. The bill covers images sent via any social media. While all of this sounds good, readers will recall that it is easy to send messages anonymously. With enough technical savvy, some will be able to route their messages so that backtrack will be next to impossible. Until we see successful prosecutions and a reduction in such practices, the partying will have to wait.

What this means now with respect to privacy and social networks should at this point be clear. All social networking sites will argue that they are mere channels through which others provide and post information. They are neither the "publishers" nor the "creators." Conversely, social networking sites also see that content, created by others, as their own, which they can use to attract advertisers and generate revenue while enticing more users. Some would say this is having your cake and eating it, too. Social networking sites remain immune to litigation with respect to all content so long as those sites act as pass-through channels. But with respect to that content as a revenue generator, the sites own it, not those who created it. It is win-win for social media, a lose-lose proposition for individuals. At the very least, we need a law with sharp teeth that will put an end to the non-consensual posting of nude pictures.[20]

Social Media Eggs Us On to Disclose

In order, therefore, to insinuate themselves into the lives of individuals, social networks must extract as much data as possible in the form of registrations or profiles. This process asks for detailed information about the user: name, interests, even, in some cases, where one lives (if not the street, then often the city and state). Users are encouraged by the sites to fill out these profiles in detail in order to be better able to relate individuals to one another. Young people are especially prone to fill them out fully. Indeed, as anyone using them can attest, when the profile is incomplete, users are repeatedly reminded to fill in the missing blanks. For example, a user might see the following after logging on to her social networking site of choice: "Your profile is only 35 percent complete." These profiles are important, even essential, to the success of social networks. Some of that success is quite beneficial. It is thanks to these profiles and their associated "folksonomies" (or people-created tagging or cataloging) that those stranded in Katrina were found as quickly as registrants could get online and post detailed information about missing individuals.[21]

But the practice of profile creation has a downside as well. The process of profile creation leads inevitably to the disclosure of personal information that would not be shared in other contexts. Today's social networking users think they can lock down their information easily. They are confident that by using checkboxes on profiles that they can share certain kinds of information with some, while hiding it from everyone else. Two MIT researchers, Carter Jernigan and Behram F.T. Mistree, in a 2007 unpublished study beg to differ.[22] In "Gaydar," the researchers discovered that finding out one's sexual orientation may be as easy as checking an individual's friends list. Members who listed known homosexual or lesbian friends proved more likely to be gay themselves. Although Jernigan and Mistree do not claim 100 percent accuracy on every person examined, they claim a high degree of predictability. Setting aside the degree of accuracy for a moment, the study reveals that the company one keeps online is important if one wishes certain information to remain private. Whatever terms of service statements say about privacy, it is clear that even if one "locks down" his or her information, a degree of public exposure remains, and that exposure may not be to the individual's liking. How are users' interests protected? Social networking sites rely heavily on terms of service agreements (TOS) to protect the sites themselves and the members using them.

Terms of Service Agreements

Social networking terms of service (TOS) agreements appear when an individual decides to join a social network. Typically, the user is asked to accept or reject them, but if he rejects them, that user is denied access. Some terms of service agreements are as short as half a page; others contain numerous tightly printed pages in barely comprehensible legalese. Such statements are designed to protect the users of the service, certainly, but more importantly, to shield the social networking site from various legal entanglements. Unfortunately, many users do not read terms of service agreements. They simply click yes, or at most read a sentence or two and then move on.[23]

The Electronic Frontier Foundation (EFF), a watchdog group for online users' rights that draws on the expertise of lawyers, policy analysts, activists, and technologists, concurs that most social networking site users do not read terms of service agreements. To underscore their importance to users, EFF created a special page in November 2009 to monitor them and examine how those agreements are holding up in the courts.[24] According to EFF, the standard "I agree" buttons on social networking sites should be replaced with an "I have no idea what this means" button. We could all click such a button confidently!

TOS agreements vary from site to site, but nearly all of them contain something like the following:

- restrictions on use
- membership rules and guidelines
- password information
- miscellaneous information
- rules regarding how to use the service
- monitoring (if any)
- user contents and user rights regarding that content (i.e., intellectual property rights)
- ownership of content
- various disclaimers
- limitation and liability statements
- privacy statements
- termination of service conditions
- use of the service by minors
- infringement
- specific state notifications, as required.

While terms of service agreements appear to cover every contingency, they can be changed at will by the social networking sites that create them. For the most part, these agreements work close to the line of the law, until social media decide to step over it. Where that line is is anyone's guess. But it is not the existence of these agreements that is the problem; it is the enforcement. For example, social networking sites' terms of service agreements warn against abusive language, racial slurs, sexual harassment, and sexual nicknames, but violations of same by members can be found on just about any social networking site chosen at random. Warnings against spamming and phishing (phishing is a scam meant to get a user to reveal much about his or her personal profile in order to use that information at the expense of the victim) occur in terms of service agreements, but they occur so often that it is now considered an epidemic on social networking sites in the United States.[25] But remember, social networking sites are "only channels" for this information, not the creators, so there is no real incentive to police it. In fact, it is possible that strict monitoring might well appear to the courts as ownership and therefore open them up to liability charges.

Minors are prohibited from joining most social networks, but again no mechanism exists to prohibit minors from joining or to let the social networking site know if they had. As the saw goes, "On the Internet, no one knows you're a dog."[26]

Readers will note that terms of service agreements include privacy statements, but these, too, can be (and routinely are) changed by the social networking site at will. Although creating fake profiles is prohibited, again, no mechanism prevents one from doing so. Perhaps the routine violation of terms of service agreements is one reason why most users do not read them. Terms of service agreements are, however, very important, as what they promise to prohibit or avoid routinely shows up in social networking legal entanglements.

Effectiveness of Terms of Service Agreements

TOS agreements "work" in the sense that social networking sites are able to clear legal hurdles during their formation. By inserting "terms of service agreements" in a Google search, one can get ready-made terms of service agreements than can be applied with modifications to any social networking site. This simply means that terms of service agreements are easy to write. Unfortunately, terms of service agreements are quite difficult to enforce, especially since the enforcement must take place in cyberspace, a "location" that readers know has no real geographical address. Moreover, it may not be humanly or technically possible to enforce them. For example, how could LinkedIn enforce its terms of service agreement for all of its 100 million-plus U.S. users, let alone its worldwide following, or Facebook for its billion-plus users, equitably? The agreements, while important, satisfy social networking sites' legal departments, but not much beyond that.

Social networking sites usually provide information about privacy matters in their terms of service agreements, but security measures are not very effective. Young people, both minors and the college-aged, provide so much information on social networking sites that others (mainly predators) are able to construct social security numbers, hometowns, and even street addresses from their profiles. Researchers at Carnegie Mellon University, Ralph Gross and Alessandro Acquisti, report that with the profile information of many young people it is possible to stalk individuals, especially if the victim and the stalker are in the same zip code.[27]

Even if the social networking site has good privacy controls, problems remain. And it is not just what users add about themselves. It has come to light recently that those billions of cat photos on the Internet mentioned above can also be tracked back to their users' locations using their longitude and latitude. According to the professor who studies the relationship between data and the public who discovered this tidbit, Owen Mundy, sites are "riding the wave of decreased privacy for all."[28] Social networking sites themselves do not abide by the privacy rules they spell out. At the beginning of 2014, Facebook found itself being sued for mining private messages with the intent of selling that mining to its advertisers, all without the permission of users.[29]

Privacy: Is It Really That Bad on Social Networks?

According to James Grimmelmann, University of Maryland law professor and affiliated with the Institute for Information and Law and Policy, "Facebook is Exhibit A for the surprising ineffectiveness of technical controls, especially in light of its recent actions. It has severe privacy problems *and* an admirably comprehensive privacy-protection architecture."[30] In other words, although Facebook attempts to manage security and privacy concerns well, it remains surprisingly ineffective in its attempts. If the security measures of the largest of social networking sites in the world are ineffective, it is not very likely that smaller social networking sites are any better. But solving security and privacy problems by using better technical controls can make matters worse, as Facebook discovered.

Facebook is a case in point on privacy matters. In late 2007, Facebook decided, without warning to users, to change its terms of service agreement and begin tracking users' purchases and alerting their "friends" via emails. The message might read, "[User name] just bought *A Tale of Two Cities* and thought you'd like to know." Facebook also changed what would appear on its "news feed" application. To say it created a firestorm of protest is an understatement. Users expressed their discontent over the social networking giant's control of content breach of security and loss of privacy. Almost immediately, more than 50,000 Facebook users signed a petition, essentially a virtual "cease and desist" order. While social networks have always reserved the right to change their terms of service agreements without notice (it is part of the boilerplate language), Facebook suffered a negative publicity backlash. In the end, Facebook scaled back, but did not retract, some of its initial changes. While users expressed their displeasure and logged comments in protest, Facebook did not change its privacy policy. Moreover, it did not stop Facebook from attempting a similar move later. And finally, with now more than a billion users, it really did not matter in terms of appeal to its clientele, now did it?

In what many industry observers consider an even bigger blunder, Facebook once again changed its privacy approach in 2009, this time with respect to access to users' content. Until this change, users thought Facebook deleted all online evidence if users chose to deactivate their accounts. But in early 2009, users discovered that Facebook kept copies of their messages even after they had signed off and "deleted" their accounts. The change resulted in an avalanche of complaints once again. Because of the volume and strength of complaints, Facebook issued a statement on its site explaining to users that it "had received a lot of feedback about the new terms" and so reverted back to the old policy "until we resolve the issues." But this should have come as little surprise as even deceased Facebook users' sites continued to be visible. Of course, Facebook would like us to believe it is a fitting testimony to those who have passed on. More likely it is a poignant reminder to loved ones of their loss.

Users are not entirely satisfied with Facebook even today. Lawyers, bloggers and others who commented on the matter are concerned about the legal implications with respect to security and privacy. Media and technology specialist Frances Anderson argues, "Even after [these changes and the subsequent hue and cry] Facebook still retains archive material—there is a lack of clarity of what the policy actually is."[31] In December 2009, Gawker.com's Ryan Tate argued that the new privacy settings are so hard to figure out that Facebook's CEO, Mark Zuckerberg, spent a month fiddling with his privacy settings to get them right. But Zuckerberg hardly has a leg to stand on since he is the one who argued that the "era of privacy is over."[32] Interestingly, when the privacy shoe was on the other foot and kicking rather briskly at Mr. Zuckerberg, his privacy seemed very important. When the documentary Terms and Conditions May Apply filmed Zuckerberg without his knowledge, his candid views were painfully familiar to all of us: we don't like it when our privacy is treated lightly, and neither did he.[33]

The dissatisfaction with Facebook's privacy controls, or lack thereof, continues. Facebook gadfly Max Schrems got more than 20,000 people to join his privacy class action suit against the social media giant in Austria. Schrems claims he has more than 20,000 people from 100 different countries. Because he must verify each claim, the number will be capped at 25,000. This class action suit in Austria is a little different from what it would have been in the United States. In Austria all the participants use one person—in this case Schrems—as their proxy litigant.[34]

Social media users provide the content free of charge that social networking sites use to generate revenue. Free of charge is overstated. In August 2013, a class action suit for $20 million against the social media giant brought to an end users' likes and dislikes for sponsored ads that appeared on their feeds.[35] In 2011, Facebook began "sponsored stories." If you liked a product, that company used your image and your "like" in an ad without asking you, not to mention without paying you, either. The ads proved almost 50 percent more effective. As usual, at places like Facebook your privacy matters, especially when it generates revenue. The class action suit was for $20 million, which sounds like a lot of money. It is not. Experts say that it cost the company about 1/5000th of its worth, so, in order words, pocket change. Let's be clear: *those* users were paid for their content after all.

Hardly six months later, Facebook came back with another approach that allowed users to opt out of some ads (good luck trying to find out how) but preventing opting out of others.[36] Facebook's view is a simple one. If you are a user, you "automatically" consent to social ads. A non-profit advocacy group, Public Citizen, is trying to pressure Facebook to change its approach and has filed a brief in the Ninth Circuit Court of Appeals in San Francisco. Since among Facebook's billion-plus users, some are minors, the suit seeks protection, forcing the company to get parents' permission. The settlement at this writing is for Facebook to develop a system for adolescent users that will allow parents to control how likes and dislikes are used. Parents fumed over the intrusions. Margaret Becker, a parent of a 16-year-old represented in the suit and a nonprofit lawyer for the Katrina Hurricane Relief Fund, expressed a sentiment shared by many: "They're turning [the teen's likes] into an advertisement for whatever she happens to like. I think there needs to be disclosure as well as explicit consent."

Facebook did make some adjustments in 2014 after the purchase of Whatsapp, a private messaging app that has global users. Zuckerberg indicated that "there are only so many photos you're going to want to share with all your friends."[37] This is a step in the right direction and a far cry from Zuckerberg's original claim that privacy was no longer a social norm. But it is not that he now believes it is a social norm as much as he may be hearing that users do not like everything out for public view. One can only hope so. But we shouldn't get too excited just yet. Some observers believe that while this change is important, it may well be that this will allow privacy information to become more exposed elsewhere.[38] As Tracy Mitrano points out, Facebook's privacy terms and principles run counter to the U.S. Constitution. It is, according to her, the "new world order."[39]

Social media platforms continue to make the case that using their sites, whether they are general sites or "niche" ones, is voluntary. But that should not be carte blanche for the loss of privacy. "The use of social networks, and thus the sharing of all this information is completely voluntary," writes one observer. "No one requires that anyone sign up for [a social networking site]. Even if you do, you need not use much of the privacy-deteriorating functionality it offers." At least this is the theory of users who sign on. But the tension is created when the site offers great value but also exposes colossal privacy risks to everyone, but especially minors:

However, online social networking has become a powerful trend. As social networking sites become more popular, it may be harder or even impractical for individuals to avoid them. A legal regime that addresses privacy concerns on social networks should not limit the ability of individuals to willingly give up traditionally private information. After all, the popularity of [social media] means that social networking sites provide a service that users actually value. In fact these sites can be extremely efficient modes of communication. But in a world where so much private information lies in the hands of others, how does the law protect abuse?[40]

It is just this tension that makes the issue of privacy so difficult. To lock down privacy is to, in effect, cut off the social network from its ability to operate. To leave it as it is exposes users to the loss of privacy, the loss of reputation, and the very real chance at loss of identity.

The Electronic Privacy Information Center (EPIC), a watchdog group that monitors privacy issues, filed a complaint against Facebook in late December 2009 with the Federal Trade Commission (FTC) over the changes. The Center for Digital Democracy joined EPIC in the complaint, along with the American Library Association and the Privacy Rights Clearinghouse. The complaint charges that the changes violate user expectations while diminishing user privacy. In order for users to "lock down" their information, a twenty-step process is required and can be found only by "googling" "privacy settings on Facebook."[41] All the negative publicity did put Zuckerberg on the editorial page of the *Washington Post*, May 24, 2010, asking for forbearance but not necessarily for forgiveness. The next day, Facebook announced it would develop new privacy settings. Will the "love affair" with Facebook sour over all these privacy problems? With a billion-plus users worldwide (and counting), it does not appear to be an issue that much concerns Facebook or many of its members.

It is not just Facebook but all social media. Even Google is facing a privacy lawsuit at this writing. A federal judge recently denied Google's claim to dismiss a privacy claim. Google had commingled user data from its various products and given that data to advertisers without users' permission. Google amassed about fifteen and a half billion in advertising revenues during the first quarter of 2014. The search giant had dispensed with various privacy policies ("policies subject to change without notice") and patched together an overarching privacy policy, mostly to its benefit and its advertisers, not so much for individuals' privacy.[42]

This is a bit amusing because Google, with all its data mining and sell-back to advertisers, is as responsible as any social medium for undermining our privacy.[43] Eric Schmidt, formerly of Google, promises us that in the future we may be able to buy our privacy. In a colossal case of the pot calling the kettle black, Facebook CEO Mark Zuckerberg took President Obama to task on the *government's* intrusion of privacy via the NSA. In other words, Facebook can treat your privacy as cavalierly as it pleases, but it's hell and high water if the government presumes to snoop into the activities of those with backpack bombs they plant at internationally respected road races.

Content Is King

Is this the end of the matter of content and who owns it? Hardly. Social media claim all content is theirs to do with as they please. Users must understand that whatever they place online is really not private in any pre–Internet sense of that word. Privacy problems continue even today. Four years ago, in April 2010, Senators Charles Schumer (D–New York), Michael Bennett (D–Colorado), Mark Begich (D–Alabama), and Al Franken (D–Michigan) wrote Facebook CEO Mark Zuckerberg a formal notice of concern over its privacy policy and attendant changes. Did anything change? No. Facebook has not backed down much, and even with privacy gaffes more public than ever and social media suffering considerable negative publicity, nothing changes beyond small corrections on the periphery. When Google released its social networking site, Buzz, in early 2010, it lasted about sixty days before privacy complaints all but shut it down. In other words, we users must demand our privacy from social media or lose it completely.

Mellon researchers Gross and Acquisti have found that users' approach to privacy is simply "quite oblivious, unconcerned or just pragmatic."[44] In its annual 2010 "State of the Net" report, *Consumer Reports* indicated that 53 percent of social networking users post risky information online that compromises their privacy. Scott McNealy, co-founder of Sun Microsystems, a well-known computer technology company, made the now famous in-your-face-comment when he said, "You have no privacy anyway, get over it."[45] McNealy argued that the invention of the web ended all questions of privacy and its related security for everyone. For social media, individual privacy is a concern only insofar as it generates negative publicity, but not so much that it changes the way social media collect and use information and/or content. In a famous let-them-eat-cake moment, social media spokespersons repeatedly reminded users that if they are uncomfortable sharing online, then don't.

While some would dub these comments as cavalier views of privacy, many Internet users really are not concerned about privacy. According to a 2007 Pew Internet Report, rising generations "are not concerned about the amount of information available about them online, and most do not take steps to limit that information. Fully 60 percent of Internet users say they are not worried about how much information is available about them online."[46] YouGov BrandIndex (http://www.brandindex.com/), a company that studies "consumer perception," says that concerns about privacy are mainly from those 35 years of age and older, not with the young. The combination of a carefree attitude about online personal information as well as the ubiquity of that information on social networking sites to anyone who wishes to use or misuse it, means that privacy will remain a security concern for the foreseeable future. Even the most careful social media user who guards her privacy carefully is not really safe. The more exposure one has on social media, the more likely he or she will be victimized by scammers, a practice known as catfishing. Catfishing occurs when someone purports to be a person he or she is not, using social media to propose money, romance, or an emotional relationship for some gain.

Social media's privacy policy is really a public-by-default policy. But, to be honest, it is public-by-default with little chance of making it private. For adults, this public-by-default may be the "price of admission," so to speak. But with young adults (and even those who are not supposed to be online but are), it becomes a serious issue. Teens share information about where they live, how old they are, and even personal information about how lonely they may be. This inadvertently makes them perfect targets for miscreants and worse. Although adults are known to use them too, check-in apps like Foursquare are problematic in the hands of young people. Not only do they make it easy to identify where a person is, thus making it easy for those seeking harm to know where their victims are, but they also make it easy for burglars to plan their next burglary.[47] In 2014, Foursquare essentially divided its app into two—one for discovery, now called Foursquare, and one for check-in, called Swarm. Whatever it is called, the check-in feature is one more way that social media expose us to unnecessary risks, risks that we users place ourselves in all too eagerly. It is not that teens do not care about privacy, but they do not understand fully what it means to share so much, and they still think they can maintain some semblance of a private life. The more we share on social media, the more we become like would-be celebrities, giving up whatever privacy we may have wanted in return for oversharing.

Some readers will argue that *any* sharing on social media puts their privacy at risk. Even signing on may expose users to unnecessary and unwanted intrusion. But social media have become so critical to communication that opting out is no longer considered by many as a legitimate choice. It would be much like telling people fifty years ago that if they did not like the news, avoid buying a paper or watching television. Indeed, social media are now the virtual news, for all intents and purposes. Social media connect us to events, to others who share similar values, help law enforcement, and provide a vehicle for those who are unable to communicate easily with the outside world. Moreover, they connect those suffering from illnesses or other maladies with those who are suffering in similar situations. They can even provide an effective means for discovering treatments that may not be known in Peoria but are known in New York City. Our choice should not be between staying off social media and signing off on our privacy, our reputation, and our identity. Users have certain recourses, like blocking certain sites, disabling third-party cookies, even encrypting instant messages and unfollowing those that violate one's principles. But even doing all these things provides no guarantee because the Internet's security in general and social media's security in specific are like Swiss cheese: full of holes wherein those who want to can intrude.

Some observers believe that those who care about privacy are simply those who are too old for social media. This is only partly true. Many social media users over 45 are concerned about privacy, and perhaps far more concerned about it than younger generations. But as this chapter has shown, young users are not unconcerned about it at all. They are very concerned about it, but not enough to forgo using social media. As far as getting one's privacy back following exposure (or overexposure) on social media, the answer is, yes, it is too late. Regardless of what terms of service promise, what social media practice is nothing short of the exploitation of users' privacy for the sake of that media's attractiveness to advertisers and therefore that social media's potential revenue. Clearly a social media site that locked down privacy tightly would be of little interest to advertisers.

Congress is not likely to get into this business of privacy too carefully since social media sites represent a large block of voters and a tremendous amount of potential campaign contributions. Users can lock down this or that setting, unfriend those who are careless about their privacy, and do whatever else they may be instructed to do. But what users must come to grips with is that by signing on to social media, they are giving up much, if not all, of their privacy. While social media will regularly remind us how concerned they are about our privacy, they will do little to jeopardize what has made them so successful: the sharing of personal information.

Much of this chapter has been harsh on social media, and rightly so. But users are as much to blame as social media. We like talking about ourselves, our plans, our families, our vacations, and so on. Whether we will tire of this in the future is anyone's guess. But if past behavior is any predictor of future performance, our presence on social media will be at the expense of our private selves.

And we users are apparently fine with that for now.

EIGHT

#IdentityTheft#Phishing

"You've Won!! Like Us on Facebook to Claim Your Winnings!"

Aren't phishing, identity theft, and/or fraud simply other forms of privacy intrusion?[1] Certainly. Then why a separate chapter? Because they represent a particularly virulent form of privacy invasion, unlike the quotidian annoyances of privacy erosion that social networking users experience routinely. Some forms of even these more virulent kinds of privacy invasions, like phishing, may or may not lead to a full frontal assault on an individual's identity. But all too often they do, and no matter how many times users are warned, they still seem to fall victim; sooner rather than later, the phishing attacks are successful.

It is true that identity theft and fraud, of course, took place long before computers and social networks ever saw the light of day. Phishing, or whatever it was called before computers, took place routinely. Dumpster diving is what it sounds like: going through reams of paper from a bank or other company's dumpsters, looking for bank account numbers, social security numbers, or any other identifying markers. John Hanneke Nelson may well be the poster boy for this form of identity theft, stealing more than 500 identities through his routine dumpster diving at a Wells Fargo Bank.[2]

After obtaining the information, a person might well make a phone call, and if the fraudster is a smooth enough talker, he or she could eventually get enough information to fulfill his or her wishes. But crimes such as dumpster diving take time, patience, and several phone calls before the criminals get what they are looking for: an easy target. Social networking sites, however, have made these crimes like taking candy from a baby. The targets have identified themselves, and nearly no interaction is necessary. With a computer and a little—but not very much—technological savvy, the tools necessary to commit the crimes of identity theft, phishing, and fraud can be performed in a matter of minutes. Often criminals reap a return that far exceeds what they could have accomplished before social networking sites appeared.

Social Media: Easy Crime of Opportunity

One reason why they are so successful is that these are crimes of opportunity. Social networking users put so much helpful information online that this low-hanging fruit begs to be harvested, and it is to the tune of billions of dollars annually, more than $25 billion in 2013 alone.[3] Social networking sites are like fat wallets left on busy sidewalks, waiting for someone to pick them up. In this case, the sidewalk is not filled with good-hearted people, but hardcore individuals who are already out there looking for those so-called wallets. The damage that can be done in a matter of a few minutes can be so devastating to the victim that fixing it is like putting toothpaste back in the tube: messy, inefficient, and pointless.

The victims are often children, but the elderly, the deceased, and young adults are also targeted. In fact, it really can happen to anyone. Making one's settings private does not help nearly so much as putting less and less information out on the Internet. Over the last few years, too, fraudsters have learned to use the information more quickly, making catching them in the act harder and harder. Often, the criminals have used the information, wreaked their havoc, and gone before the victim notices it. Fraudsters are more likely to use information gleaned from social networking than they are from making up names because the identities have already been established and can be easily verified. Fraudsters wisely think that the time spent in trying to create a legitimate-seeming identity can be better spent bilking the funds of a real person. Make no mistake about it: Once caught in the theft's web, retrieving one's identity can take years, even though the crime took place over only a few hours.

Identity theft as it relates to social media is a fairly recent crime, and its criminalization is less than two decades old.[4] With the passage of the 1998 Identity Theft and Assumption Deterrence Act (P.L. 105–318), the act became a federal crime. The rapid rise of the World Wide Web, coupled with the explosion of social media, made it hard for users to understand that placing so much personal information in public might not be a good idea. Users learned too late. The crime, as far as crimes go, is easy to perpetrate. A criminal needs only a person's uniquely identifying information—an address, social security number, phone number, credit card, or driver's license—to begin his potential wrecking-ball behavior. With this in hand, a criminal can do serious harm in a matter of minutes. The problem is further magnified through the Internet because anyone anywhere in the world, with access to a computer, can scan social media for possible victims, exploit them, and then move on before the unsuspecting user knows what hit him.

Social Media Crimes Are Easy and Ubiquitous

Social media sites, because they are open to anyone, anywhere, with computer access, make it simple for fraudsters to track unsuspecting victims easily. We log onto our social media accounts at restaurants, cafes, in busy airports, on flights, and even just waiting in line at the grocery store or for a movie to begin. Because we are all so hyperconnected, we are not only vulnerable to the loopholes in social media security, but also multiply the risks in which our identities can be taken. Like porn sites that often display the latest in web technology and graphic interface, so also do criminals have some of the best technology available for tracking down easy prey. Some readers will complain that, yes, it is easy for the unwary to be caught. But they will point out, in defense of social media, that just as these criminals are tracking individuals online, so can police track them down. Some will cite well-known stories of lost phones being recovered or criminals found because police have gone hi-tech, too. All of this is true, but identity theft can happen so quickly and so surreptitiously that by the time the victim knows her identity has been compromised, the criminal is long gone. Tracking down criminals even with hi-tech equipment will not generally work, at least not in the same way that it did to steal the identity, because the crime is realized long after the "trail" has gone ice-cold. Once your identity has been stolen, getting it back proves ever more difficult.

Laissez-Faire Security

So why are social media companies at best laissez-faire about security? Social media companies are not dismissive of security. But security costs money, and the tighter they lock down these sites, the less users will be able to share with others, the less advertisers will want to advertise on them, and the fewer dollars social media companies will be able to generate in revenue. If Facebook, for example had to tighten its controls to eliminate much of the threat to privacy, the company would go broke in a matter of months. Keeping access open keeps advertisers on board. If this sounds like social media's security is sacrificed for revenues, that's only because it is. No social media company, large or small, can afford to keep controls too tightly constrained. Further, by remaining open, users and social media sites can keep the interchange going 24 hours a day, 7 days a week.

Wormholes Galore: Geotagging

Using metadata, geotagging identifies where something is located. Geotagging has a useful purpose. If you are in a new town or city, you can find stores or points of interest near you in a matter of seconds. This saves time and effort and is a tremendous help. But if the geotagging can find you or help locate where you are in an area, so those seeking to do harm can track you down just as easily as you can track down a restaurant.

On the web, however, for every good idea using some form of technology, there is a bad one, or one in such dreadful taste that it defies belief, or so it would seem. For example, one particularly nefarious and stupid geotagging app is called "Girls Around Me." The site drew on location services provided by Foursquare and Facebook and then returned to users of the app women who were in the vicinity. While the Russian developer did not think he had done anything wrong, Apple, Foursquare, and Facebook acted quickly to remove the app, thereby killing it.

Or did they? The fact of the matter is that with some finagling, one can still find women or men by using the general features of many social media sites. The app itself proved too straightforward and perhaps a bit too blatant in its intentions. Yet some features of it remain on social media sites that can be gamed to offer a similar result if one is inclined to look for them. If geotagging became widespread, individual privacy would be destroyed, and possibly forever. Still, would that stop us from using it? It's a good question but one we likely know the answer to already.

Identity Theft as Revenge

Identity theft using social media does not have to involve an exchange of money, though it often does. One reason why fraudsters are trolling social media sites is to find easy victims. But identity theft can also occur because someone is angry with another person, because someone wants to get back at another, or because someone wants to prove a point to others at the expense of the victim he or she chooses to use. A New Jersey woman, Dana Thornton, used Facebook to set up a profile of her ex-boyfriend, a narcotics detective. Apparently the relationship soured very badly, as she depicted him as a sexual deviant and a drug addict. Thornton posted that he used drugs, hired prostitutes, and had herpes. She also posted comments from him such as, "I'm an undercover narcotics detective that gets high every day."[5] Although the case is going to court, proving guilt will be difficult because of the way the law has been written in New Jersey.

In California, a teenager stole a classmate's Facebook password in order to post sexually explicit material about the victim.[6] Ira Trey Quesenberry III was a high school student at Sullivan Central High School. He decided to make light of his school director, Dr. Jubal Yennie.[7] Quesenberry set up a Twitter account that appeared to come from Yennie. Then the 18-year-old began sending out tweets of a graphic and unprofessional nature. After Yennie contacted police to let them know the account was fake, Quesenberry was discovered as the perpetrator and booked to appear in court. While some social media pundits see these as "merely" high-tech pranks, they seem to forget just how public and how widespread such things can become in a matter of minutes. Thirty years ago, young people like Quesenberry might have drawn a caricature of the director and placed it in a public place within the school. Perhaps as many as a few dozen students would have seen it before it was taken down. But in today's high-tech world, it does not take any time before thousands have seen it and a reputation is compromised. Sure, it can be cleared up

Social media are the "low-hanging fruit" to cyberthieves (courtesy Shutterstock; used with permission).

as a hoax, but the web is far more likely to share the dirt as it is to correct it. To reinstate a good reputation takes a great deal longer than it does to destroy one.

Phishing's Damage

Phishing is used to gain access and/or establish communication in order to access private information, be it credit card numbers, passwords, or just a way to get into a person or a company's network. Once inside, the criminal can use that communication to harm or even destroy a company's reputation or an individual's private information. No money changes hands, of course, but it provides a quick and effective way to disable the competition. Geotagging, as mentioned above, identifies where you live, where you work, and even where you are any time of the day, if the tags remain enabled. By searching through social media sites, fraudsters can find important information like favorite colors, pet's names, and any other information that would enable them to combine whatever information they have on hand to hack into important public or private systems. Bank accounts have been drained using this method, email accounts hacked, and even changes made into important saving accounts or other financial arrangements that harm the victim.

Identity theft is big business, and it pays the criminal effort well. The likelihood of being caught is also small since the mischief can be done and over, long before the victim understands what has happened. Unraveling the mess can take months if not years. Often, once the damage is done, full credit or restitution recovery is not always possible.

Phishing occurs when enticing information is entered online, in a social media site, or via emails to individuals asking for information in return for either monetary or other rewards. Most readers are familiar with the now infamous "Nigerian" email scams. According to recent information, these scammers look through Facebook pages for "lonely old women with money."[8] These phishing expeditions used to net about $12,000 a job, but with as much knowledge as these cons now have available, they now net "only" about $200. Still, in a country where the average person lives on $2 a day, these scammers who are making more than $50,000 annually can live like proverbial kings.

Altruism Plays a Role

Why is it still possible for phishing scams like this to work? Because people want to believe they are helping others, for one thing; they are credulous, for another. By playing on one's naïve altruism, they are able to get others to fund their crimes. And the scammers have nothing to lose. If they can get someone to play along, even if it costs them several hundred dollars, they will keep up the ruse for the possibility of a larger gain. The credulity, along with, it must be admitted, some greed, plays right into the hands of those seeking to make some quick money. With access to much of what they need already on social media, the crime is easier and easier to commit.

Phishing attacks via social media can and do happen to anyone, even the tech-savvy.[9] The ploy usually begins not with some silly Nigerian scam, but with a note about a party or some common event from an individual the victim knows. This kind of phishing uses a person's known friends and the note, say from Facebook, or even from Twitter, is familiar-sounding enough to entice the victim to click on it. Brian Rutberg had his Facebook account hacked in this manner. Messages were sent to his "friends" that he was in urgent need of help: he had been robbed and needed to get from point A to point B. The cry for help was URGENT, in all capital letters.[10] How many of us, if we saw the message from a dear friend, would automatically ignore it? Probably not many. In Rutberg's case, his friends came through with more than a thousand dollars in a matter of minutes. Once people click on the indicated link to help, the message may reveal slightly more information that requires a further click of some kind and perhaps some sort of pass-through that allows a long enough delay for the message to install whatever hacking mechanism is required to complete the attack.

In the end, it doesn't take much to make any of us a victim of these clever ploys: a message from a "friend" who is not a friend, but a name taken at random from our list of social media friends; an urgent message from another "friend" about being stuck in another geographical location and without a phone but in need of money; or, a cry for help from a stranger. All it takes is enough information to hook us, to appeal to our altruism, friendship, greed, or just stupidity, and the miscreant has us. When the criminal combines what he has learned from the social media with what he can glean elsewhere, perhaps some commonly reused pass-words, the damage is done. As David Hannum, a critic of P.T. Barnum, once famously said, "There is a sucker born every minute."

In the Case of Social Media, Less Is More

The more information users put in personal profiles, the easier it is to gather enough data to phish for (fraudulently request) additional infor-

mation. While all ages using social networks are at risk, a group of researchers at MIT and Indiana University found that younger age groups are most
vulnerable.[11] If the data have been gleaned from a social network, securing
identity theft is four times more likely. According to Kelly Higgins of Dark
Reader, a security firm that reports on this and other web-related security
activities, social networking phishing attacks from 2008 to 2009 increased
240 percent, surpassing email scams. Real identities are pilfered from
social networking sites, and fake identities are created. Privacy Rights
Clearinghouse, an organization that monitors all types of breaches, reports
that since 2005 over 355 million breaches have occurred in which "sensitive personal information" was taken, including everything from credit
cards to social security numbers.[12] In some cases, those stealing identities
are able to combine social media data with other personal information
found on the web to home in on where individuals live or work. Fraudsters
have a prime venue of attack on social media sites because the information
is rich and the security easy to disable or work around.

Sadly, with the proliferation of social media also came skyrocketing
cybercrime and especially identity theft. While many of us may be immune
to requests via email, as we have seen above, the request through some
social media may be too intriguing to ignore. While there are some ways
to avoid identity theft, there are too many loopholes in social media to
make any protection failsafe. Are users left with no other choice but to
stay away? That really is not an option, of course, but it should provide
enough hyperventilation for anyone on social media to do everything she
can to limit her exposure.

More Crime: Slander and Libel

Under the heading of slander and libel, social networking sites are
replete with potential problems. The problems happen routinely, but often
only the well-known prove newsworthy. The WBA welterweight boxing
champion Amir Khan and his promoter, Frank Warren, hired lawyers in
2009 to threaten Facebook with legal action over the use of images and
names associated with the boxer that the pair believed were defamatory and racist. Warren is fighting Facebook to develop a more responsible policy.[13] Stephen Taylor Heath, the head of sports and media at
Lupton Fawcett, a prestigious law firm in Leeds, points out that a quick
search of Facebook reveals materials that, if published in a printed source,
would be subject to defamation of character charges. He believes Facebook
does not take the problem seriously. Although this incident took place
outside the U.S., legal actions against social media sites, regardless of

geographic location, will eventually impact them because they "exist" everywhere.

Legal experts are divided over whether such sites are liable for posted comments (again owing to Section 230 of the Communications Decency Act), or whether defamation applies in every context regardless of the format. Complicating this matter are terms of service agreements that promise to remove materials that are abusive, vulgar, hateful, or racially and ethnically objectionable. If social media sites claim that such behavior is prohibited and promise to remove it when it occurs, they open themselves up for potential legal risk when they do not.

In the 2007 case of *J. S. v. Blue Mountain School District*, a student created a MySpace page and charged that his principal, Mr. James S. McGonigle, "is a married, bisexual man" whose interests include "f*cking in his office and hitting on students and their parents." When his identity was discovered, the student was suspended for ten days, but he later brought legal action for a violation of his First Amendment rights. While the court agreed he did have those rights, he did not have the right either to state falsehoods or to cause a disruption at the school. The court denied the injunction and did not order the school to overturn the suspension.[14]

But when Anna Draker, a principal at Clark High School in San Antonio, Texas, discovered a fake profile of herself on MySpace that was full of defamatory information, the court decided her case differently. The two students who had invented her profile, Ben Schreiber and Ryan Todd, had been disciplined by her several times. Ostensibly they were out for revenge, and they got it in spades. Once the site appeared, Draker took the students and their parents to court in 2006 (*Anna Draker v. Benjamin Schreiber* (a minor), *Lisa Schreiber, Ryan Todd* (a minor), *Lisa Todd and Steve Todd*, 2006). She claimed that the parents were at fault for allowing unsupervised access to the Internet and for negligent supervision. The court granted the negligence claim in 2008 but dismissed the rest of Draker's case on the grounds that the profile claims could not be proven (the students made claims about Draker's sexuality that were untrue). Draker appealed, but the Texas appeals court upheld the lower court ruling. Forget the fact that Draker has had to repair her reputation about the sexuality claims that went worldwide.

In Henry County, Georgia, high school teacher Robert Muzillo sued a fifteen-year-old student for slander because of a MySpace profile filed under his name. The student implied that Muzillo was gay. After being caught, the student claimed he only meant it as a joke. Just days before the suit was filed, Muzillo gave the student three days of in-school suspension for the incident. The suit later failed because it relied on a statute that the Georgia Supreme Court had already declared unconstitutional.[15]

What makes these and other cases like them so interesting is that under "traditional" circumstances (i.e., before social networking sites), the infractions might never have occurred, or if they did, would have been known only to a small circle of people. They would have died a relatively quick death, too, from lack of exposure. Because social networking sites give instant access to tens of millions of people simultaneously, silly "pranks" go viral, suits get filed, and attorneys are hired. Social networking sites have changed much about the way we not only conduct our lives, but also about the way we *can* conduct our lives.

What frustrates many who look at these and other cases is the courts' inconsistency in deciding these cases. Perhaps the courts need a new legal benchmark to decide matters in light of the very new means of communication.

Remaining Somewhat Safe

Is there anything that social media users can do to remain safe? There is, but nothing will keep you as safe as staying off social media altogether or severely limiting exposure by connecting to only one or two and making your profile as private as possible (and thereby defeating its purpose). But even this isn't failsafe, and the suggestions below will work only so far.

It would appear to go without saying that one should never reveal his or her social security number, driver's license number, or bank routing numbers to anyone but those individuals who must have it and to give out this information in person, never online. Thirty years ago, it was common to find checks with social security numbers on them, and even as late as 1999–2000, the university at which I work still used social security numbers very much like PIN numbers are used today. Social security numbers often ended up on the backs of checks or other documents routinely, and driver's license numbers were and still are used more often than they should be. Increasingly that is being discouraged, and it should go without saying that these numbers should never appear on a social media site, be given out in an email, or ever given to anyone who asks for it online.

Of course users should change passwords regularly, they should consist of letters and numbers, and they should be long rather than short. As the saying has it, change your passwords as often as your underwear. A password generator can help, but what trips up most people is their need for a few dozen passwords. They tend to use the same ones over and over because it's easier to remember two or three than thirty or forty. Of course, writing them down on a piece of paper is not a good idea. Google is working on a plan that will eliminate the need for passwords by linking them to a sound that only your phone can hear.[16] To access sites in this manner one would hold up a phone to listen to the website's ultrasonic sound. The sound is encrypted with unique required confirmation that only the phone can detect. The timetable on the rollout for this is not yet set. Until then, other measures like changing passwords and making them more difficult to decode are necessary. Using programs like Keypass to keep track of multiple passwords is also helpful.

It is important to remember that those seeking to break into accounts use things like dictionaries and other tools, all automated to make the process easier and quicker. Longer passwords made up of both letters and numbers will be more secure than shorter ones with only letters or numbers.[17]

Once these passwords are secure, be sure not to use them over and over again or give them out to anyone else. Resist the temptation to believe that giving them out makes connecting with others easier. It is better not to connect everywhere if it means you can remain safe somewhere. When signing up online, do not overshare. Social media sites try to lure you in by reminding you that your profile is only 30 percent complete, as if you are some sort of slacker who cannot fill out his profile the right way. Some will also remind you by asking you simple questions, such as where did you go to school or what is your favorite pet? Resist the temptation to answer. The more you tell about yourself, the more open you will be to someone stealing your identity.

Keep on top of your credit report by using something like Experian or another security company that tracks both your credit and intrusions to same. Such companies do not charge much and do a reasonably good job of protecting you and letting you know when someone has attempted an unauthorized access of your accounts.

While these things can work to make you safer online, they cannot protect you fully. The fact of the matter is that when you choose to sign up to a social media site, you are in essence saying that you are happy to risk your security for your ability to connect to these individuals, some of whom you know and many you do not. Making common-sense decisions about your social media presence will make your online presence a pleasant one, not one you'll live to regret.

NINE

#CyberDoctorsAre4Real

"Listen Up. If you think you're having a heart attack, start coughing as hard as you can. It'll stop the heart attack."

One of the places in which social media shine is in the area of medical advice or symptom diagnosis. Social media link patients with illnesses to other patients across cities, states, and even countries. Patients and/or families post treatments for various illnesses allowing others to benefit from the collective wisdom of crowds.[1] For crowdsourcing authors like James Surowiecki and David Weinberger, social media, the Internet, and the World Wide Web are now the collective geniuses of our age.[2] We no longer need to remember, to collect facts, or to try to keep chronologies straight. All of that is on the web, and social media keep us connected with one another, acting as a kind of checks and balances. Medical advice is yet one more place, say proponents, where we all benefit from this collective wisdom. Unsurprisingly, crowdsourcing is beneficial but not without some strong qualifications. Crowds do become mobs and are often subject to group-think. In the case of medical advice, this can be both good and bad, as we shall see.

Social media have placed at the fingertips—literally—of many what they need to know about illnesses they or their loved ones have. Furthermore, these sites disambiguate medical tests or provide second, third, or even twenty-fifth opinions, all completed without anyone ever having to leave home. In fact, in some cases, researchers are encouraging the government to get more involved with social media, to use it more, and to use it more effectively. Few, for example, doubt the usefulness of sites like WebMD.

Researchers from Boston Children's Hospital, Harvard Medical School, and Brigham and Women's Faulkner Hospital have asked the Federal Drug Administration to use social media to explain in more detail

127

drug interactions and contraindications.[3] One of the complaints of the researchers is that, while the advice is on the web, the connections between the various sites the Food & Drug Administration (FDA) hosts are not obvious and are hard to find. Social media would be a way in which, with very little effort, the FDA could make more information available to patients, explain drug interactions in a more apparent manner, and promulgate correct information to everyone faster and more thoroughly. Wikipedia is another place in which medical researchers wish could be made more effective. Wikipedia is now the first or second choice for anyone looking for information about an illness, whether for drug or treatment options. But drug information is woefully inadequate, outdated, or both on Wikipedia. By working with WebMD, the FDA could update the information early and as often as necessary, thereby getting out to patients much needed information about drug interactions. Having such information handy would not only provide an important public service, but also even potentially save lives.

Physicians and Social Media

Physicians, too, are getting on social media, though their acceptance of it has been slow. The caution has been well-advised. Physicians have ethical obligations demanded by their profession, not to mention their patients—us. Besides, patients would not want a doctor treating them who later tweeted, "Whoa! Just saw #giantmole." "Digital communications and social media use," writes Dr. Phyllis Guze, Chair of the Board of Regents, ACP, "continue to increase in popularity among the public and medical profession. [But physicians need] guidance on best practices to inform standards for the professional conduct of physicians."[4] While these technologies do provide physicians new and exciting ways to connect with patients, possibly in ways that provide greater openness on the part of both patient and physician, they are not without pitfalls. "Digital media use for nonclinical purposes," warns the American College of Physicians, "may affect societal perceptions of the profession, especially when questionable content is posted by physicians in their personal use of the web. Maintaining separate personal and professional identities in web postings may help avoid blurring boundaries in interactions with patients and colleagues."[5] The concerns about potential pitfalls are nothing to be dismissive about. Issues of confidentiality, the loss of face-to-face interactions, the ambiguity of digital interactions, non-peer reviewed information, scam medical sites, flaming, and the use of unsecured channels to give out personal medical advice are currently the biggest concerns related to physicians using social media to dispense medical advice.

Issues of confidentiality may loom the largest in this context. A patient's medical issues should not be public knowledge unless the individual so deems it. But discussions about one's medical health over unsecured networks mean that patients run the risk of having that information made public. There could be serious ramifications, particularly if a patient is also employed in a job that requires good or excellent health to perform. A particular medical issue that is under control but becomes public knowledge may put in jeopardy that patient's employment.

Further, the loss of the ability to look directly into a patient's eyes could well diminish the physician's ability to diagnose. Eye color, size of the pupils, skin color, temperature, and so on are but a few of the many data points needed by physicians to give their best assessment. While it is true that many medical units now offer "Skype-like" appointments, many of these occur after there has been a full face-to-face medical work-up.

In addition to the lack of eye-to-eye contact is the ambiguity of digital interactions. How many times have a nudge and a wink been misconstrued as something else entirely? And how many times have we misread someone's accidental cap lock for anger? When talking about someone's dinner, or last evening's night on the town, digital ambiguity may be a plus. When trying to ascertain whether a symptom is nothing to worry about, or whether it warrants an ER visit, getting the right answer is supremely important. A simple "that may not be a bad sign" can be read, literally, as either "don't worry about it" or "it sounds bad but perhaps it is not." Even humor can be misplaced. Unfortunately, the ambiguity of digital interactions is part of the warp and the woof of being online. Yet it is also something physicians cannot afford to get wrong. Moreover, a misplaced modifier or a simple misspelling can lead to the wrong diagnosis, the wrong treatment, or the wrong advice. This is certainly one reason why medical sites are chock-full of various disclaimers and the ubiquitous "No advice given on this site is a substitute for seeing your personal physician." All too often, however, patients are looking for free advice and an easy way out. Add to this the plethora of non-medically trained voices chiming in, and the recipe for disaster is there for the taking.

While patients are certainly better informed about medical issues than they were only a decade ago, their newfound knowledge may not always be in the best interest of the attending physician. When social media were younger than they are today, patients often went to their physicians with their diagnosis in hand and their treatment predetermined. When these patients were confronted with an entirely different diagnosis, they were not always agreeable to the explanation and either skipped that new diagnosis or went to another less qualified physician or quacksalver for the answer they wanted. That happens less frequently now than it once did, but even television commercials predispose patients to the treatment they want, not necessarily the one they actually need.

Non-peer-reviewed information can also send patients down blind alleys. Everything from the treatment of AIDS or the treatment of arthritis, to the treatment of terminal illnesses gives patients hope where there isn't any.[6] At one time, sites promised cancer cures for patients who took shark cartilage! While amusing now, those who found this as their last hope did not laugh, especially those patients or families who spent their life savings for treatments that did not work or for lab work from sites that were abandoned or that never existed in the first place. The good news is that the FTC strongly recommends that users steer away from non-government-related sites. It also warns individuals to avoid sites that claim cure-alls for multiple illnesses or that make outrageous claims that cannot be documented elsewhere. It's a safe bet that if consumers have never heard of a cure on a site, and if they cannot find it documented on multiple, physician-approved sites, the information must be viewed as dubious. The sad fact of the matter is that just as fraudsters seek to "make you rich quick" if they can have your bank routing numbers to deposit "your lottery winnings," so also are the quacksalvers and their sites promising cures underway at nonexistent labs if you'll just give them enough money.

This by no means is a reason for not using the web to check a symptom or a treatment. But it is ample warning that whatever one finds on the Internet in general or on a social media site in specific needs to be treated *cum grano salis* until it can be corroborated.

Social Media: No Silver Medical Bullets

Many social media sites will help patients to understand their diagnoses, or to read the lab results that their own personal physicians have not clearly explained. But there really are not any silver bullets for serious medical illnesses; even the advice found on ever-reliable sites like WebMD is not failsafe without personal physician intervention. But the web is ever versatile. In the 1992 film *Lorenzo's Oil* with Susan Sarandon, the medical establishment fails to find a cure for her son, afflicted with the deadly disease adrenoleukodystrophy, ALD. Sarandon and her husband embark on their own treatments, using bulletin boards, emails, and whatever else they can find to get their son the treatment he needs. Apart from the cheap political shots throughout the movie, the true story shows what determination and a never-give-up attitude can do. But for every *Lorenzo's Oil*, which has a somewhat happy ending, there are dozens more where family fortunes are spent hunting "snipes."

Scam medical sites abound on the Internet and are abundant on social media. The FDA provides excellent advice about many of these scams, and patients can sign up to receive alerts on the FDA site, in addition to receiving recalls and other important medical advice. The FDA is also policing fraudulent pharmacies on the web. It is a matter of life and death because many of these quack cures can lead to misdiagnosis, mistreatment and even death.[7]

Furthermore, the simple "flame wars" so prevalent on the web can lead to the wrong medical information. Well-meaning but non-medically trained individuals can give very adamant and smart-sounding advice that can lead patients astray. Two individuals engaged in a tit-for-tat verbal tug of war often sound like scientific-based advice to the unwary. When that advice sounds like hope for the hopeless, it becomes even more dangerous. Ill-informed but desperate patients can view these as "important" discussions and be misled.

In all these cases, patients can avoid both loss of dollars and loss of important treatment by taking a little extra time to be careful and verify the information through a medical authority. For example, bee pollen, an often-advertised cure-all for various illnesses but especially for debilitating diseases like arthritis, is not only useless in most cases, but can in some cases exacerbate the illness its proponents claim to cure. Checking out any social media medical advice with a few more clicks on authoritative medical sites helps patients find what they are looking for or, at the very least, avoid something that harms. The problem is that we all know the exceptions to this rule. Famed basketball star Ervin "Magic" Johnson got his AIDS treatment by bypassing conventional medical wisdom, and his treatment has saved his life and given him a quality of wellness once unknown among some AIDS patients. But we all know such stories because they are the exceptions. Yes, the FDA is slow to approve treatments. And yes, people do die waiting for them. We cannot, however, make the leap that *all* conventional medical advice is wrong. Identifying scam sites is not altogether a shot in the proverbial dark. Sites that promise "smart drugs for longer life," "arthritis will vanish like magic" or "new scientific breakthrough" are almost always more fiction than fact. The old adage, "if it sounds too good to be true, it probably is," is good advice to follow.[8] This is particularly true when it comes to those who are 65 and over, the age group found by government studies most likely to be the victims of such targets.

Patients can avoid becoming victims by avoiding sites that claim quick fixes and promise cures when no known cures have yet been found by medical science. Particularly suspect are those sites that ask for money up front or that provide only the flimsiest of background but promise the full advice when payment is received. Often these sites will have testimonials from "patients" who cannot be tracked, who have no real information for contacting them, or that are really no more than simply quotes from undocumented sources.

Patients who have been through several medically sound treatments without any change in their condition are often at their wits' end and willing to try anything. A local librarian can help patients work through many of these sites by showing them simple ways to compare bogus sites with those that have valid scientific backing. Patients are likely to discover that they are using a site that may well have been written by someone who never leaves home, has never graduated from college, or has no medical training at all. All of this is easy to say when sitting in an armchair and relatively disease-free. But patients need to know that unsound medical advice abounds on the Internet, and guard-ing oneself against bogus treatments will save time, money, and false hope.

Regardless of what even our government tells us, medical information over social media is not really privacy-proof. The Health Information Technology for Economic and Clinical Health Act (HITECH Act) protects the privacy of patients' medical records. As the American Recovery and Reinvestment Act of 2009 encouraged the adoption of health information technology, the HITECH Act sought to protect patient confidentiality. The idea behind the act was to create electronic health records nationwide as a prelude to Obamacare. Since then, however, more than 29 million heath record breaches have been noted.[9] While about half of all breaches are theft, about 20 percent are for unauthorized access. Unfortunately, the stress of the Obamacare rollout to make medical records available electronically has helped to put all patient records more at risk. While more and more organizations are able to note the breaches after they occur, few are able to prevent them until the loophole or entry point is exposed.

Getting out accurate medical advice via social media cannot be overstressed. Even medical schools are now providing guidelines on the use of social media when it comes to medical advice.[10] Medical schools and medical associations now realize that individuals will look to social media first before looking to a medical practitioner. Whether this is the best of all possible worlds or not is a moot point. It is the world in which we now live. If correct medical information is to get out to patients, and patients are repairing to social media for answers, the only way to provide them with useful information is for medical practitioners to provide that information where those patients are: social media.

Wikipedia, Social Media and Medicine

It has become a favorite pastime of some academics to beat up on Wikipedia, a primary source for those who use social media and want to prove a point or provide some point of reference.[11] The problem is not so much that Wikipedia has bad information. On the whole, it is reliable, or rather it can be. And there's the rub: users often can't tell when it is and when it isn't.

Unlike traditional encyclopedias that employ only the best scholars to write their articles, Wikipedia is crowdsourced, allowing most anyone to write an article, regardless of his or her expertise in the area. Thus, its reliability largely depends upon who has written the article.[12] Wikipedia proponents, however, do not make this distinction, arguing it is the best source for any information. Much has improved in the last decade in Wikipedia, including the gatekeeping for its "editors." No longer is it *as* easy for just anyone to write or edit an article (but it is still astonishingly easy). Anyone with a little persistence can edit or write an article, whether or not they know anything about the subject matter.

Witness a very minor case in which two admittedly "stoned out of our minds" editors chose to write "total bullshit" about the children's book series Amelia Bedelia.[13] After getting stoned and heading to McDonald's for a munchies fix, the authors in question came back and edited articles about the then little-known children's series, claiming that the literal-minded maid was based on a character from Cameroon who wore outlandish hats. Not only did the edit fool many (including a relative of the author of the books), but it remained on Wikipedia for five years.

This is not the first time this has happened to Wikipedia. War battles that never occurred, as well as assassination plots involving people who were never involved, have appeared in the pages of Wikipedia. Apart from damaging reputations or passing along misinformation, most have viewed these as no-harm-no-foul incidents. When it comes to medical information, however, that is definitely not the case.

Dr. Robert Hasty of Campbell University in North Carolina led a team of researchers to investigate Wikipedia's medical information. Their conclusion is that it is simply *not* a reliable source. The study calls into question the more than 20,000 medical articles in the online source. Researchers found that 90 percent of the articles randomly chosen contained false or misleading information.[14] The articles examined a variety of illnesses, such as lung cancer, major depression disorders, osteoarthritis, chronic pulmonary disease (COPD), diabetes mellitus, back pain, and hyperlipidemia (high cholesterol). Nine out of the ten entries on these diseases had errors of fact, misleading statements, wrong information, or simply bad information when compared to the peer-reviewed literature. The physician-researchers doing the study concluded that Wikipedia is not a safe source for medical information. Since Wikipedia is a favorite source to use when citing medical information on social media, social media users should be aware of Wikipedia's weakness in this area.

Wikipedia Knows Its Limitations. Do Users?

While this information is very helpful, it did not need a study. The site itself provides the following disclaimer:

Wikipedia contains articles on many medical topics; however, no warranty whatsoever is made that any of the articles are accurate. There is absolutely no assurance that any statement contained or cited in an article touching on medical matters is true, correct, precise or up-to-date. The overwhelming majority of such articles are written, in part or in whole, by nonprofessionals. Even if a statement made about medicine is accurate, it may not apply to you or to your symptoms.

The medical information provided on Wikipedia is, at best, of a general nature and **cannot substitute for the advice of a medical professional** (for instance, a qualified doctor/physician, nurse, pharmacist/chemist, and so on). **Wikipedia is not a doctor.**

None of the individual contributors, system operators, developers, sponsors of Wikipedia or anyone else connected to Wikipedia can take responsibility for the results or consequences of any attempt to use or adopt any of the information presented on this web site.

Nothing on Wikipedia.org or included as part of any project of Wikimedia Foundation, Inc., should be construed as an attempt to offer or render a medical opinion or otherwise engage in the practice of medicine.[15]

This seems clear enough, but it is not, and the number of social media users who resort to Wikipedia and then repeat what they find there (with or without attribution) in their posts, tweets, blogs, and so on is enormous. Getting social media users to understand that Wikipedia in specific and the Internet in general are not reliable medical resources is, at this juncture, nearly impossible. And it isn't just Wikipedia or nonprofessionals, either.

Physicians, too, make the same kinds of mistakes on social media. One tweeted to about 150,000 users of a popular health site that when chest pain is present, "If movement, deep breaths, swallowing makes [sic] pain worse or better, it is NOT a heart attack."[16] Many of those following the tweet thanked the doctor because they worried about the kind of chest pain he described. Of course it is possible that the pain is simply of nondescript origin. The majority of all chest pain is not indicative of a heart attack. But distinguishing between nondescript chest pain and an actual heart attack is what doctors are for. Most physicians would require a full work-up of a patient before making that diagnosis.

Social Media Are Killing Us

Mentally debilitating diseases, too, are often not helped by social media. Elliot Rodger, a young man with a serious mental illness, killed six people in Santa Barbara. But before doing that, he chronicled his pain, envy, and self-absorption on tweets, Facebook posts, and short videos, claiming that while he was in pain, others were together, having fun. While he suffered, others enjoyed life. He had to put an end to that, and so he did, but not before chronicling it in 137 self-absorbed pages he posted to the Internet, then filming his angst and then posting it to YouTube.[17] Rodger, a young man whose affluence enabled him to want for nothing and receive everything, including expert medical care, turned to the Internet for help during his crisis and found none. His postings, tweets, and other statements are now part of the "crime scene" that is our brave new world. Rodger isn't the only one, of course. A young married woman and mother committed suicide after reading offensive and defamatory posts to her Facebook page.[18]

Eliminating bad medical advice on social media sites is not always as easy as it might seem. Making a disclaimer does not always work. Oftentimes, the bogus information will appear everywhere on the web, but only a handful of retractions will appear later, if any at all. For example, an email circulated in 1999 about the "coughing technique" to prevent a heart attack, a version of which heads this chapter. Later this same heart attack advice appeared on a social networking site called Blogher. Following that, the bogus technique began to get widespread additional media coverage, including some television exposure and appearance on numerous social media sites. The question was not its effectiveness but the erroneous notion that something other than emergency treatment should be considered in the case of severe, persistent chest pain. The matter became so serious that the American Heart Association (AHA) issued a statement to the contrary. AHA pointed out that any persistent chest pain should be investigated by one's personal physician or in an emergency room.

Do social networking sites have a responsibility for bad advice that appears on their sites? Section 230 of CDA argues against affixing blame. This is the legal quagmire that faces the courts when social networking sites come before them, and this perhaps partially explains why Section 230 provides an easy solution.

Is Social Media Usage Itself an Illness?

Not only is the appearance of bad medical advice on social media a medical problem, but so are the sites themselves. More and more research is appearing about the addiction some now have to social media. As alluded to in an earlier chapter, we like talking about ourselves and telling our stories, however boring and mundane. But some of us have taken this to an addictive level.[19] Rameet Chawla, a computer programmer, proved this point when he created a bot to look like every single picture of every person he followed who posted on Facebook or Instagram. His

Physicians are warming up to social media but fear their viruses (drawing by Joe L. Boyd).

followership skyrocketed. Everyone liked him and/or followed him, and one person even approached him on the street "to commend his Insta-magnificence."

We create these needy personalities and some, though not all of us, are so connected we cannot be without either our phones, laptops, iPads, or tablets so we can like, follow, or post to our thousands of faceless "friends."

Clearly there is a phenomenon called "Internet addiction" that some social media users exhibit.[20] The research is still teasing out whether this represents a pathological behavior or a communication problem, but whatever it is, it harms those who suffer from it. And getting those addicted to social media to relinquish their tight grip on it proves most difficult. Proponents of social media will dismiss this as a problem; opponents of social media argue it is a bigger problem than is so far admitted. Those who work in university settings will tell you it is a huge distraction when trying to teach a class. High school students will take out-of-school suspension rather than give up their phones for mere hours.[21] Suffice it to say that while we may not yet know to what extent this is a problem, we know that some percentage of social media users cannot function well without hourly visits on social media.

Does Social Media Use Lead to Obesity?

Perhaps more logical is a link between the frequent use of social media and obesity. Researchers at Columbia University found that repetitive use of Facebook could lead to rising levels of obesity in social media users.[22] The Centers for Disease Control and Prevention in Atlanta reported that of the 470 participants they surveyed, those who reported higher uses of Facebook also had higher and unhealthy body masses. What the researchers found was that those who stayed connected to Facebook also reported more binge eating, and most often those foods were associated with higher body fat. The study contained a good news-bad news conclusion. Those who used Facebook routinely often exhibited an increase in self-esteem. But apparently this rise in self-esteem also gave them permission to snack on unhealthy food options. The research is rudimentary at this point, but one thing is certain. Social media can be used anywhere at any time, but it is most difficult to engage in this while exercising unless the user limits himself to stationary bikes. Adolescents may be at the highest risk since their use of social media and gaming often replaces outdoor activity of any kind. Ironically, some studies show that social media can reduce obesity.

Other studies find that social media may increase our feelings of inadequacy and anxiety. More recent studies show that using Facebook may make us feel miserable. The first study, reported in *Medical News* in 2012, showed that use of social media can make us feel overwhelmed and less secure. Although the study was a small one, the results were important enough to cause some concern. The anxiety comes not only from trying to keep up with others, but also from trying to keep up with our gadgets to the extent that we cannot turn them off even to sleep. Ethan Cross of the University of Michigan conducted a small study in 2013. Over a 14-day period, participants responded to a series of questions relating to how users felt, whether they felt lonely, and how much direct contact they had had with people in face-to-face interactions. The results, tentative, of course, given the sample size, did provide an interesting conclusion: the majority felt increasingly awful over time. Although the researchers admitted that Facebook provided an important social connection, it had a downside: "[R]ather than enhance well-being, we found that Facebook use predicts the opposite result: it undermines it."[23] We are simply becoming too addicted, too reliant upon social media for our social interactions, something that Robert Putnam, mentioned in an earlier chapter, warned about in his *Bowling Alone* over a decade ago. While some proponents will dismiss such claims, the Diagnostic and Statistical Manual for Mental Disorders is considering adding "Internet Addiction Disorder" to its list of real mental disorders in its most recent addition.[24] It is hardly any wonder. In a Harvard University study, researchers found that disclosing information about ourselves triggers that part of the brain associated with pleasure. With so many of us now on social media in some way, Facebook, Twitter, Instagram, Google, and even LinkedIn, a large portion of the world's population is connected in some manner. Constant conversation about ourselves may well be pleasurable, but it may not necessarily be a good thing for our overall mental health. In other words, too many twittergasms may lead to self-ignorance, not to mention depression.

Social Media and Suicide

This is particularly true for that part of the population that suffers from borderline but serious insecurities who need treatment by trained professionals and not the white noise of so many nameless faces chiming in about whatever happens to be on their minds. In 2008, U.S. nurse William Melchert-Dinkel was charged with aiding in suicide over the web.[25] Melchert-Dinkel encouraged at least two people and possibly as many as five to commit suicide, providing them with step-by-step instructions. The former nurse would feign compassion for those with whom he chatted and then would tell them what they needed to know to kill themselves. He told investigators that he encouraged "dozens" and that he described it as "the thrill of the chase." He said that his fascination "with death and suicide" could be considered an obsession.

Some will argue that this is not a problem with social media or the web but with very disturbed individuals. That Melchert-Dinkel is deranged cannot be gainsaid. But what also cannot be denied is that he would have had far less success with these suicides in a world without social media. His sphere of influence would have been very small, and he would have had to engage in his "obsession" face-to-face, something he may not have been prepared to do. Our brave new world is indeed brave, but it is also deadly to those whose mental health may be hanging by the proverbial thread.

Professional Medical Advice, Tweet by Tweet?

Random health tips on various social networking sites are only part of the problem. What happens when trained professionals provide medical advice on social networking sites? Medical sites are, of course, everywhere on the web, and many of them are constructed along the same lines as social networking sites: members join and exchange information. These sites have been very popular with patients suffering from various ailments who want to trade medical opinions or those who are just medically curious (e.g., Patientslikeme.com; WebMD.com). Are physicians at risk? Quite possibly, according to one medical malpractice expert, Dr. Eric Shore.

Dr. Shore explains, "Simply publishing general information on the Internet is unlikely to give rise to [a problem]." But when the physician writes a blog, or begins to express his or her medical opinion on a specific medical question, legal lines blur. "Is a physician-patient relationship formed when a doctor writes a blog or otherwise contributes to a social networking website? Sometimes."[26] According to Shore, the liability waters cloud when the physician answers a specific medical question with a specific approach or treatment. The only thing standing between the physician and a potential liability claim, according to Shore, is the site's disclaimer about seeing one's own physician. A casual survey in late 2009 of medical social networking sites demonstrates that many physicians are relying on that disclaimer.

Erroneous Information: Who Is to Blame?

If someone suffers serious harm or even loss of life, where is the blame to be placed: on the social networking sites, the Internet provider, venture capitalists who make social networking sites possible, at least initially, the person who knowingly posts incorrect information, or all of the above? It might be easy to argue that adults are expected to take pains to investigate claims made on social media, but what about minors? According to researchers at Seattle Children's Research Institute, the majority of adolescents (54 percent) are especially prone to share unhealthy or risky behaviors on social networking sites, and often without their parents' or guardians' knowledge. What are the safeguards to protect them?

The teen magazine *YM* and its related social networking site began with the idea of helping young girls come to grips with growing up by offering a wide range of advice about changes in puberty, acne, and boyfriends. The site proved wildly popular among its intended audience, but the host site discovered about six months later that some YM "fans" were posting techniques for hiding anorexia. Following the discovery, the site posted rules for discussions on the forums and even required passwords for them. Nothing slowed down the "masking anorexia" exchanges. Fearing not only possible liability issues but also increasingly bad publicity, YM removed the site.

The loss of the site did little, however, to quash the fascination for masking anorexia. "Pro-ana" sites, short for pro-anorexia, are still ubiquitous on the web. So who is to blame for this bad information, and who is responsible for taking it down or correcting it?

Right now, no one is. Social networking sites fear taking on too much editorial control because it might make them appear as editors of content. Posters who share information do not always vet it carefully before posting. Even when liability claims against social networking sites skirt constitutional issues like privacy, First Amendment rights and so on, they are not held accountable, nor does it appear that they will be in the near future.

Whether we want to admit it or not, when social media and medical advice collide, it may be disastrous for anyone caught up in the collision. Social media sites may well prove addictive to some, while merely creating a kind of "brain drain" for others. But we are all hyper-connected in ways that are not necessarily healthy. The legal ramifications are currently in favor of the social networking sites. Like some drive-by shootings, social media can dance in and out of our lives with misinformation that may well prove deadly to us. We all know that social interactions that are face-to-face are good for us, by and large. We also know that some of us have a very hard time making those face-to-face connections. Social media provide a great avenue for those individuals, and this gives them a non-threatening way to make social interactions. Many of these would-be introverts may be enticed out of their shells by these interactions, and for that reason social media are a plus.

Social media platforms also connect individuals who could not otherwise make any social connections given their illness or physical disability. As we said at the start of this chapter, they also provide countless ways for individuals suffering from debilitating illnesses or disabilities to connect with each other, share treatments, offer new possibilities, and even to connect those who are suffering with practitioners who may be able to offer some much-needed relief. But we cannot deny that social media sites have a downside in this very respect as well.

Social media venues can interfere with treatments, prolong illnesses, or interfere with a physician's ability to diagnose and prescribe correctly. Social media can provide misinformation that delays treatments unnecessarily and can in fact lead to death. On the one hand, social media are positive social goods when they connect individuals with others in a mutually beneficial way. On the other, social media are social negatives when they provide the wrong information or dispense wrong-headed misinformation. Where does this leave social media users?

Most likely it leaves them using social media. A Pew study found that 70 percent of those with chronic illnesses use social media to track down treatments, find diagnoses, or look for health answers.[27] On the whole, social media provide a great public service in this and in other respects. But when it comes to medical information, social networking sites are just as likely to provide the wrong information.

Are we left with a public service that can heal as well as kill? The answer will be debated for many years to come. But this chapter has provided some evidence that social media, at least with respect to medical information, may not be best suited to our ever-connected selves. This is not a call to put an end to social media, of course, but only to sound the clarion call for responsible, intelligent use.

Now send two tweets and call your physician in the morning.

TEN

#Cyberbullying

"You're an idiot and a fool and you ought to shoot yourself.
I know I would if I were as fat and as ugly as you."

If identity theft represents one of the more financially burdensome and intrusive unintended consequences of social networking, then cyberbullying[1] or cyberstalking, represents one of its more nefarious outcomes. The problem is not a minor one, either. Annually, there are thousands of adults and/or young people bullied, stalked, or otherwise harassed online.[2] While anyone can be bullied or harassed online, the problem is particularly internecine among adolescents. For all the good social media do, this one area is so brutal and so destructive that it calls into question much of social media's merits. Furthermore, the solutions to cyberbullying threaten the independence of social media.

Twenty-five percent of teens have reported being bullied online via social media on their phones. About half of all teens report having been victims of cyberbullying, with 33 percent of those admitting to having received threats online.[3] Unfortunately, there appears to be no quick solution once it starts. All too often, once it begins, it escalates into a more serious form of cyberbullying, such as stalking or serious bodily threats. Social media provide just the right environment in which cyberbullying can be carried out easily and anonymously, making ending it difficult and prosecution problematic.

Most states are beginning to enact cyberbullying laws. Federal law 18 U.S.C. Chapter 110 treats the sexual exploitation of children and includes language that could apply to these cyberbullying cases. The law also treats stalking and domestic violence, and most cyberstalking would come under this aegis. The law has specific language dealing with stalking and domestic violence. In both cases, however, the language does not necessarily apply to what takes place online. Even if it applied to online cyberbullying, it is further unclear whether the law would result in any convictions. There is no federal law against cyberbullying or bullying as of this writing, so laws covering similar kinds of behavior often offer a way to prosecute those who engage in this reprehensible behavior.

Cyberbullying Laws Multiply

The good news is that many states are lining up to pass bullying and cyberbullying laws, as indicated above. To date, forty-two states have both policies and laws against bullying or cyberbullying, eight with laws only. Only Montana has a policy against cyberbullying but no law as yet.[4] Make no mistake about it, however. When cyberbullying cases come to court, they are devilishly difficult to prosecute, not only because social media sites are themselves exempt from liability, but also because the nature of social media is voluntary and requires engagement from both sides. Cyberbullying rarely occurs off the cuff but begins small, only to explode later. The end result can be vicious, unending, and devastating to the victim. Too often, those who are on the receiving end of cyberbullying endure it for many weeks or months before ever saying anything about it to anyone. This is particularly true when it happens to adults. Most adults think they should be able to handle the matter themselves. But adolescents also endure the torture from cyberbullying, fearful of saying anything that might increase the awful and unbearable pressure already present.

This is a serious social networking problem, as it puts others at risk, either from cyberbullying or from criminal predation. Cyberbullying takes on various forms, but it typically involves using a social networking site to harass one person or a group of people. As is typical of the American modus operandi, for years following the rise of social networking, courts ignored or dismissed cyberbullying. This is partly due to the newness of this form of bullying, but also because bullying itself is often inevitable wherever young children congregate.

The Tragedy of Cyberbullying

Years ago, for adolescents, especially male adolescents, bullying was a problem they should solve themselves. Parents rarely got involved, and apart from a few mean-spirited comments, the bullying usually ceased over time. But not always, and some children, long before there were computers or social networking, suffered monumentally from bullying.

Today, however, ending bullying in general and cyberbullying in spe-

cific has become something of a national campaign. Parents quickly
engage, principals and teachers receive training to watch for symptoms,
and woe betide those in positions of authority who do not act immediately.
It cannot be denied that this is a better approach than the earlier one that
ignored it in the hope that it would disappear. In other words, it is a step
in the right direction. But the national trend to treat every slight, every
pique as a full-scale display of bullying may be more representative of the
American propensity to overreach.

Bullying and cyberbullying often take on gigantic proportions. Sadly,
it often does begin with a slight pique, only to explode in a kind of Brobdingnagian assault on some unsuspecting child who has been singled out
either for his or her looks, his or her behavior, or, really, no reason at all
other than to pick on a defenseless individual. Rarely does cyberbullying
today begin and end with a few comments. All too often these cyberbullying stories take on tragic proportions.

Kylie Kenney was an eighth grader when she became a victim of cyberbullying in 2004, and it continued for the next two years. She was standing
at her locker when someone asked her if she had seen "the website." She
had no idea what they were talking about. From middle school through
her sophomore year in high school, she endured the existence of a site
that proclaimed "Kill Kylie Incorporated" and contained homophobic
slander, harmful names, and sexual advances. The tag line used most often
was "Kylie Must Die." She was in the eighth grade when she found out
that this site was created to "show people how gay Kylie Kenney is." Police
eventually filed harassment charges against those responsible for the site.[5]

As Kenney explained, "I was just so ashamed, humiliated and scared.
I couldn't understand why anyone would do this." She did not have to
understand. Those behind the site wanted to make her life miserable, as
if being an eighth-grade girl who did not fit in with any of the "in" crowd
was not enough. But Kenney proved as tough as her tormentors and made
her way through school, later enrolling in a college in Vermont.

Not All Cyberbullying Ends Happily

Unfortunately, Ryan Halligan's story did not have a happy ending.[6]
Ryan Patrick Halligan was a delicate, very intelligent young boy from all
accounts. He seemed happy-go-lucky before his ordeal began. He did well
in school despite a learning disability that he struggled to overcome and did.

At some point a classmate claimed she had a crush on him and began
chatting with him online. Without his knowledge, everything Ryan wrote
to her, she shared with everyone else in his school. When his private hell

began, he endured it and did not let his parents know. But as the cyberbullying continued online, and the bullying continued at school, he asked his father what to do. His father told him to ignore it, that words could not hurt. But those words did hurt, and deeply.

In the beginning, Ryan did fight back against his bullies. He was successful, too, making friends with one of them. This proved to be a mistake. Once he gained what he thought was the confidence of his former tormentor, he shared his troubles, and that came back to haunt him. The bullying continued and became so severe that one day he rushed from a class in tears. Ashley, his putative sweetheart, began at first to defend him and was proud he stood up to his bullies. But as the bullying continued over the next *two* years, she, too, turned on him. She later used the relationship to mock him, sharing his private messages with her friends, who shared them with the school. As her popularity increased in middle school, she turned on Ryan, calling him a "loser," and joined the bullying crowd. Meanwhile, the website created to continue the torture began circulating the lie that Ryan was gay. After Ashley called him a loser, Ryan texted Ashley, "It is girls like you who make me want to kill myself." On October 7, 2003, while his family still slept, Ryan hanged himself. His older sister found his lifeless body. Ryan left no suicide note.

Ryan's parents were unaware of the cyberbullying until they examined his computer. When Ryan's father, John, discovered the extent of the torment his son underwent, he invited Ashley over to the house. He told her, "You did a bad thing, but you're not a bad person." John devoted his life to putting an end to cyberbullying and bullying of any kind. The Halligans later left Vermont.

The bully who began the rumor about Ryan being gay later made fun of the way Ryan had killed himself. John drove over to the boy's house, furious, but he got stuck in traffic and had time to think about what he would do. Rather than thrash the child, he told him, "You have no idea of the pain you caused my son. And you're still bullying him now even when he is defenseless and you're still lying to your parents about it. I refuse to believe that you are so cruel that you don't have a heart." Shortly thereafter the boy broke down in tears and apologized. It did not bring back Ryan, of course, nor did it undo what torment he had caused this young thirteen-year-old boy, but it was a start.

Are Social Media Really to Blame?

Bullying has been around as long as there have been children congregating in school or elsewhere. Would the bullying have continued without access to social media? Most likely. But would it have been as perva-sive, unrelenting, or widespread? Not at all. Ryan had nowhere to go, nowhere to get away from the relentless onslaught of the constant rumors, threats, and innuendo. Welcome to our brave new world.

Children are especially at risk, and some children's experts wonder if social networking sites can ever be made safe for them. Teens admit to being bullied online, just over 25 percent.[7] The range in Europe is more dramatic, with the fewest in Italy (10 percent) but almost half in Den-mark (45 percent) and Norway (50 percent). While not all cyberbully-ing happens on social networking sites, one in three teens admits to having experienced online cyberbullying. A California teenager, Denise Finkel, filed a lawsuit suing her former classmates, their parents, and Face-book for cyberbullying that occurred on that social network.[8] Classmates had created a Facebook profile called "90 Cents Short of a Dollar" and there posted lies, rumors, and other defamatory comments against her. The suit was filed in New York's supreme court, the same state in which Finkel later enrolled in college, at the University of Albany. Finkel filed the suit because Facebook was "grossly irresponsible" in allowing defam-atory remarks to be posted about her. Among other comments, the posters claimed Finkel had AIDS. Although the Facebook profile was password-protected, it contained numerous fabrications and defama-tory comments, and access was provided to many students at Finkel's school. Facebook's lack of robust security measures and its unwilling-ness to remove the site added to Finkel's anxieties while prolonging her agony.

But the case was DOA with respect to Facebook, as some observers noted at the time. Suing the classmates who tormented her was not at all unusual but nevertheless a long shot given the protection provided by CDA Section 230. But suing Facebook was really more for the publicity and to draw attention to the blanket protection that Section 230 of the CDA provides. Section 230 made certain the case would go nowhere.[9] Finkel hoped that her claim of content ownership would hold against Facebook, but alas it did not. She also banked on the ubiquitous nature of Facebook to spread the defamations about her to influence court opin-ion. It did not. The judge, New York Supreme Court Justice Debra James, made short shrift of the ownership claim: "'Ownership' of content plays no role in the Act's stated claim," she wrote. "The only issue is whether the party sought to be held liable is an 'interactive computer service' and if that hurdle surmounted immunity granted by 42 USC 230 (c)(1) is trig-gered if the content was provided by another party [i.e., not provided by the social networking site itself, but a third party]."[10]

The case against the classmates did go forward, but it, too, was thrown out eventually in 2010. Finkel hoped that the notion of negligent entrustment would hold against the parents or the children, since all involved were minors at the time. Negligent entrustment occurs when the parent or guardian of a child neglects to oversee that child who takes a gun or steals a car. But the judge found that computers are too commonplace, and parents could not be held accountable for their children when those children would have access to computers wherever they went. Finkel planned an appeal after the 2010 ruling, but that too proved impotent. The judge found the classmates had engaged in puerile behavior, and that behavior did not rise to defamation. Further, even though New York had a bullying law on the books, it did not have a tort action for cyberbullying.

Legal Action Difficult but Can Be Successful

The list of these sad cases appears endless. In 2005, a Florida honor student, Jeffrey Johnson, committed suicide, but only after enduring three years of teasing, threats, and rumors had been posted about him or sent to him in emails.[11] In 2008, Florida enacted one of the tougher laws prohibiting social media bullying, the "Jeffrey Johnson Stand Up for All Students Act." The act prohibits teasing, social exclusion, stalking, sexual, religious or racial harassment, threats, and public humiliation of any public school students or employees either online or off.

It did not take long for the law to be applied. Taylor Wynn and McKenzie Barker were arrested for setting up a false Facebook page with photographs of classmates whose photoshopped faces they placed on nude men and women. A parent of another student alerted authorities, who traced the IP addresses back to the two students. Both were charged under the Jeffrey Johnson Stand Up for All Students Act.[12]

Academics and Cyberbullying

It does not have to be high school children, either, though it is just as likely to be. Even academics are subject to bullying, as are college students. College students may also encounter it on faculty-assigned websites, especially if those are more public than something like Blackboard.[13] The cyberbullying can come in the form of hostile responses to what others have written, threats, or other comments made on other social media. University professors are not immune either, especially when they are starting out. Hence, bulliedacademic.blogspot.com. Many of these take the form of tenure-track professors encountering roadblocks or other forestalling measures, but even here straightforward bullying is not unheard of.

More than one faculty member has complained about the "rate my professor" (mentioned in an earlier chapter) site on which students can rate their professors, both for content and teaching skill, but just as often for their appearance—that is, whether or not the professors are "hot." The site can be demeaning as well as insightful, sexually abusive as well as complimentary.

The site will rate professors on everything from their drab or frumpy dress, their bad breath, whether or not they are boring, good-looking, etc. Some ratings border on the sexually suggestive if not straightforwardly assaultive.[14] Scrolling through the site, one can see why some academics are unhappy. Too often some comment about a professor's appearance will crop up, and the comments are either none too complimentary, or all too suggestive. Moreover, it is clear that some students look at this site before signing up for a course. The number of students who do this is certainly small. Still, the idea that one's education is predicated on whether a professor is "hot" and entertaining is demoralizing and sinks American higher education to an all-time low. In at least one case, professors struck back with a kind of "rate my students," complaining about how students dress, smell, and act in class.[15]

Some professors do see the value in tools like "Rate My Professor," and some even admit to changing what they were doing. But too often the site commenters seem hell-bent on making a hurtful comment. What difference does it make whether or not a professor wears "up-to-date" clothing or is trying to recover her youth? Comments about physical appearance, good or bad, are out of bounds and certainly within the realm of cyberbullying.

Cruel teasing has always occurred in schools. But social networking sites have the potential to expose ridicule not merely to a small circle of known antagonists, but to every person in the school, the neighborhood, the school district, and across the globe. Bebo, now defunct, was a well-known site that aimed its appeal at the school-aged, became the target of many such assaults, and was eventually banned by some school districts. While some teasing is to be expected among teens, social media cyberbullying has reached dramatic proportions. Child psychologists and sociologists are unified in their denunciations of cyberbullying. Conventional bullying is bad enough, they warn, but the ability of social networking sites to broadcast that bullying essentially worldwide creates greater anxieties for the victims.

Cyberbullying bedevils many adolescents, sometimes fatally (drawing by Joe L. Boyd).

Types of Cyberbullying

As noted throughout this chapter, cyberbullying can take on many forms. Flaming (when an online discussion turns nasty and abusive) and harassment have been mentioned most often, as have threats and rumors. But denigration also occurs, along with trickery, impersonation, outing, and exclusion.[16] Trickery involves revealing information that one person gave to another in confidence. Exclusion involves setting aside an individual or individuals and barring them from an online group. Outing occurs when information about a person that has been kept secret by that person is placed online without consent. Most often this involves one's sexual orientation or a sexual secret. In some cases, the latter has been accomplished merely though the use of the social network and not by any individual.

While social networks are immune from third-party content postings, what is not immune is the criminal behavior of those who use social media to broadcast their crimes. In *Rios v. Fergusan* (2008), the Superior Court of Connecticut granted a restraining order on a temporary basis against North Carolina resident Christopher Fergusan after he posted a rap video on YouTube showing him waving a handgun around and threatening to harm the mother of his child. Because the parents no longer lived together or even resided in the same state, the mother, Stacy Rios, filed the restraining order in her state of residence, Connecticut. Judge Stephen F. Frazzini ruled that Connecticut had jurisdiction and granted a six-month injunction, subject to renewal as warranted.[17] The case is interesting in many ways but especially because it is clear that there is no evidence Fergusan ever set foot in Connecticut. He threatened virtually, so to speak.

A similar case occurred in *Harkness v. Larrieu* (2009), in which a California court of appeals granted a protective order against Edwin Larrieu, who had used a social networking site to harass and otherwise threaten his former girlfriend. The judge issued the order because Larrieu not only sent threatening electronic messages and kept changing his profile so he could "friend" Harness, but also because he posted to a social networking site (not specified in court documents) that Harkness was dead. He continued his threats even after she blocked him by using various aliases.

Recalling a case mentioned briefly in an earlier chapter, cyberbullying reached new extremes when Amanda Tatro was banned from the University of Minnesota in December 2009 for posting to Facebook threatening comments that three of her mortuary science professors thought serious enough to report. Tatro had recently been through a bad breakup and used her posting to discuss an upcoming class in which she could "update her Dead List #5" and stab "a certain someone in the throat with a trocar."[18] The University of Minnesota mortuary science student posted to her feed that she was "looking forward to Monday's embalming therapy.... Give me room, lots of aggression to be taken out with a trocar." A trocar is a sharp instrument used in embalming. Tatro later said something about getting in touch with the "crematory guy" and wanting to use the trocar to stab "a certain someone" and that she would perhaps hide the trocar up her sleeve to get it past security.

When she appeared for class the following Monday, she was met by the police, patted down, and then questioned. While she complained that she was merely venting, administrators did not take it that way and banned her from the university.[19] The case did not end well, no matter how one views it. Although the ACLU took up Tatro's case, she was found dead at age 31, just days after her lost appeal in June 2012. Her tragic death is linked to her struggle with RSD, Reflex Sympathetic Dystrophy, a nerve disorder that causes searing burning sensations and complicates circulation. She had struggled with the disease for six years. She had just had surgery in January of that year to ease her difficulties. Her attorney said they were preparing a Supreme Court appeal when she was found dead by her husband, Joel Rand.

Social Media a Cover for Cyberbullying?

Are social networking sites providing cover for cyberbullies? Or is it the law, or lack thereof? The answer is not an either-or, but perhaps both. Cyberbullies can blast an individual with hundreds of texts, comments, and "likes" simply by setting up a social media profile. While the law protects the website, and anonymity, more or less, protects the bullies, no one is protecting the victims. They must fend for themselves, endure the torment, or, as in the cases above, commit suicide. There ought to be a better way, a better approach. But too many fear that to tighten the law would hamstring social media. Moreover, there are many who think that to tighten the controls would also cast a chill over First Amendment rights. But the First Amendment is not absolute. It does not protect slander or threats, nor can you claim there is a fire when there is not one, sending a crowd into unnecessary and dangerous panic.

Nevertheless, it would appear that social media sites violate all of these concerns and yet remain immune, with rare exception, to any recourse by the thousands who are victims of cyberbullying. In the cases mentioned above and the ones below, criminal charges were brought. But it is the rare case that ends in legal action of some kind. While some perpetrators may experience some humiliation at being caught, few feel the pinch of their crime by having to pay some sort of restitution, or by serving long stretches in jail. It would appear that social media sites provide protection only for the perpetrators. If you are a victim, look for protection elsewhere and hope for the best.

Cyberbullying on the Rise

The inability to do anything substantive about cyberbullying may also have given rise to its increase over the years. Daniel Patrick Moynihan once famously quipped that you get more of what you subsidize. In this case, it would appear you get more of what you do not deter. ChildLine, a well-known charity in Great Britain, reported "a large increase" in the number of children contacting it about cyberbullying.[20] Young people are facing cyberbullying more and more often, and the ability of adults to help them through it appears to be increasingly negligible. Unless adults make a concerted effort to intercede for young people to stop or at least impede the cyberbullying, it appears that it will not stop until serious damage has been done.

But it isn't just teens and young adults who are subject to cyberbullying, of course. Adults often take one another to task on social media, especially when divorce is in the mix. Too often unhappy divorces get played out on social media, often to the painful embarrassment of everyone associated with the main parties: children, friends, coworkers. Anthony Elonis began writing posts on Facebook after his wife left him and took their two young children with her. In one post he wrote, "There's one way to love ya but a thousand ways to kill ya."[21] Elonis went on to fantasize about killing his wife, leaving her body in a bloody mess, and also attacking her co-workers. The case, *Elonis v. United States*, is now before the Supreme Court. The justices are struggling with whether the threats were "true ones" and so are no longer under the protection of the First Amendment.[22] The case may well be the first to create a fissure in Section 230.

The Special Case of Megan Meier

Cyberbullying might never have become a household word had it not been for Megan Meier.[23] Minors Megan Meier and Sarah Drew were eighth-grade friends in Missouri, living the life that eighth-graders are supposed to live. Meier transferred to another school. Meier and Drew had a falling-out. Megan had some of the troubles that many eighth-graders have: self-esteem issues, braces on her teeth, weight problems. She also suffered from attention deficit disorder that led to some mild learning disorders. But her newfound love, Josh Evans, a 16-year-old who had recently contacted her, had helped lift her spirits and also provided her with the added incentive to lose twenty pounds. Although the "dating" took place most often on MySpace, Megan's mom was ever the watchful parent.

Josh had moved to the area from Florida recently and was being home-schooled. While Megan basked in the attention, Megan's mother began to get suspicious: Josh never called, never came over. When he said he didn't have a cell phone, yet they talked over the Internet, Megan's mom began to worry about who this Josh really was.

Just as soon as the relationship bloomed, it quickly began to fade. Suddenly Josh did not want to be friends any more, claiming that Megan was not a very good friend to her own friends. Now Megan began to wonder how Josh would know, not being in public school and not having a phone. And what did he mean that she was not a very good friend? In late October 2006, Megan sent out invitations to her birthday party and asked her mother to sign on and see if Josh replied. Megan's mother had to take her other daughter to the orthodontist. She couldn't stay but she could tell that Megan was upset. She asked Megan to sign off, and Megan said she would.

When Megan's mother returned, she noticed that Megan had not signed off, that Josh and others had begun calling Megan "fat" names and asking others if she was a "slut." Many had chimed in. Megan had responded in kind, and Megan's mother chastised Megan for her vulgarity. Megan ran upstairs crying that no one was on her side. Megan's mother prepared dinner, and a short twenty minutes later found that Megan had hanged herself in her closet, just a few weeks prior to her fourteenth birthday.

Megan Meier's story isn't one of "puppy love" gone sour. Sadly, the story has a much more nefarious cast to it. As the events of the story became known, it shocked not only the community in Missouri, but people around the world. It turned out that Sarah Drew's mother, Lori, created a fake profile on MySpace after her employee, Ashley Grills, showed her how. She planned to spy on Meier to see what she might say about Sarah after Sarah and Megan had their falling-out. Under the alias of a 16-year-old boy named "Josh," Lori Drew befriended this 13-year-old Missouri girl and established what Megan thought was a serious romantic relationship. "Josh" later unceremoniously dropped Meier and began to harass and make sport of her. Just days before her suicide, she told "Josh," "You're the kind of boy a girl would kill herself over." The last message "Josh," really Lori, sent to Megan read as follows: "Everybody in O'Fallon knows who you are. You are a bad person and everybody hates you. Have a shi**y rest of your life. The world would be a better place without you." As the case unfolded, Sarah Wells, a woman following the social networking goings-on, posted Lori Drew's name and address on her site allowing others to link and circulate it on MySpace and other social networking sites.

Lori Drew, the harasser, became the harassed. After Megan Meier's suicide, her parents took Drew to court. Drew defended herself by arguing she did not intend any harm (no one ever does, of course). Drew's defense collapsed when Ashley Grills detailed in court how she had pitched the idea of creating a fake persona to Drew so that Drew could find out what Megan said about her daughter. The prosecutor, in what many considered a far-flung gamble, filed against Drew for three counts of fraud under the Computer Fraud and Abuses Act (CFAA). Legal experts saw it as an unprecedented attempt to use fraud statutes to bring a conviction over an episode that occurred on the popular social networking sites. Each fraud count carried a maximum of five years.[24]

CFAA says in part that is it illegal to "knowingly [access] a computer without authorization or exceed authorized access, and by means of such conduct [obtain] information ... determined by the United States Government pursuant to an Executive order or statute to require protection against unauthorized disclosure...." Most legal observers found this prosecutorial approach "novel" at best since CFAA is typically used to prosecute terrorist-type activities.

The case ended up being tried in California where the MySpace servers reside, not Missouri, where Drew lived. A jury found Drew guilty of the minor counts in November 2008. But U.S. District Judge George Wu overturned the guilty verdict in July 2009.[25] Wu worried that it would set a bad precedent for a social networking site to be linked to a conviction for failure to live up to its TOS agreement, and it would have a chilling effect for all other social networking sites. The overall impact on all social networking sites, he feared, would be to severely limit open and free discussion. In September 2009 an appeal was filed, but most observers thought it unlikely to be heard.

Bad behaviors left undeterred often multiply. A case too hauntingly similar to that of Megan Meier is the tragic suicide of Phoebe Prince. Prince, an Irish immigrant who moved to Massachusetts in 2009, was found dead in her home in January 2010. As the case unfolded, officials discovered what they described as a pretty young girl with a beautiful accent who had been harassed literally to death by two different groups of her classmates. According to the police, after she dated a very popular boy, her classmates began relentlessly mocking her on Facebook, texting threats to her, and spreading rumors about her character throughout the school. In some cases the threats called for her death. The comments cast aspersions on her character, on what she did on dates, and why she was so popular. The cyberbullying was unrelenting and ubiquitous. At the height of all this cyberbullying, Prince took her life. She hanged herself in the stairwell of her family's apartment, her body discovered by her 12-year-old sister.[26]

Her suicide led to the criminal prosecution of the six teenagers who harassed her. The case also sparked more robust laws against cyberbullying in Massachusetts. A statewide cyberbullying task force assembled and came forward with legislation that the governor signed into law in May of 2010. The trial of the six teenagers occurred the next year. In return for guilty pleas, the teenagers received probation and community service. The convictions were a step in the right direction, but certainly probation and community service do nothing for the lovely young woman, Phoebe Nora May Prince, whose life cannot be reclaimed. The six miscreants will go on with their lives, their options constricted somewhat by the conviction. But with some effort and relocation, and perhaps even a name change, these six individuals can lose themselves in the crowd. The Prince family can never get back their daughter, never see what her life would have become.

Congress attempted to strengthen cyberbullying laws when, in April 2009, Rep. Linda Sanchez (D–CA) submitted *Megan Meier Cyberbullying Prevention Act*. The act tried to define cyberbullying as "repeated, severe and hostile attacks of harassment." The act fines each convicted perpetrator, adding up to two years of imprisonment. After Sanchez made her act public, negative web reaction was immediate. Many expressed fears that it would constrain verbal exchanges on social networking sites. They worried that when those exchanges heat up as they inevitably do, participants might be subject to criminal prosecution. The bill languishes in Congress.

States, however, have not waited for Congress to settle the matter. Not surprisingly, those states that have seen the most terrifying acts of cyberbullying (e.g., Missouri and Massachusetts) have passed laws. In response to the Prince case, in May 2010, Massachusetts Governor Deval Patrick signed into law what many legal experts are calling the strongest cyberbullying law to date. According to *Cyberbully Alert!* (www.cyberbullyalert.com), a blog devoted to discussing cyberbullying law and policies, at least ten states have passed, or are in the process of passing, cyberbullying laws. In addition to Missouri and Massachusetts, Idaho, Rhode Island, Oregon, New Jersey, New York, Arkansas, Vermont, and Iowa have also passed cyberbullying laws.

The Especially Heinous Case of Ask.fm

Is it wrong to charge social networking sites with incitement to suicide? They are, after all, only vehicles. One site in particular has been associated with a large number of suicides. Ask.fm, a relatively new site, emerged with one particular feature: the ability to send messages anonymously. Begun in 2012, the site jumped to five million users, then fifteen million, and finally about sixty million users worldwide. The site's niche is the ability to ask questions, either under your own name or anonymously. The anonymous feature has the putative benefit of allowing users to ask any question at all and not be associated either with their own ignorance or with the content of the question. It is, however, now being blamed for a number of suicides: Hannah Smith, Jessica Laney, Ciara Pugsely, Amanda Todd, Erin Gallagher, and Shannon Gallagher are among some of the names associated with suicide on a site noted for dreadful cyberbullying.[27]

Hannah Smith, a fourteen-year-old, took her own life after receiving numerous messages on the order of "get cancer and die" or "drink bleach." Sixteen-year-old Jessica Laney was found dead in her home after messages on Ask.fm inquired, "Can't you just kill yourself already?" One of the sadder cases involved the Gallagher sisters. Erin, a thirteen-year-old, faced horrific messages about her weight and her looks over numerous months. She took her life in October. Her sister, Shannon, brokenhearted over the loss, took her own life two months later in December 2012, deepening the family's tragedy with two suicides. And so it goes.

The anonymity of the site can be set to block those who seek not to be known, but users have to know to do this. Even after doing it, a user is never really protected. Furthermore, the anonymity feature is what terrorists may have used to find out answers in order to carry out their own nefarious ends.[28] Another individual not blocked may well bring to the attention of users what others are saying about them. Some argue that it is not the sites we should blame; it should be the bullies. But these bullies would never have the arena, the world's stage really, to transact their awful business in the absence of social media. The only silver lining is that Ask.fm has suffered financially from this crop. MySpace saw its own fortunes rise and fall with unchecked cyberbullying, and now Ask.fm may suffer a similar fate. It may not be able to recover quickly enough.

Recently, Tinder and Ask.com bought out Ask.fm with the intention of making it safe.[29] Ask.com CEO Doug Leed is intent on eliminating the cyberbullying so rampant on Ask.fm. The company said it will invest millions to make the site safe, eliminate cyberbullying, and still provide a first-rate and appealing service. That remains to be seen, since Ask.fm has been overrun with cyberbullying that has resulted in numerous suicides in the UK, Canada, and elsewhere.

Some readers will complain that the MySpace suicide of Megan Meier is tragic, and the multiple suicides linked to Ask.fm are horrific, but U.S. social media sites have a better track record, Phoebe Prince notwithstanding. If only that were true. In May of 2014, former Marine Daniel Rey Wolfe posted pictures of his suicide as he bled to death. Family members pleaded with Facebook to remove the bloody, graphic, and sad pictures, but Facebook refused, at least initially.[30] This isn't the first time, either. In 2013, a horrific decapitation appeared on Facebook. At first Facebook took it down but then put it back. Following member outrage, it took it down once again.[31] The decapitation occurred in Mexico as a man determined to "punish" his wife for her cheating. Amanda Todd, a Vancouver teen, posted her sad story on cue cards on YouTube after being cyberbullied by an older man on Facebook who had befriended her. Her body was later discovered in Coquitlam, British Columbia, Canada.[32]

These sad stories multiply on social media no matter who begins them or where they are located. There may be, as some proponents of social networking have argued, wisdom in crowds. Crowds may be well-informed, no doubt, but crowds can also become unruly, rush to mob mentality, and nearly attack the innocent without reason. A few years ago, we sank an apple juice industry over alar, a substance found in apple juice at the time. The outrage occurred because alar proved carcinogenic. Although a person had to eat 700 alar-treated apples per day for 70 years to increase the risk beyond what merely living in the world does anyway, alar had to go, for the children, we cried.

Where are those cries now, for the children on social media? Why is it that social networking creators do not think first about the impact and later about their potential billions? Why is it always the money first, lives later, if at all? Is it because we think First Amendment rights are absolute?

Using Social Media to Commit Murder

Social networking sites are blamed for suicide, and now they are being implicated in murder. Such was the case when in 2009 Phillip Markoff, a 22-year-old Boston University Medical School student, used Craigslist to meet women. Craigslist is a networking site that allows members to post services, to communicate with one another regarding those services, or to join in discussions to pass judgment on services for members' benefit. In 2006, even amid much negative publicity, Craigslist allowed "erotic services" to be advertised on its site. That is how Markoff came to meet the women in question.

Markoff met at least two unnamed women, both of whom he robbed. Later he met Julissa Brisman, an "erotic masseuse," in a Boston hotel. He murdered her there in what police described as a calculated and brutal killing. A grand jury charged Markoff with first-degree murder, armed robbery, two counts of armed kidnapping, armed assault with intent to commit robbery, and two counts of unlawful possession of a firearm. The gun he allegedly used at the scene he carried in a hollowed-out copy of *Grey's Anatomy*, a standard classic medical text.[33] Other emails captured as evidence suggest he had solicited sexual favors from men and transsexuals via the Craigslist erotic venue. Markoff pled not guilty to the crimes.

The irony of the case is that the social networking site linking the alleged killer to his victims is also responsible for his capture. For all the ease with which Markoff allegedly tracked his victims via Craigslist, it proved easier still to track him down via his Internet activities. At every URL he visited, he left a telltale cyber fingerprint. For example, hotel security services where he stayed routinely tracked the goings-on of Craigslist members just to see what sort of erotic traffic they got. They quickly discovered Markoff and what he had been doing. When his trail stopped at a wireless router, the investigation didn't. Although anyone within several hundred feet could have been using the site, the police did what anyone would do: they looked up the name they had on Facebook and Google. To say they were surprised when they found the *summa cum laude* graduate, medical student, and member of Boston's social elite, Markoff, is an understatement.

Markoff had everything going for him. As part of Boston's elite, he was engaged to Megan McAllister, a beautiful young woman who remained clueless about his activities until they came to light in a kind of flash bomb. Even after his capture, Megan wrote to the *Boston Globe*, defending him and asserting in her letter that this was not the man she knew or that her family knew and that the Phillip she loved "is a beautiful man inside and out. He is intelligent and loyal, and the best fiancée a woman could ask for. He would not hurt a fly."[34]

According to police files, after Markoff robbed a woman at gunpoint in a Boston hotel, he jumped a plane to Baltimore less than eight hours later to celebrate Passover with his grandparents. Forty-eight hours later, he murdered Julissa Brisman in a Back Bay hotel. Following another crime he committed in Rhode Island, he called to chat with his fiancée and gamble at nearby casinos.[35] Markoff, son of a prominent dentist, led two very separate lives. In a seven-day stretch he went on a crime spree that included murder without hesitation. Like some modern-day Raskolnikov, Dostoevsky's murderous intellectual who also lived two separate lives, killing pawnbroker Alyona Ivanovna while struggling with the guilt, Markoff was a medical student by day, a murderous villain at night.

After his capture, Markoff, while awaiting trial, tried to commit suicide early on. After his fiancée broke up with him, he redoubled his efforts. On the day that was to be his wedding day, Markoff wrote his ex-fiancée's name in his blood, severed major arteries in his neck, legs and ankles, covered his wounds in plastic, covered his head in a plastic bag, swallowed toilet paper to prevent his resuscitation, and then wrapped himself in a blanket. When prison officials checked on him later, they discovered the bloodbath much too late to help.[36]

No one knows why Markoff did what he did. Could he have done it without Craigslist? Probably. Could he have done it as easily? Hardly. The existence of social networks made it so much easier for him to make contact, to set up his visits, and then to commit his crimes.

Famed comedic genius Robin Williams tragically committed suicide in 2014. Social media were there, chronicling his career, reposting his many famous quips, and linking us to his various brilliant routines. Often, social media beat the news outlets to the punch, offering not only up-to-the minute news, but just as often far more background than small cadres of reporters could get to. When everyone has a phone connected to social media, everyone is a reporter on events like these.

But social media also gave us pause. Mr. Williams's daughter, Zelda Williams, announced shortly after his death that she was signing off social media. It had grown too mean-spirited, provided too many lurid details, and snooped where it should not. The onslaught from social media proved so intrusive and abusive that at least one social media giant is reconsidering its policies.[37] Even in the face of such grand tragedy as death, and death by suicide, social media cannot leave us alone. It must harass to the grave and even beyond.

Where Do We Go from Here?

So where do we go from here? Are we stuck with social networks that encourage cyberbullying, that enable cyberstalking, and that facilitate cyber-mischief to the extent that some commit suicide, some plan murders, and others make eternal nuisances of themselves? Are social networks the be-all and the end-all of connecting us to one another, all at the cost of exposing us, literally, to the overexposure of the few for the eternal annoyance of the many?

It appears that way. No one would dare gainsay the value of social networking sites. They connect us to friends, allow us to make new ones, connect us with interesting people, and answer many of our burning questions, answers that might take us weeks if not months to uncover on our own. They recommend movies to see, books to read, restaurants at which to eat, and clothes to buy. They offer insights into symptoms we may be experiencing, giving us just enough information quite possibly to dismiss those symptoms, or hie ourselves to a physician forthwith. We get all of this for free, or rather for the cost of Internet service. If we cannot afford it, it is provided for us, through our local libraries, free of charge, or rather at the cost of taxes to those who pay them.

In any event, we can have this service and these many amenities at a fraction of the cost they would be if we had to do it all ourselves. Let's face it. Many of us would not be able to do so. Our social media act like so many personal librarians, gathering information for us and putting it at our fingertips while we lollygag the day away in our pajamas.

Or, given the ubiquity of our devices, we do not have to lollygag in our pajamas but can go to work, to the beach, to the park, for a walk, for a run, or even go for a drive and still stay connected, though the latter is, of course, not only taboo, but illegal now in many states. The point is, we can have all this service and access with very little effort on our part. It is there for the taking.

But the price of admission is sometimes too high. In return for all this access, must we endure cyberbullying, cyberstalking, and other forms of cyber-menacing just to have the opportunity to partake of the riches of the crowds? Perhaps those crowds are not called "madding" for nothing!

CDA Section 230, notwithstanding, it would appear that we could reach some common ground between unadulterated immunity on the one hand and a little civic and social responsibility on the other. Yes, some readers will argue that we should expect that of people. No doubt we should, but in other crowd-like settings, we allow for some policing. For example, when large crowds gather, we assume there will be a police presence. In our now terrorist-laden age, we not only assume it, we demand it. Crowds, as we all know, become unruly easily and quickly. Further, we have many benefits from public transportation, but we not only hold drivers accountable, we also hold those who provide that transportation accountable when they act irresponsibly: the airlines, airplane and car manufacturers, highway divisions, and so on.

Recently, we have held accountable not only those who smoke but also tobacco manufacturers who made that tobacco so omnipresent, so glamorous. Furthermore, we are not only holding drunk drivers accountable, but also bars that irresponsibly contribute to their inebriation. In every case, we hold those who contribute to the delinquency of minors culpable in some way.

Why then do we give so public a vehicle as social media carte blanche to trample us and our children? Surely there is some common ground in which we could make them at least marginally responsible for miscreants who repeatedly offend, or who, with their first incursion into social media, make the few or the many feel assaulted virtually. Why should social media be exempt from a civic duty to which we hold every other producer of some good accountable? Indeed, when social media in specific and the Internet in general enjoy its content solely from those of us who contribute to it sans remuneration—without us, social media are nothing—the least they could do is police their airways for the flotsam and jetsam of cyberabuse. The price of our use should not be our potential abuse.

It is the very least we should be able to expect from a multibillion-dollar industry that has made those multibillions from our content. Without that content, social media have only the worst offer, the awful underbelly of our society.

Isn't that the least we could expect?

Cybercitizens of the cyberworld unite! You have only the cybersleaze bonds to lose!

ELEVEN

#AyenbiteOfInwyt

"In the future we'll be able to think our tweets!"

The chapter title comes from a little-known Middle English text that can be translated as the "prick" or remorse of conscience, according to how some modern English translations handle the obfuscated (to us, anyway) phrase. If modern readers are at all familiar with the phrase, it is probably from reading James Joyce's *Ulysses*, in the part of that book known as "Telemachus." Granted, Joyce had a bad habit of drawing phrases from just about anywhere and writing around them. In his autobiography, Samuel Beckett, who once acted as an amanuensis for Joyce, recalls a time when he took dictation and recorded a conversation between Joyce and his maid. Beckett took dictation with his head down, almost never looking up, and so he did not see the maid enter. When he read it back to Joyce in the afternoon, as was his habit, he apologized profusely. Joyce only laughed and told him to leave it in, as the critics would never figure it out.

In our case, Ayenbite of Inwyt (also spelled *Agenbite of Inwit*) has relevance for social media, notwithstanding its obscurity. The phrase, literally translated, means that the inner working of the mind can come back and bite you. My point in bringing it forward in this connection is simply to raise the question of whether we will allow our conscience about social networking to come back and haunt us or bite us into doing what is right for the good of the whole. We do not have to settle for social media that control us; we can control them if we want to.

Given our penchant for reality shows, it may well be laughably Puritanical of me to think something like a discussion about conscience will resonate with anyone else in the modern age, but hope springs eternal. Some of the issues raised in this book have helped us see, I hope, that the full immunity accorded social networking sites is not always in the best interests of civil discourse. As the late Irving Kristol once famously wrote, "If you care for the quality of life in our American democracy, then you have to be for censorship."[1] What Kristol meant, and what I endorse, is that if we want to continue our freedoms, some restrictions are necessary. It may sound counterintuitive, but wholesale freedom without boundaries will result in libertinage, hardly what we call democracy. In every avenue of life, we require some boundaries, and without them, we end up with some form of anarchy. Daniel Defoe makes this clear in his timeless book *Robinson Crusoe*. Crusoe's goats, as they are sometimes referred to, lived in a pen so large that they became as wild as goats that roamed freely outside the fence. What I think Defoe cleverly shows is that we can draw our boundaries so wide and so large that the difference between civil order and anarchy is a distinction without a difference.

Another artist, Stravinsky, put it in a similar manner:

> [I]n art as in everything else, one can build only upon a resisting foundation: whatever constantly gives way to pressure, constantly renders movement impossible.
>
> My freedom thus consists in moving about within the narrow frame that I have assigned myself for each one of my undertakings.
>
> I shall go even further: *my freedom will be so much the greater and more meaningful the more narrowly I limit my field of action and the more I surround myself with obstacles. Whatever diminishes constraint, diminishes strength. The more constraints one imposes, the more one frees one of the chains that shackle the spirit.*
>
> *The more art is controlled, limited, worked over, the more it is free.*[2]

To put it another way, unbridled, unrestrained freedom of a thing leads as quickly to anarchy as overmuch restriction leads to revolution.

It will doubtless appear odd to some that a librarian by profession favors some form of censorship. It will not be the first time this has been brought to my attention. But that is just the point. Having spent a career in this profession, I am more convinced than ever before that if we intend to preserve the freedom we have been vouchsafed, then we must favor some small form of censorship to protect and to preserve our democracy. If we want something different, something other than the democracy (and yes, I know, it is really a republic) which our founders entrusted to us, then we may well want to dispense with all restrictions.

Before pursuing that line of inquiry, the conscience of social media, let's establish why it may be necessary. If social media are merely a pastime, a novelty, we should not bother. But since they are fast becoming the central focus of our lives, then perhaps the question is worth asking after all.

The Good, the Bad and the Ugly

The ubiquity and value of social media cannot be gainsaid, of course, and I have tried to make that clear. To review: We use these sites for everything. Wikipedia, once the bane of online encyclopedias and the punchline to any joke about research, is now the most used online encyclopedia on the Internet.[3] It will come up most often in specific search terms, such as science terms, history, biography, and so on. While Wikipedia continues to have its problems with reliability, as pointed out in chapter nine, it remains the first choice among most users. The endgame seems to be that if you can get it quickly and it sounds plausible, go for it. Users appear to be saying, "Don't confuse me with details; just give me the answer, and quick!" It would be wrong to say they do not care if the answer is wrong, but it is not too far off base to say they are unconcerned if the answer is debatable.

Young people use social media incessantly. As recently as 2008, young people used social media in some manner close to 1,750 times a month. By late 2010, they were using it well over 3,000 times a month, according to Nielsen.[4] To say we might be addicted to social media may be an understatement rather than an exaggeration. As mentioned earlier, there is talk about social media addiction making it into a future volume of the DSM (*Diagnostic and Statistical Manual of Mental Disorders*). We love our social media, and we will not abide anyone telling us that something is wrong with their use, even if there is. In fact, we love them so much that for most of us, but especially young people, these are the *only* places to go to find information or reply to an inquiry.[5] Although many wish they could disconnect more than they do, most teens (two-thirds) admit to connecting at least once a day. Clearly, for colleges and universities, if they are not connecting with potential students via some form of social media, they are not connecting with them at all.[6] Often trying to get a young person to answer the phone or even an email is out of the question. If, however, you tweet them...

This may be why so few Americans are concerned about the downsides of social networking. Experts disagree. *Freakonomics* authors Stephen Dubner and Steven Levitt (their book investigates world truths via economic understanding) held a forum in which a handful of experts were asked about the overall positive and negative aspects of social networking.[7] Some believed it to be an unqualified good, others had serious reservations. Any new technology has both good and bad effects, latent or manifest outcomes. For example, most would argue that cars have revolutionized individual travel. But no one can deny they have also come at great and tragic personal cost to some, at extraordinary cost to the environment, and at great geopolitical costs owing to the oil required to run them. Would Americans give up their cars?

Hardly, and it would be silly to ask them to. Much the same is true for social networking, it must be said, philosophical musings notwithstanding. Social networking sites have created many benefits in communications, improved the ability to share information among professionals, and even made it possible for revolutions to occur in countries under oppression. But social networking sites have also cost the lives of some, pushed the limits of decency and good taste, cost businesses billions, wasted the time of countless millions, and made it possible for repressive regimes to put a quick and effective end to needed revolution. In the same way Americans have regulated their cars, one can only hope they will also eventually come to see the need for stronger regulation of social networking sites.

Social Media's Popularity Grows

The number of social networking users and their enthusiasm for social media is undiminished. While total social networking site users rise and fall on a given platform, overall numbers have continued to grow over the last five years. According to Mashable, Facebook accounts for almost half of all social media activity, but Twitter is quickly catching up. According to Nielsen Online, activity on social media is up 82 percent worldwide. At least for the short term, social networking is here to stay, and it will likely continue to grow and flourish.

But tensions with this mega-use are already causing difficulties. Most universities employ a majority of non-digital natives, professors who are between 45 and 65. Even accounting for post-traditional students, most universities have a majority of 18- to 22-year-olds who matriculate annually. And therein lies the problem. Most of the over–40 professors still use the acroamatic or lecture method to teach. They rely on very expensive textbooks and a tried and proven means to impart knowledge. But young people, the very ones paying their salaries, some of which are quite high, have little patience for these things. More and more college-bound students are looking for other avenues to complete their educations. Their confidence in a college education grows less and less each year, and it is certainly far less than the value their parents placed on their education.[8] Students complain that their college educations are too low-tech, too "boring," and too dependent on peripheral matters in which students have little or no interest. Even parents of these children who value the traditional college course of study often find the costs too high and the return too costly, or at least taking too long to return any real value.

Not all of these ills can be laid at the doorstep of social networking, of course, but some surely can. Students' interest in the interactive, the flashy, the inexpensive (save for smartphones and plans they purchase) is so ingrained now that they abhor any medium without these accoutrements. Anyone who has taught at the university level can attest that students in the 2000s do not like to read long texts, do not like to contemplate complex ideas, and do not like to spend long stretches of time thinking about thinking, as it were. They want answers instantly—as in 2.5 nanoseconds—and they want to have fun while finding out. It is too early to say whether this is a trend that will eventually unravel higher education, or if it is merely a bump along the digital superhighway.

One effort to address the boring is Massive Open Online Courses (MOOCs). MOOCs have not only not caught on, but they also appear to be crashing and burning with surprising regularity. Tweed-coated professors should not, however, gloat. MOOCs may not have begun to work as well as some hoped (and hyped) early on, but what is clear from many students is that the lecture method approach causes many of them to seek other options—*any* other options. Likewise, it would appear that no matter how abusive social media become, or how severely they trample their privacy, young people are willing to make almost any accommodation to keep social media close. As in the case of MOOCs, so also in social media, we need to do what it takes to make them better.

Social networking is now more popular on mobile devices (such as smartphones) than it is on desktops, and that trend is one that will continue, according to experts at Read Write Web. Young people, ages 15 to 24, are among those who drive this trend, but it is moving to the next age bracket, 25 to 34, as well. This only highlights one change in social networking connectivity: it is far more likely to be carried out over a phone than on a conventional computer, meaning that sites like Twitter will increase in the near term.

This Is Your Brain on Social Media

We still do not know how much of this is a step in the right direction, the wrong direction, or in a neutral direction. Gary Small, a researcher at UCLA, points out that "...the brain's neural circuitry responds to every moment to whatever sensory input it gets, and that the many hours people spend in front of the computer—doing various activities, including trolling the Internet, exchanging email, videoconferencing, IM'ing and e-shopping—expose their brains to constant stimulation."[9] It is what the author later refers to as "techno-brain burnout." Apparently, when we are plugged in for so long and so often, our brains begin to get fatigued and simply shut down, or slow down, stymied in a kind of "digital fog." This fog or miasma will cause the brain to function at a slower pace until it recharges or is reinvigorated by spending time away from the continuous "plugged in" state. That is the good news. It does not take too long for the brain to redeem itself when rested. But therein lies the problem. We stay connected for nearly all our waking hours, turning off, if at all, for only a few hours of sleep. The long-term effects of this are not really known, but Small and other researchers believe that our brains will evolve and adapt to these new stresses. Most readers, too, will want to be quick to argue that various kinds of online activity actually improve our brain function, especially in activities like video games and other mind-engaging activities. The long-term effects may well be absorbed by our brains and, a decade or so from now, or certainly after a generation of complete online engagement by digital natives, this will be another "age" in our evolutionary growth. What is not quite clear now is what will get left behind.

For proponents like Clive Thompson, little or nothing gets left behind in the longer term. If his example of Gordon Bell, a septuagenarian lifeblogger who is endlessly logged on, is an example of where we are going, this author does not want to go.[10] But others might. Bell has a fish-eye camera about his neck that snaps pictures every sixty seconds and a tiny recorder that tapes most conversations. Software on his computer saves a picture of every webpage he visits, and he also captures every email he reads or sends, as well as every conversation he has, though whether this is illegal is unimportant in the grand scheme of "remembering" every-thing. Bell's "memory" is better than most human memories, of course, because computers do not forget unless forced to. But they can be devil-ishly difficult to search, something that is not all that hard for our brains until old age overtakes them. Even if this is the "brave new world" of the future, having a computer memory really does not have the same kind of appeal to everyone, even it if can be perfected and miniaturized so as not to be very obtrusive. The cyberborg feel of it also has a nonhuman aura. Thompson thinks we will land in the middle of the road of this artificial memory highway. I am not so sure any part of it is an overarching good. If the full frontal assault by Bell and others is too much, the middle of the road appears to be the next place to get hit solidly in the face. Our digital world is simply too much with us, but perhaps that will change as digital natives grow up and as evolution overtakes the resistant or the uncom-mitted.

Gordon Bell is not the first hyperconnected human, or as well known as Ray Kurzweil. Although Bell may be more connected literally, futurist Ray Kurzweil may be more obsessive, or simply more dedicated. Among his many celebrated inventions, Kurzweil is also known for his book on the singularity.[11] The singularity is a Gladwell-esque point in which technology and invention and all of human progress ramp up so quickly and at such a pace that we transcend biology, discovering a way to cure all sickness and even death, and become, for all intents and purposes, immortal. The 660-plus-page tome covers, among other things, molecular computing, bending the speed of light to go back in time, nanobots, artificial intelligence (AI) and brain circuitry that is secondary to computer circuitry. If computers do not prove to be the Antichrist, then they will prove to be God, at least in the Kurzweil economy. But all of this pales in comparison to Kurzweil's tracking of his own health. Kurzweil has tracked his eating and his consumption habits so carefully that he knows what he ate on a given day at a given time, including how many grams, for almost the last *three* decades.[12] Part of Kurzweil's obsession or diligence, depending on how one views these things, has to be his own inherited genes for heart disease and Type–2 diabetes. His tracking has allowed him to outlive his father's 58 years, but as a prescription for our future, it is doubtful that many people would be this meticulous.

No one questions that machines are smarter than we are, even though we created them. But can they replace us, or make us so much better that we will eventually live forever? The supercomputer Watson (currently on a quest to cure cancer) proved that it is incredibly smart but also incredibly dumb. When it went up against Jeopardy's three best champions, it won hands-down. While the show may well have been slanted in Watson's favor (easily searchable answers), the computer also came up with some surprisingly idiotic responses. In the category "U.S. Cities" with the final answer, "The largest airport named for a World War II hero and the second largest WWII battle," both humans responded correctly with "What is Chicago [O'Hare and Midway] but Watson responded, "What is Toronto?"[13] Sure, these sorts of things can be fixed by *humans* who can reprogram them. Yes, computers are said to be on their way to recoding themselves, but until then, it may not be the best idea to put all our eggs in one basket, or all our socializing into one or three or five social media platforms.

Are Social Media Making Us Posthuman?

Other proponents argue that we are entering a new phase of what it means to be "posthuman."[14] We have never really been "in control," and digital realities force us to confront the true nature of our reality. Our posthuman existence may well catapult us into a new way of thinking and understanding that allows us to avoid repeating the mistakes of the past.

If we work hard to define what it means to be posthuman, we may well be able to avoid the more anti-human scenarios that continue to plague the landscape of the future. All of this may be true, but it is for the philosophers to ponder. From this coign of vantage of naïveté, becoming, being, or even moving toward posthuman sounds too much like becoming something that is after humanity, or beyond humanness, not ensconced in it. Perhaps, as Simonides once said, when people begin to talk in this wise, it may be best to speak (and think) otherwise.

One thing is for certain, however. Our brains are very flexible with respect to all this brave new cyberworld. We know, for example, that when a person learns to read, the very plasticity of our brains allows for this activity to take place, but it also changes our brains forever.[15] Online activity is yet another very different kind of activity in which the "plastic nature" of our brains allows our brains to adapt. For some, this simply means that we will be fine. All we have to do is wait for the transformation. For others, it appears we may be adding something that could short-circuit the process. Society is always changing, and we change with it; we adapt. On the other hand, not every change in evolution has been for the better, and we call those mutations. Not all of them rank high on the evolutionary scale of things, and some of them, like the mutations in our cells that cause cancer, we have not yet been able to adapt to. It could well be that for some of the online changes, we will simply have to wait and see. In the meantime, we can say with some assurance, what does not kill us will make us stronger.

The Zuckerberg Revolution

We know from the changes that took place when we humans moved from the oral to the written word that our minds were radically transformed.[16] We are in a kind of new Gutenberg Age that Naughton humorously calls "Zuckerberg" for a good reason. While Facebook may well be declining among some users, it still holds the highest number of members. One study argues, for example, that Facebook could lose as many as 80 percent of its users by as soon as 2017.[17] (Facebook countered by using the correlation-is-causation argument to show that Princeton will close its doors in 2021 based on the same principle.)

Although the report was widely commented upon, no one really believes it, and Facebook continues to thrive. Ello, the invitation-only "anti" social network, is gaining ground on Facebook by offering social networking without the loss of privacy. It is also offering this without ads, at least for now.[18] But as its fame grew, so did its first denial of service outage. Further, the adoption of Instagram and Pinterest, as well as Vimeo, appears to mean that any new social media will attract "some" users, here meaning "millions of." Obviously, since this is the case, we know that there will be a transformation of some kind. How much and to what extent is anyone's guess. We simply do not know right now. And even what we do know now in no way means it will be important going forward. But it does mean we need to keep an eye on it, and keep watching it. Social media will continue to be important in our lives in the near future, and that will impact our culture and our communications, at least in the near term.

Current and Future Trends: More to Prick the Conscience

Current and coming trends that affect social networking include mobile computing, or computing that can be carried with the user, according to New Media Consortium and EDUCAUSE's Learning Initiative *2013 Horizon Report*.[19] For social networking this is likely to mean more devices capable of delivering a satisfying online social networking experience from tablets, smartphones, netbooks, and iPad-like devices that are likely to proliferate. The report also underscores gamification, at least as it touches upon classroom learning, and 3D wearable technologies. As prices continue to drop for technology, we should also see more Google glass-type technologies. Social networking thrives on openness in everything, including open access and "remixable" information. This does not necessarily mean it will be free, although it may be free to the user. Someone will be footing the bill, but for social media anything that charges users beyond current data cost will be DOA.

Simple augmented reality, a feature that once required special non-portable equipment, will become more common, but it is still maturing. Augmented reality takes the physical world view and adds or augments computer-generated enhancements. So, for example, one may use a smartphone to view a street. Augmented reality populates that view with restaurant locations, area events, or special regional features. Some of these features are already possible on some social networking sites but are likely to become more common and more numerous. Gesture-based computing, or computing controlled by one's natural arm, finger, or hand movements, will also increase, though again, its perfection is still several years away. While gesture-based computing is more commonplace in gaming, it will also become important for other aspects of social networking connections.

Certain social media will continue to gain market share. Pinterest and Instagram, mentioned above, will continue to expand their user base. Social media users like being able to do everything they want to do in one place and not be hamstringed by what those users see as restrictions. Social media users like to post images, videos, pictures, and messages all at once. Any social media platform that allows them to do this seamlessly will continue to attract users by the millions. Pinterest's well known "pin it" lure will find users drawn to it as a first choice. Not only does that social network make it easy to post whatever is on the user's mind, it also helps steer traffic to that user's website. LinkedIn will continue to grow, and sites like Sobrr that help to erase a user's unpleasant past will also gain a foothold. Sobrr thinks its niche will be helping people recover from their own stupid social media posts. Certainly there is a need for such a service, as witnessed either by the numerous drunken posts by Anthony Weiner–type politicians, or like Justine Sacco, the PR staffer who tweeted in a colossally forgettable moment, "Going to Africa. Hope I don't get AIDS. Just kidding. I'm white!"[20]

Sites like Facebook and Twitter may not grow as quickly, as both continue to work to monetize what they do. In the spring of 2014, authors Adrienne LaFrance and Robinson Meyer wrote a long piece for *The Atlantic* on how Twitter is twitching its last.[21] According to LaFrance and Meyer, although Twitter experienced growth (14 million new users and its revenues were up), its users have become noticeably less active. Twitter says this is because everything is more streamlined. The authors think it is more Twitter's twilight. It used to be, according to the authors, more a "surrogate barroom" around which one could organize one's own ideas in the smelting crucible of others. But lately, it appears to be suffering from the "eternal now" syndrome, a kind of modern-day Nietzsche gone madder. Users are going to Twitter if only to post why they do not plan to stay. This may mean something, or it simply may prove that the authors' contention is wrong. Whatever it is, Twitter announced its first ever decline in timeline views earlier in 2014.[22] It did not help that in March 2014, a Twitter snafu reset millions of passwords—not a hack or a DOS, but a company glitch. In any event, more Twitter usage may have more users but fewer posts, leading the authors to contend that it has changed, or perhaps just the authors have.

In addition to losing views, or perhaps in response to this, Twitter is also adding to timelines tweets from people whom users are not following.[23] Twitter explained that if there is a very popular tweet from someone a user may not be following, they may add if it's "relevant." The idea behind this is to put in front of users brands they may want to follow. This is doubtless helpful to those who are only just discovering the social medium, but for those who have spent the time and energy weeding out all they do not want to see, the move is not appreciated. From Twitter's perspective, it is a business decision: advertisers can be assured of getting before some number of users whether those users are following them or not. Users, especially new ones, may find it helpful, even if only temporarily, to follow a new tweet or retweet from someone they were not following. For Twitter, it is a win-win so long as long-term users of the social network do not revolt.

Social Media's Reach Expands

Both Facebook and Twitter may be protesting too much about the fact that there is user decline in access to those accounts, while there may well be an increase in users. It does not help their case that nothing is wrong when Facebook shelled out $14 billion for Whatsapp, a mobile messenger service that skyrocketed to the top of message volume with 19 billion sent and 34 billion received in a matter of months, quickly exceeding SMS volume worldwide.[24] Facebook and Twitter will argue it is making the company better, and perhaps it is. But Whatsapp was unknown by many in this country until Facebook made it a household word.

Whatever is going on with those two social media giants, the fact of the matter is that social media are growing at every turn, at every level of use, from elementary school students through retirees.

Let Your Conscience Be Your Guide

Having said all that, social media will need to address more seriously the ease with which they can be hacked and users' privacy (and identities) can be compromised. In other words, they need to acquire a conscience strong enough to do something about it. The rise in the denial of service attacks (DOS) will continue to grow. DOS or DDOS attacks (distributed denial of service attacks) have also been a problem. DDOS attacks come from multiple computers and have a particularly disrupting influence. These attacks are measured in gigabits per second (GPS), and a user of 100 GPS can disrupt a corporate network. In February of this year, Cloudfare, a company that tracks these sorts of things, tracked 400 GPS attacks.[25] That kind of an attack, one of the most massive to date, will shut a network down. While it is not always easy to see where the attacks come from, we do know they go after the weakest networks, or the easiest ones through which to gain entrance. Increasingly, hackers are finding social media among the more attractive. The reason is obvious: social media sites are more public and will garner the hacker the most attention. While social media sites are becoming more savvy to these intrusions, they still have work to do in this area. Addressing these attacks will be important but will also be difficult, not because social media sites do not know what to do, but because this kind of protection is not glamorous or very visible. Think of it as replacing your mattress and bedsprings. We all know this is important and even critical to our well-being. But mattresses are expensive, finding the right one is like shopping for a car, and they aren't exactly the kind of thing that you rush out and tell people about: "Oh, we just spent $5,000 on a new mattress. Do come by and see it." Likewise, preventing a DOS attack is unglamorous, not exactly cheap, and really something you cannot see until it fails.

A new study of radio and television and online media by Radio Television Digital News Association (RTDNA) and Hofstra University found that newsrooms will increase their use of social networking, especially following disasters when news outlets crowdsource (when groups do the job of independent contractors) pictures onto social networking sites. For example, following a recent meteor shower in Wisconsin, news outlets crowdsourced pictures and uploaded them to Twitter to share with viewers. The same was true with the disastrous oil spill in the Gulf of Mexico in April 2010, as news outlets shared aerial photographs and some pictures from satellites. Expect more of this in the future, as more and more individuals will naturally turn to social networking for updates on news events.

It is expected that television shows will seek tie-ins with social networking audiences, too. According to a report by *Forbes*, television is seeking to make connections over social networking with audiences by allowing them to interact with each other on ten-foot screens instead of screens only 10 centimeters wide. This only makes sense, as social networking ads are better at reaching audiences than ads on television. Television will need to find a way to incorporate social media into what they do, and early indications are that they will do it via the social networking sites themselves. Talk shows make a great deal of sense by allowing millions of followers to connect with each other in real time as they watch a given broadcast. It does not hurt either that so many characters text and get online and talk about "posting" or "following" or even "tweeting" as second nature to them. These are not too subtle reminders that this is how we communicate now. Certainly Jimmy Fallon has proven that television can make tie-ins with social media to the benefit of both.

Trains, Planes and Automobiles

Social media captured train usage easily enough with smartphones. Plane use continues to be controversial, but it has already been pushed to widespread use. But now cars? So it would seem. The University of Michigan, in conjunction with Ford, Microsoft, and Intel, is making a marriage all right, but whether it is heavenly or hellish remains to be seen. Caravan Tracker is an application that allows multiple cars traveling together to trade information about remaining fuel, places to stop and eat or sleep, or places of interest, all on dashboard-embedded screens, and all while driving. Another application on the horizon allows cars to consume fuel more efficiently and avoid congestion via crowdsource mapping. Many new cars are also now made with social networking connections built in, so to speak. Since texting and driving are now as much an anathema as drinking and driving, and equally as dangerous, having these controls on the wheel or nearby so the driver does not have to look away is, one must suppose, safer. And all of this is "hands-free," as we have come to call it. The emergence of Navdy, the transparent, heads-up display, is certainly an improvement, but how much improvement remains to be seen.[26] None of these features are, however, attention-free. Until they are, can we claim that it is safe? Is it really a good idea to have one more distraction for the driver beyond those like music, smoking, soft drinks, and snacks? Of course, we should do everything we can to discourage texting and driving, but voice-activated, hands-free texting is not any safer since it still distracts the driver from the road. It still requires the users to put their attention on something other than the road. In fact, early reports indicate that all of these features are still distracting drivers, even when hands-free.[27] Apparently, it is the distraction of being connected as much as it is whether or not they have to use their hands.

Businesses will create stronger social networking policies with a more punitive measure of enforcement behind them. More gaming will occur via social networking sites, and mobile connections will play a much bigger role than ever before. No business has figured out whether all these tweets and posts and what-have-yous really increase the bottom line. For every ten articles that say it does, there are ten more that say it does not and five that say if it is not driving up business, you must be doing it wrong. The latter sounds more like a heads-I-win-tails-you-lose proposition. Still, businesses are spending a great deal of time with social media, and it is clear that if you are going to reach the millions who use social media, you had better be on it. But sophisticated ROI studies have not so far proved that social media are a terrific investment.

Email will eventually give way to social networking site communications as smartphones offer more sophisticated features. But if content is not going to be shared as freely as users want, email may remain. For the last decade, articles have cropped up about the demise of email, but as yet it has not disappeared. Another ten years may prove the point of these early predictors.

In conclusion, social networking will have an even more central and integral role in the lives of all Americans. The only less-than-rosy picture appearing for the future of social networking is its ability to generate revenue. According to Mobile Marketing Watch, a site that monitors all aspects of social networking news, revenues for mobile social networking will explode in 2016 to $9.6 billion and are forecast to reach $15 billion in 2018. That sounds like very good news. But the fact of the matter is that when companies look more closely at their returns, they are not exactly dancing in the streets. Ads on social media still do not translate into an increase in sales, having little or no influence at all about 90 percent of the time.[28] Rather, users go onto social media to chat with friends, make new ones, and renew acquaintances, not to shop or look for bargains. Having a lot of followers means only that you have a lot of followers; it doesn't mean those followers translate into buyers. Perhaps the only companies making a great deal of money on social media are social media companies.

Social media revenues will continue to escalate, but what troubles some observers is the time it takes a social networking site to make a profit (only over the last few years has Facebook turned the corner on profitability). Additionally, user loyalty to a social networking site is not guaranteed. Failures even of giant companies give pause. Facebook's recent privacy disaster and Google's social networking site disasters are two examples. Facebook's privacy stance created a small exodus of members and leaves the door open for a new site that takes privacy seriously. Google continues to work on social media after its colossal failure with Buzz in 2010. The service was discontinued the next year, owing mainly to a lack of attention to privacy issues. After Facebook purchased Oculus Rift for $2 billion, a steep price for a game-headset that is no more than a screen right now, its stock dropped almost 6.5 percent. All of which is to say that as fast as companies can hit record heights, they can just as quickly hit rock-bottom.

Are social networking sites making us smarter or more stupid? This is a debate that is not going to end. On the one hand, proponents say that being connected makes us smarter because we are more aware of the world and everything that is going on in it. Opponents, on the other hand, argue that it makes us overly dependent and robs us of exercising our memories; thus we become increasingly less attentive to details and more likely to be forced to resort to social media for answers (something most social media companies probably hope is happening). One school of thought tends to argue it is making us less civil while it is also making us more self-censoring.

Could it be all of the above? Probably. Some researchers found that we are made smarter in the short term, but dumber in the long term.[29] They contend that observing others and copying them is a recognized social learning mechanism that helps us adapt. But too much social media engagement in a continuous and uninterrupted fashion leads to a reduced capacity for reflective and analytical reasoning. We develop an "unreflective copying bias." In other words, our reflective abilities need exercise. Without exercise on a regular basis, the muscles, in this case our brains, become flaccid and unable to perform as needed. A great deal more research needs to be done with respect to this issue, but even at this stage, it is clear that we are becoming less and less the kind of people who can tolerate long stretches of quiet time.

In a series of eleven studies done by psychologists Timothy Wilson and his colleagues at the University of Virginia and Harvard University, "most people" find sitting quietly by themselves with their own thoughts an intolerable predicament. Others would rather apply electrical shocks to themselves than sit alone with their thoughts for even six minutes.[30] While only rudimentary, these are most disturbing studies and ones that do not bode well for our future. Are we so afraid of thinking that we would much rather shock ourselves than to be forced to deal with what is inside our own heads? Apparently the participants in this study would say yes. They preferred to fiddle with smartphones, listen to music, or do just about anything rather than sit quietly and think about whatever came to mind. The silence is deafening, and we must whistle past the graveyard in order not to think too carefully about ourselves. Excogitation in the new age is impermissible by choice.

The study included individuals who ranged in age from 18 to 77, from a wide range of backgrounds. Apparently Neil Postman was right after all: we are amusing ourselves to death.[31] If nothing else, these studies at least prove some indication, however small, that we are becoming less reflective and less willing to think through issues on our own, a far cry from the tradition that made Western Civilization the darling of the world.

Regulation on the Horizon: Conscience de Jure?

After the flurry of activity in the mid–2000s, as Congress tried and failed to craft a bill that would not only curb pornography on the Internet but also pass Supreme Court approval, little regulation of that kind has since surfaced. It is not that we are no longer concerned about it—many are—but crafting a bill that will meet the approval of the First Amendment absolutists is most likely a losing battle. Perhaps pornographers will suffer the same fate as Ask.fm, and users will revolt. One can dream, right? Besides, what would FCC employees do if they could not surf X-rated sites all day?[32]

What has surfaced instead are numerous net neutrality bills. Net neutrality, in its most simple definition, is a principle that argues broadband network providers should not favor one information content over another, that no information should take priority over any other. This would probably be the case were it not so lucrative for certain kinds of information to get to users first. In the same way that Google ranks information, providers want to rank some content above others. This has both up and downsides. It is good for the company that is willing to pay for that priority, bad for anyone else who cannot. Some argue that it is bad for users, too, but that often depends on what the prioritized information happens to be. Perhaps if tech companies were not making billions overnight, companies like Verizon and Netflix would not want to be part of that game, too. In any event, companies like Verizon and Netflix, some fear, would have the *real* superhighway on the Internet, while everyone else will be unable to pay the higher fees and will be forced to travel what are essentially backwater web "roads." The FCC (Federal Communication Commission) has twice tried to establish net neutrality only to be turned down by the Supreme Court. It is now back for a third time but with the same result staring them in the face: the FCC just doesn't have that authority, or so the Court said.[33] Net neutrality would protect the Internet from becoming a tiered system. In early 2015, however, the FCC voted for a strong net neutrality rule and President Obama promised to defend it. In principle it sounds so simple; in execution, where billions are at stake, it often turns out to be more complicated.

Net Neutrality Bills

Several bills made their way through Congress since 2009, but all eventually failed. ISPs (Internet service providers) oppose net neutrality because they want to be able to charge more to users whose activity takes up lots of bandwidth. Net neutrality proponents argue that a bill is needed because telecommunication companies are seeking to charge for a tiered service. To do so would allow, as indicated above, one provider to block or restrict the content of another provider by having what opponents see as roadblocks. The streamlined route would be superfast, but everything else would travel at a snail's pace, or noticeably slower at any rate. Berners-Lee and Vinton Cerf (sometimes referred to as the father of the Internet) favor net neutrality, while Bob Kahn, engineer and computer scientist who, with Cerf, created the protocol for web transmission opposes it. Passing a net neutrality bill received a severe blow in April 2010 when the District of Columbia Circuit Court rejected the FCC's authority to sanction Comcast, a major telecommunications provider, for attempting to interfere with Comcast's peer-to-peer trafficking and reversing the FCC's first attempt to enforce net neutrality. Peer-to-peer (commonly abbreviated P2P) refers to any network's architecture that allows a portion of its resources (e.g., disk storage, bandwidth) to be directly available to other network participants. Most observers viewed this decision as the death knell for net neutrality. But the FCC announced in early May 2010 that it would seek to reclassify broadband as a transport service that would allow the agency to enforce network neutrality and implement some parts of a national Broadband Plan. But the move also opens the door for court battles and fierce lobbying as Internet service providers fight to prevent regulation and allow for fast/slow lanes.

President Obama campaigned hard in favor of net neutrality in 2008 but remained largely silent on the matter until August 2014. He questioned the FCC's new net neutrality rules that would favor being able to charge more for faster Internet delivery of services.[34] But his responses up to this point had been ambiguous and weak, or at least that is the view of those who favor a neutral Internet.[35] Whether Obama's summer remarks will lead to a different FCC approach remains to be seen. The matter is not tangential to social media. As social media begin to ramp up their delivery of services, an Internet that would allow richer companies to make their content first would have a leg up on the competition. As late as October 2014, President Obama reaffirmed his opposition to FCC chairman Tim Wheeler's net neutrality plan.[36] But he also made a decided point to remain out of the actual fight.

But then came the shellacking he and his party took in the November 2014 elections. One week later, President Obama came out strongly in favor of net neutrality, providing the FCC a roadmap to the goal of his broadband policy. FCC Chairman Tom Wheeler remained noncommittal. The roadmap the president laid out is not, of course, a law, nor is it a sure indication of where this controversy will end. But it does get the White House off the fence a little farther than it has so far been in this debate.[37] While the news is music to the ears of companies like Netflix, it caused cable stocks to tank.[38] While the plan promises to help keep the Internet "free and open," as the president put it, it remains unclear what the ripple effect might be.

It is very likely that some form of federal cyberbullying regulation will emerge, but when is anyone's guess. For now, the states are stepping forward while Congress continues to consider it. Antonio Orsini, a principal at Benjamin Franklin Middle school, made headlines in May 2010 when he called for a voluntary ban on social networking sites in elementary and middle schools. Orsini believes social networking sites cannot be made safe for children. Further, they facilitate cyberbullying and are a distraction to the education of youth. Many agree.

In its baseline report issued in 2008 by the National Cyber Security Alliance (NCSA), Education Technology, Policy, Research, and Outreach (ETPRO) indicated that teens (ages 10 to 14) spend more time on the Internet than they do watching television. But only a handful of states have educational curriculum requirements for teaching children how to protect themselves, and 90 percent of all educators have received fewer than six hours of professional development on cybersecurity (no doubt this has changed some since the baseline study). Such daunting odds make it highly likely that minors will run into trouble eventually while online. The report also highlights that some law will be forthcoming regarding cyberbullying. The research of University of Arizona Professor Sheri Bauman and professional school counselor Tanisha Tatum indicates that the number of children online between the ages of three and twelve is growing exponentially and that their participation in social networking sites (especially children in elementary and middle school) remains a problem because they falsify their ages. They point to the need for greater parental and school proactive measures to make certain that children have safe online experiences. Given the best intentions of well-meaning adults, is it possible to provide a safe social media experience for adolescents when the very nature of the Internet—no quality control, please—precludes it? Meanwhile, in Great Britain, Cultural Secretary Andy Burnham hopes to impose a ratings system for websites. He argues that whatever content is on the web, it should not be available for anyone to view without some sort of rating, such as those for movies. But good luck with that!

Parents and educators of young children are showing a greater interest in and growing concern for stronger Internet policing. Whether this can be done without imposing on social networking sites to monitor themselves both here and abroad is doubtful. The sharp horns of this dilemma are piercing. On the one hand, the need is obvious; on the other hand, how to effect the desired result while not also infringing upon rights of others, especially adults, is not. While many Internet advocates argue for teaching minors online responsibility, critics complain that it is easier said than done. Stronger social networking site regulation appears to be the only sure solution, a solution that there is little will to implement.

Social media sites are here to stay. No one disputes that. But the form in which they will exist and the regulations that will govern them are likely to be far different in the coming years than they are today. Are we doomed to have our social media inundated with baby pictures, cute cats, another espresso drink with very intricately swirled milk, and yet another cupcake, pie, or watercress salad? Or will these media grow up to provide more important information than just the day-to-day musings of ordinary users going about their ever so ordinary lives?

The parody online magazine and video site *The Onion* ran a piece on how the Internet was about to collapse under the sheer weight of baby pictures.[39] Like all its parodies, this one was hilarious. But it got attention not just because it was funny; it had a strangely resonate quality about it, as if this could really happen. It certainly feels that way. Between the baby pictures and the five tips on how to sleep better, plus a post about the "fantastic" shrimp at some restaurant, social media often feel frivolous and hollow. When Facebook chose to bury brands that had not paid to appear in posts, it only made matters worse.[40] The company changed its algorithms to highlight posts from individuals while allowing those with free advertising brand posts to sink into virtual oblivion. Can media this in tune to their own internal and, at times, frivolous interests be made to rise to the level of a true public online forum?

Proponents will say that this criticism misses the boat on two counts. Social media do not want to grow up, and besides, they do, from time to time, catch criminals, commence revolutions, help serious political candidates win elections, or enable those same candidates to shoot themselves in the foot. What more do we want?

Opponents will say that is too generous to social media. Yes, they stumble into the serious, but often in the wrong way, and just as often in a way that mucks up things repeatedly (see how Redditt announced the wrong Boston Marathon bomber), or aid in the sinking of potential revolutions while making it decidedly worse for those who choose to revolt online, in their own names. How this will be managed and still allow for the very features that make social networking an exciting and vibrant means of communication is anyone's guess.

We began this chapter asking the question whether social media could get a conscience and police themselves; that is, when will they feel the "prick of conscience" enough to want to address their serious downsides. The purpose of the foregoing survey is to show its wide reach in every facet of our lives and therefore all the more reason we should want social media to acquire something on the order of a conscience. What remains is whether social media will remain more indecorous than necessary. Key to that will be whether we can fashion them into something that will be more vital and enduring rather than indiscreet and intrusive.

It will certainly appear silly to some to think of social media as having a conscience. Some will believe that is much like anthropomorphizing an inanimate object. Since, however, social media are, like the famous 2006 *Time* magazine cover "Person of the Year, You, or Rather, Us," then why can't we demand that we act more responsibly?[41] Why is it impossible to demand that social media act more like a public forum that encourages civil discourse, not the flotsam and jetsam of every good or bad idea every person on them has? The only thing standing in the way of this is not so much social media platforms but those of us who make them work—their users. This is not a question of whether we can do this. We have proven we can. The question is one of an entirely different sort.

Do we have the will to make it happen?

Chapter Notes

Introduction

1. Kathryn Zickuhr, "Who's Not Online and Why," *Pew Research Internet Project*, September 25, 2013. http://www.pewinternet.org/2013/09/25/whos-not-online-and-why/.

2. Pew Research, "Social Networking Use," *Pew Research Data Trend*. http://www.pewresearch.org/data-trend/media-and-technology/social-networking-use/.

3. Bill Gates, "Why Inequality Matters," *Gate Notes*, October 13, 2014. http://www.gatesnotes.com/Books/Why-Inequality-Matters-Capital-in-21st-Century-Review.

Chapter One

1. Lev Grossman, "You—Yes, You—Are TIME's Person of the Year," *Time*, December 25, 2006. http://content.time.com/time/magazine/article/0,9171,1570810,00.html.

2. Patrick Tucker, *The Naked Future: What Happens in a World That Anticipates Your Every Move?* (New York: Current, 2014), xv–xviii.

3. Samuel C. McQuade, ed., "Internet." *Encyclopedia of Cybercrime* (Westport, CT: Greenwood Press, 2008), 124.

4. Barry M. Leiner, et al., "Brief History of the Internet," Internet Society. http://www.internetsociety.org/internet/what-internet/history-internet/brief-history-internet.

5. While the glossary can no longer be found, it still appears on several sites referenced (and not) as here: http://libraryandsocialnetwork.wikifoundry.com/.

6. " Social Networks," *Wikipedia*, http://en.wikipedia.org/wiki/Social_networks.

7. "Social Networking Site," *Pcmagazine*, http://www.pcmag.com/encyclopedia_term/0,2542,t=social+networking+site&i=55316,00.asp.

8. danah boyd and Nicole B. Ellison, "Social Networking Sites: Definition, History and Scholarship," *Journal of Computer-Mediated Communication*, Vol. 13 (1) (2007). http://onlinelibrary.wiley.com/doi/10.1111/j.1083-6101.2007.00393.x/full.

9. danah boyd, *It's Complicated: The Social Lives of Networked Teens* (New Haven: Yale University Press, 2014).

10. Randi Zuckerberg, *Dot Complicated: Untangling Our Wired Lives* (New York: Harper One, 2013).

11. Amanda Lenhart, Kristen Purcell, Aaron Smith, and Kathryn Zickuhr, "Social Media and Young Adults," *American Life Project*, February 3, 2010. http://pewresearch.org/pubs/1484/social-media-mobile-internet-use-teens-millennials-fewer-blog.

12. Amanda Lenhart, "Young Adults, Mobile Phones and Social Media: Technology and the Transition to Adulthood," May 7, 2013. http://www.pewinternet.org/2013/05/07/young-adults-mobile-phones-and-social-media-technology-and-the-transition-to-adulthood/.

13. Joshua Porter, *Designing for the Social Web* (Berkeley, CA: New Riders, 2008), 19.

14. Lenhart, Purcell, et al., "Social Media and Young Adults," *Pew Internet & American Life Project*. http://pewresearch.org/pubs/1484/social-media-mobile-internet-use-teens-millennials-fewer-blog.

15. Amanda Lenhart, "Young Adults, Mobile Phones and Social Media: Technology

and the Transition to Adulthood," May 7, 2013. http://www.pewinternet.org/2013/05/07/young-adults-mobile-phones-and-social-media-technology-and-the-transition-to-adulthood/.

16. Tom Standage, *Writing on the Wall: Social Media: The First 2,000 Years* (New York: Bloomsbury, 2013), 22–28.

17. Erin Allen, "Update on the Twitter Archives at the Library of Congress," *Library of Congress Blog*, January 4, 2013. http://blogs.loc.gov/loc/2013/01/update-on-the-twitter-archive-at-the-library-of-congress/. Today, there are more than 170 *billion* tweets archived and growing daily.

18. Standage, *Writing on the Wall*, 47ff.

19. Actually it wasn't the *Ninety-Five Theses* that originally caused all the trouble but his gauntlet two months earlier, *Disputation Against Scholastic Theology*. See Arthur Herman. *The Cave and the Light: Plato Versus Aristotle and the Struggle for the Soul of Western Civilization* (New York: Random House, 2013), 307.

20. A very good effort to make that point can be found in John Naughton's *From Gutenberg to Zuckerberg: Disruptive Innovation in the Age of the Internet* (New York: Quercus), 2012.

21. Porter, *Designing for the Social Web*, 7.

22. David Weinberger, *Everything Is Miscellaneous: The Power of the New Digital Disorder* (New York: Times Books, 2007), 190.

23. Berners-Lee, Tim, *Weaving the Web: The Original Design and Ultimate Destiny of the World Wide Web* (New York: Harper-Collins, 1999), 123. (Italics mine.).

24. Christoph Wieser, "Tim Berners-Lee: We Need Data on the Web to Work Better Together," *The Semantic Puzzle*, April 22, 2009. http://blog.semantic-web.at/2009/04/22/tim-berners-lee-we-need-data-on-the-web-to-work-better-together/.

25. Thomas Blass, *The Man Who Shocked the World: The Life and Legacy of Stanley Milgram* (New York: Basic Books, 2004), 284–285.

26. Albert-László Barabási, *Linked: How Everything Is Connected to Everything Else and What It Means* (New York: Plume, 2003), 30. Barabási is credited with resurrecting the work of Milgram.

27. Many books and places on the Internet recount this history. For example, see "The BBS Corner," http://www.bbscorner.com/users info/bbshistory.htm.

28. Fred Turner, "Where the Counterculture Met the New Economy: The WELL and the Origins of Virtual Community," http://www.stanford.edu/~fturner/Turner%20Tech%20&%20Culture%2046%203.pdf.

29. For much of this history see Howard Rheingold, *The Virtual Community: Homesteading on the Electronic Frontier* (New York: HarperPerennial, 1993), 39–59.

30. George Mannes, "Spinning the Globe: The Net Bubble Through the Eyes of Callow Youth," The Street.com, September 1, 2001. http://www.thestreet.com/tech/georgemannes/10000562.html.

31. boyd and Ellison, "Social Networking Sites: Definition, History and Scholarship," *Journal of Computer-Mediated Communication*, http://onlinelibrary.wiley.com/doi/10.1111/j.1083-6101.2007.00393.x/full.

32. The Winklevoss twins are Cameron and Tyler, who complained in court that Facebook was really ConnectU and had been stolen from them by Zuckerberg. Just because the court gave them a settlement of $65 million (down from the original $140 million claim) doesn't necessarily mean they were right, but only that Zuckerberg preferred to settle the case rather than go forward. Of course, the settlement also doesn't mean the Winklevoss twins were wrong, either.

33. Sascha Segan, "Why I Don't Want My Daughter to Work in Silicon Valley," *PC Magazine*, March 17, 2014. http://www.pcmag.com/article2/0,2817,2455042,00.asp.

34. Nick Bilton, *Hatching Twitter: A True Story of Money, Power, Friendship and Betrayal* (New York: Portfolio/Penguin, 2013).

35. The search giant has had more than one notable flop when it comes to social networking, something that doubtless worries Google as Facebook is beginning to eclipse it in driving traffic on the Internet. For more on the flops, see Harry McCracken, "A Brief History of Google's Social Networking Flops," *Time*, July 11, 2011. http://techland.time.com/2011/07/11/a-brief-history-of-googles-social-networking-flops/.

36. boyd and Ellison, "Social Networking Sites: Definition, History and Scholarship," *Journal of Computer-Mediated Communication*, http://onlinelibrary.wiley.com/doi/10.1111/j.1083-6101.2007.00393.x/full.

37. Lev Grossman, "You—Yes, You—Are TIME's Person of the Year," *Time*, December 25, 2006.

38. Marcus Wohlsen, "The Next Big Thing You Missed: Email's About to Die, Argues Facebook's Co-Founder," *Wired*, January 21, 2014. http://www.wired.com/2014/01/next-

big-thing-missed-facebook-co-founder-says-email/.

39. Andrew Keen, *The Cult of the Amateur: How Today's Internet Is Killing Our Culture* (New York: Doubleday, 2007), 7.

40. Weinberger, *Everything Is Miscellaneous*, 108.

Chapter 2

1. James Grimmelmann, "Saving Facebook," *Iowa Law Review* 94 (2009). http://works.bepress.com/james_grimmelmann/20.

2. I am greatly indebted to Captain Jeffrey J. Krohn, ROTC, Winthrop University, for help in clarifying my understanding of this issue. Any errors are of course my own.

3. "Responsible and Effective Use of Internet-based Capabilities," Department of Defense, DTM 09-026. http://www.dtic.mil/whs/directives/corres/pdf/855001p.pdf. See also Erika Morphy, "The Military Has Legitimate Reasons to Ban Social Networking Web Sites," in *Should Social Networking Web Sites Be Banned?* edited by Roman Espejo (Farmington Hills: MI: Greenhaven Press, 2008), 66–67.

4. "Mafiaboy Hacker Jailed," *BBC News*, September 13, 2001. http://news.bbc.co.uk/2/hi/science/nature/1541252.stm.

5. Noah Shachtman, "Military May Ban Twitter, Facebook as Security Headaches," *Wired Magazine*, July 30, 2009. http://www.wired.com/dangerroom/2009/07/military-may-ban-twitter-facebook-as-security-headaches/. However, Captain Krohn has been an officer on active duty since 2002 and does not recall a ban on social media. Personal communication with the author, 5 November 2014.

6. James Dao, "Military Announces New Military Policy," *New York Times*, February 26, 2010. http://atwar.blogs.nytimes.com/2010/02/26/military-announces-new-social-media-policy/?_php=true&_type=blogs&_r=0.

7. Phoenix Cosmopolitan Group, "Social Media's Role in the 21st Century Military Family," *PC Impact*, October 13, 2013. http://pcgimpact.com/blogpress/article/10/14/2013/social-medias-role-in-the-21st-century-military-family.

8. It's no wonder. Captain Krohn tells me of an incident in 2007–2009 in which a soldier's Facebook page contained photographs of rooftop security, weapons systems, and even how the vehicles were parked near an Iraqi police station. The Facebook view was reported by someone 4,000 miles away. Personal communication with the author, 5 November 2014.

9. Erica Morphy, *Should Social Networking Sites BE Banned?*, 67.

10. Todd Garvin, "The Military Ban on Social Networking Web Sites Lowers Morale," in *Should Social Networking Web Sites Be Banned?* edited by Roman Espejo (Farmington Hills: MI: Greenhaven Press, 2008), 71–73.

11. Daniel Fisher, "Cybersquatters Rush to Claim Brands in the New GTLD Territories," *Forbes*, February 27, 2014. http://www.forbes.com/sites/danielfisher/2014/02/27/cybersquatters-rush-to-claim-brands-in-the-new-gtld-territories/.

12. Gady A. Epstein, "Web Site Owner Links City to Smut," *The Baltimore Sun*, January 14, 2002. http://articles.baltimoresun.com/2002-01-14/news/0201140317_1_domain-names-gregory-links.

13. "Why Issaquah Can't Be Trusted, Part 1: Mayor Admits Cybersquatting Water District to Redirect Customers to City Websites," *Sammamish Comment*, September 13, 2013. http://sammamishcomment.wordpress.com/2013/09/13/why-issaquah-cant-be-trusted-part-1-mayor-admits-cybersquatting-water-district-to-redirect-customers-to-city-websites/.

14. Missy Graham and Elizabeth Johnson Avery, "Government Public Relations and Social Media: An Analysis of the Perceptions and Trends of Social Media Use at the Local Government Level," *Public Relations Journal* Vol. 7 No. 4 (2013). http://www.prsa.org/intelligence/prjournal/documents/2013grahamavery.pdf.

15. Matthew Ingram, "So Facebook Controls the Way Millions of People Get Their News. What Should We Do About It?" *Gigaom*, October 27, 2014. https://gigaom.com/2014/10/27/so-facebook-controls-the-way-millions-of-people-get-their-news-what-should-we-do-about-it/.

16. U.S. Government Service Administration, *GSA 2013: The Social Media Navigator: GSA's Guide to Official Use of Social Media.* http://www.gsa.gov/portal/category/101299.

17. Lee Raine and Aaron Smith, "Politics and Social Networking Sites," *Pew Research Internet Project*, September 4, 2012. http://www.pewinternet.org/2012/09/04/politics-on-social-networking-sites/.

18. Rob Nikolewski, "Social Media Blunders 2013," *New Mexico Watchdog*, December 29, 2013. http://newmexico.watchdog.org/19982/editorial-social-media-blunders-of-2013/.

19. One of the scores of such stories appears here: Craig Agranoff, "Social Media Mistakes Learned from Anthony Weiner," *The Huffington Post*, September 9, 2013. http://www.huffingtonpost.com/craig-agranoff/social-media-mistakes-lea_b_3852050.html.

20. International Association of Chiefs of Police, "2013 Social Media Survey of Results," http://www.berkeleyside.com/wp-content/uploads/2014/02/2013SurveyResults.pdf.

21. Robert D. Stuart, "Social Media: Establishing Criteria for Law Enforcement Use," *The FBI Law*, February 2013. http://leb.fbi.gov/2013/february/social-media-establishing-criteria-for-law-enforcement-use.

22. Ken Bryon, "Avon Police Officer Fired Over Social Media Interaction with Students," *The Courant*, October 14, 2013. http://articles.courant.com/2013-10-14/community/hc-avon-akerly-1015-20131014_1_police-chief-mark-rinaldo-todd-akerley-complaint.

23. Jessica Chasmar, "Dallas Police Chief Fires Officers on Social Media," *The Washington Times*, January 9, 2014. http://www.washingtontimes.com/news/2014/jan/9/dallas-police-chief-fires-officers-social-media/.

24. Tyler Simpson, "Social Media Proves Important Resource for Law Enforcement," *The State*, March 26, 2014. http://www.thestate.com/2014/03/26/3348456/social-media-proves-important.html.

25. Anarka. "Government Working on Draft to Restrict Social Media in Turkey." *Hurriyet Daily News*, June 18, 2013. http://www.hurriyetdailynews.com/governement-working-on-draft-to-restrict-social-media-in-turkey.aspx?pageID=238&nID=48982&NewsCatID=338. Accessed June 2014.

26. Saiyai Sakawee. "Under Martial Law, Thailand Will Shut Down Some Websites and Monitor Social Media." *Techinasia*, May 22, 2014. http://www.techinasia.com/martial-law-sites-shutdown-social-media-watched/. Accessed June 2014.

27. Calum MacLeod, "China Shuts down 16 Websites in Effort to Curb Rumors," *USA Today*, April 2, 2012. http://usatoday30.usatoday.com/news/world/story/2012-04-01/china-internet-crackdown/53935178/1.

28. Jak Phillips, "'The Civil Disobedience of the 21st Century': How Vietnamese Bloggers Evade Controls," *Time*, September 30, 2013. http://world.time.com/2013/09/30/the-civil-disobedience-of-the-21st-century-how-vietnamese-bloggers-evade-controls/.

29. Mike Isaac, "Vietnamese Government Passes Law to Fine Social Media Critics," *All-things D*, November 29, 2013. http://allthingsd.com/20131129/vietnamese-government-passes-law-to-fine-social-media-critics/.

30. Evgeny Morozov makes this point in two of his books. First, in *The Net Delusion: The Dark Side of Internet Freedom* (New York: PublicAffairs, 2011), he chronicles how governments have restricted, blocked, and otherwise made access impossible to their own countrymen for various reasons. Most recently, he continues this line of thought, expanding it to other areas, in *To Save Everything, Click Here: The Folly of Technological Solutionism* (New York: Public Affairs, 2013).

31. Beina Xu, "Media Censorship in China," *Council on Foreign Relations*, February 12, 2014. http://www.cfr.org/china/media-censorship-china/p11515/.

32. *Ibid.*

33. Reporters without Borders, "Press Freedom Index 2013: 203 World Press Freedom Index: Dashed after Spring," *Reporters Without Borders for Freedom of Information.* http://en.rsf.org/press-freedom-index-2013,1054.html. The U.S. ranks *Below* 31 other countries, including the likes of Slovakia, Costa Rica, Czech Republic, and Namibia, so it's hard to assess whether China's ranking is as execrable as it seems.

34. Dana Liebelson, "Map: Here Are the Countries that Block Facebook, Twitter, and YouTube," *Mother Jones News*, March 28, 2014. http://www.motherjones.com/politics/2014/03/turkey-facebook-youtube-twitter-blocked.

35. "The World Social Networking Ban Race," *Investingtech*, n.d. http://www.investintech.com/articles/theworldsocialnetworkingbanrace/.

Chapter Three

1. *Tinker V. Des Moines Independent Community School District (No. 21)*, 393 U.S. 503. *Legal Information Institute*, Cornell University Law School. http://www.law.cornell.edu/supremecourt/text/393/503.

2. *Ibid.*

3. Although, depending on which teacher you talk to, they love it or loathe it.

4. Teenage Research Unlimited, *Teen Internet Safety Survey*, National Center for Missing & Exploited Children and Cox Communications, 2006. http://www.netsmartz.org/safety/statistics.htm. See also Natalia Waechter, et al., "Youth Connecting Online," in *Emerging Practices in Cyberculture*, edited by Daniel Riha and Na Maj (Amsterdam: NLD Editions,

2010), 54–160. http://site.ebrary.com/lib/Winthrop/Doc?id=10404071&&ppg=161. Subscription required.

5. This is the more familiar name for the Telecommunications Act of 1996.

6. Adam Thierer, "Technopanics and the Great Social Networking Scare," *The Technology Liberation Front*, July 10, 2008. http://techliberation.com/2008/07/10/technopanics-and-the-great-social-networking-scare/.

7. Phillip Elmer-Dewitt and Hannah Bloch, "On a Screen Near You," *Time* Vol. 146 (1), July 3, 1995, 38–45.

8. *Child Online Protection*, http://epic.org/free_speech/censorship/copa.html.

9. Richard J. Greenstone and Robert G. Pimm, "The Difference between COPA, COPPA and Copa Cabana," *The License Journal*, May 2001, http://www.rjg.com/copa.html.

10. *United States V. American Library Assn., Inc. (02–361)*. http://supct.law.cornell.edu/supct/html/02-361.ZS.html.

11. "An Update on the Children's Internet Protection Act (CIPA)," *Thumann Resources*. http://thumannresources.com/2008/11/03/an-update-to-the-childrens-internet-protection-act-cipa/.

12. "Text of *Deleting Online Predators Act of 2006*," HR 5313 (109th Congress, 2005–2006). *Govtrack.US*. https://www.govtrack.us/congress/bills/109/hr5319/text.

13. Sean Cavanagh, "U.S. Court Ruling Raises K–12 Concerns About Internet Access," *Education Week*, January 28, 2014. http://www.edweek.org/ew/articles/2014/01/29/19neutrality.h33.html.

14. Maria Sacchetti, "Schools Use Social Networking Web Sites to Catch Athletes Who Break Rules," in *Online Social Networking*, edited by Sylvia Engdahl (Farmington Hills, Mich.: Greenhaven Press, 2007), 143.

15. Jamie Sarrio, "Tennessee Teen Expelled for Facebook Posting," *The Tennessean*, January 28, 2010. http://usatoday30.usatoday.com/news/nation/2010-01-28-student-facebook-expelled_N.htm.

16. Some argue that Cummings's plight wasn't his post but his violent anger. But no one would have heard it had it not been posted to Facebook.

17. See danah m. boyd, *It's Complicated: The Social Lives of Networked Teens* (New Haven: Yale University Press, 2014). Now pregnant with her first child, boyd may feel very differently seven years from now, especially when she sees how her own "innocent" uses social media.

18. Rosemarie Emanuele, "Math Geek Mom: Internet Safety and Young People," *Inside Higher Ed*, January 16, 2014. http://www.insidehighered.com/blogs/mama-phd/math-geek-mom-internet-safety-and-young-people#sthash.VIohMdpO.dpbs.

19. Jack Dickey, "Meet the Brothers Behind the Web's Most Controversial Social Network," *Time*, June 26, 2014. http://time.com/2923146/ask-fm-interview/. See also Jack Dickey. "Ask.fm: The Antisocial Network," *Time*, June 16, 2014. http://time.com/2926428/ask-fm-the-antisocial-network/#2926428/ask-fm-the-antisocial-network/.

20. For more on parents, teens, and schools, see Lynn Schofield, *The Parent App: Understanding Families in the Digital Age* (Oxford: Oxford University Press, 2013). See especially chapters 1, 3.

21. National Society for the Prevention of Cruelty to Children, "Children, Young People and 'Sexting': Summary of a Qualitative Study," May 2012. http://www.nspcc.org.uk/Inform/resourcesforprofessionals/sexualabuse/sexting-research-summary_wdf89270.pdf.

22. "Teen Sexter Convicted for Child Porn," *BBC News*, January 13, 2014. http://www.bbc.com/news/technology-25711938.

23. Rhea R. Borja, "Social-Networking Sites for Schools Promote Safety, Education Benefits," *Education Week*, October 10, 2006. http://www.edweek.org/ew/articles/2006/10/11/07network.h26.html.

24. "Imbee.com Settles FTC Charges Social Networking Site for Kids Violated the Children's Online Privacy Protection Act; Settlement Includes $130,000 Civil Penalty," *Federal Trade Commission*, January 30, 2008. http://www.ftc.gov/news-events/press-releases/2008/01/imbeecom-settles-ftc-charges-social-networking-site-kids-violated.

25. For more, see Marian Martens, "COPPA-Compliant Participatory Sites for Young Readers," *ALSC Blog*, March 3, 2014. http://www.alsc.ala.org/blog/2014/03/coppa-compliant-participatory-sites-for-young-readers/.

26. John Schafhauser, "How Sexual Predators Are Targeting Children Using Google+: Part I—The Facts," *Prevent Child Abuse New Jersey*, February 2014 http://preventchildabusenj.org/blog/2014/02/04/sexual-predators-targeting-children-google-part-facts-by-john-schafhauser-patty-mojta/.

27. "Tucson Man Arrested for Luring Juvenile on Social Networking Website," *Arizona Daily Independent*, February 19, 2014. http://www.arizonadailyindependent.com/

2014/02/19/tucson-man-arrested-for-luring-juvenile-on-social-networking-website/.

28. "Tucson Man Arrested for Luring Minor," *Arizona Daily Independent*, June 14, 2014. http://www.arizonadailyindependent.com/2014/06/14/tucson-man-arrested-for-luring-minor/.

29. "Man Arrested for Using Social Networks to Trick and Extort Young Children," *KEYT-KCOY-KKFX Television*, May 1, 2014. http://www.keyt.com/news/man-arrested-for-using-social-networks-to-trick-and-extort-young-children/25763070?view.

30. See, for example, "Anorexia Blogs Nearly Killed Me," *Daily Mail*, August 21, 2013. http://www.dailymail.co.uk/health/article-2398749/Pro-ana-Anorexia-blogs-nearly-killed-Starving-girl-17-says-thinspiration-sites-encouraged-her.html.

31. Alexis C. Madrigal, "Why Did 9,000 Porny Spambots Descend on This San Diego High Schooler?" *The Atlantic*, November 24, 2013. http://www.theatlantic.com/technology/archive/2013/11/why-did-9-000-porny-spambots-descend-on-this-san-diego-high-schooler/281773/.

32. Chris Blank, "Missouri Teachers Sue over Facebook, Social Networking Law," *Huffington Post*, August 19, 2011. http://www.huffingtonpost.com/2011/08/20/missouri-teachers-sue-ove_n_932261.html.

33. Lori Grisham. "Teachers, Students and Social Media: Where Is the Line?" *USA Today*, April 9, 2014. http://www.usatoday.com/story/news/nation-now/2014/04/09/facebook-teachers-twitter-students-schools/7472051/.

34. Especially helpful on these and related questions is Dorothy G. Singer and Jerome L. Singer, eds. *Handbook of Children and the Media* (Thousand Oaks, CA: Sage Publications, 2012).

35. I say officially, because clearly it is happening without permission.

36. In a nearby school system, iPads were purchased for all students. Fees were charged for lost iPads, about one fifth the actual cost. Quickly, students declared them lost, paid the small fee, and then sold the iPads for a hefty profit.

Chapter Four

1. Jeff Seaman and Hester Tinti-Kane, *Social Media for Teaching and Learning*, October 2013.

2. See, for example, "50 Most Social Media Savvy Professors in America," *Online Colleges*, n.d. http://www.onlinecolleges.net/50-most-social-media-savvy-professors-in-america/.

3. One cannot list them all. Here are representatives from each of the groups. Bad grades: Riley Davis, "Social Media Use May Lead to Poor Grades," *The Brown Daily Herald*, April 24, 2013. http://www.browndailyherald.com/2013/04/24/social-media-use-may-lead-to-poohttps://www.insidehighered.com/views/2014/08/08/essay-defends-university-illinois-decision-not-hire-stevensalaitar-grades/. Good Grades: Masters in Education, "How to Get Better Grades through Social Media," June 24, 2011. http://mastersineducation.org/infographic-how-to-get-better-grades-through-social-media/. No correlation: Chuck Martin, "Social Networking Usage and Grades among College Students," n.d. http://www.unh.edu/news/docs/UNHsocialmedia.pdf.

4. Andrew Lepp, Jacob E. Barkley, and Aryn C. Karpinski. "The Relationship Between Cell Phone Use, Academic Performance Anxiety, and Satisfaction with Life in College Students," *Computer in Behavior* Vol. 31, February 2014. DOI: 10.1016/j.chb.2013.10.049. http://www.sciencedirect.com/science/article/pii/S0747563213003993.

5. For more on what follows, see this useful summary: "How Social Media Is Killing Student Success," *Online Courses*, May 22, 2013. http://www.onlinecollegecourses.com/2013/05/22/how-social-media-is-killing-student-success-2/.

6. Sandra Levy, "Texting While Walking Causes More Accidents than Texting and Driving." *Health Line News*, March 10, 2014. http://www.healthline.com/health-news/tech-texting-while-walking-causes-accidents-031014.

7. Sherry Turkle, *Alone Together: Why We Expect More from Technology and Less from Each Other* (New York: Basic Books, 2011). Robert Putnam, *Bowling Alone: The Collapse and Revival of American Community* (New York: Simon and Schuster, 2000).

8. You can also find the opposite claim being made.

9. An interesting take on this is found here: Lee Burdette Williams, "Skewered by Social Media," *Inside Higher Ed*, June 20, 2014. http://www.insidehighered.com/views/2014/06/20/social-media-threatens-civil-discourse-between-administrators-and-students-essay#sthash.YWz6uWTM.dpbs.

10. John Rowe, "Student Use of Social Media: When Should the University Intervene?" *Journal of Higher Education Policy and*

Management, Vol. 36 (3), 241–256. DOI: http://dx.doi.org/10.1080/01587919.2014.899054.

11. Many places examine this. See Farhad Manjoo, "A Bright Side to Facebook's Experiments on Its Users," *The New York Times*, July 2, 2014. http://www.nytimes.com/2014/07/03/technology/personaltech/the-bright-side-of-facebooks-social-experiments-on-users.html?partner=rss&emc=rss&_r=0. The study itself is here: Adam Kramer, et al., "Experimental Evidence of Massive-Scale Emotional Contagion through Social Networks," *Proceedings of the National Academy of the Sciences*, March 25, 2014. http://www.pnas.org/content/111/24/8788.full.pdf.

12. For those too young to remember, Emily Litella was the obnoxious character whom the late Gilda Radner made famous on the earlier days of *Saturday Night Live*. The somewhat deaf and highly opinionated Litella would appear on SNL's segment "Weekend Update" as the op-ed guest. After she had ranted about some subject that she obviously had completely wrong, the news anchor, typically Chevy Chase, would point out her error, to which she would reply, "Never mind," as if those two words made up for the ten-minute vitriol that had immediately preceded. Facebook's "sorry" sounds an awful lot like Emily Litella.

13. Cathryn Rudolph, "Unleashing Law Reviews onto Social Media: Preventing Mishaps with a Social-Media Policy," *Thomas Coley Law Review* Vol. 30: 2, 2013. http://www.cooley.edu/lawreview/_docs/2013/vol30/2/unleashing_law_reviews_onto_social_media.pdf. It *May* be possible to get law students, soon to be attorneys and presumably familiar with all that can go wrong in this context, to be willing to behave responsibly. But thirty-five years in academe have taught me that the likelihood is small with college-aged students.

14. See, for example, Rachael Rowan, "Social Media Shocker: Twitter and Facebook Can Cost You a Scholarship or Admissions Offer," *Tuition.Io*. https://www.tuition.io/blog/2014/04/social-media-shocker-twitter-facebook-can-cost-scholarship-admissions-offer/.

15. Emma Graves Fitzsimmons and Bonnie Miller Rubin, "Social Networking Sites Viewed by Admissions Officers." *Chicago Tribune*. http://articles.chicagotribune.com/2008-09-20/news/0809190659_1_social-networking-sites-admissions-facebook-profile/2.

16. "Highlights from Kaplan Test Prep's 2012 College Admission Officers Survey," http://collegeapps.about.com/gi/o.htm?zi=1/XJ&zTi=1&sdn=collegeapps&cdn=education&tm=254&gps=75_81_1920_985&f=00&su=p284.13.342.ip_&tt=2&bt=8&bts=8&zu=http%3A//www.kaptest.com/assets/pdfs/Highlights-from-Kaplan-Test-Preps-2012-College-Admissions-Officers-Survey.pdf.

17. James Grimmelmann, "Saving Facebook." *Iowa Law Review* 94 (2009). http://works.bepress.com/james_grimmelmann/20., 1166. This may be the best summary of legal problems now available.

18. "Court Case on Use of Social Networking Sites," *Ers Blog*, October 19, 2009. http://www.esrcheck.com/wordpress/938/court-case-on-use-of-social-networking-sites.

19. See, for example, Carly Brandenburg, "The Newest Way to Screen Job Applicants: A Social Networker's Nightmare," *Federal Communications Law Journal* Vol. 60 (2013). http://www.fclj.org/wp-content/uploads/2013/01/11-Brandenburg.pdf.

20. William B. Harrison III, "Do Professors Read Their Reviews on Rate My Professors?" *Slate*, December 11, 2013. http://www.slate.com/blogs/quora/2013/12/11/higher_education_a_professor_s_thoughts_on_the_website_rate_my_professors.html.

21. Scott Jaschik, "Fireable Tweets," *Inside Higher Ed*, December 19, 2013. http://www.insidehighered.com/news/2013/12/19/kansas-regents-adopt-policy-when-social-media-use-can-get-faculty-fired#sthash.fFG10OTx.dpbs.

22. Erik Voeten, "Kansas Board of Regents Restricts Free Speech for Academics," *The Washington Post*, December 19, 2013. http://www.washingtonpost.com/blogs/monkey-cage/wp/2013/12/19/kansas-board-of-regents-restricts-free-speech-for-academics/.

23. Cary Nelson, "An Appointment to Reject," *Inside Higher Education*, August 8, 2014. https://www.insidehighered.com/views/2014/08/08/essay-defends-university-illinois-decision-not-hire-steven-salaita.

24. Kathryn Cusma, "Visiting NYU Lecturer Makes Waves with Offensive Tweet About Fat People," *New York Post*, June 4, 2013. http://nypost.com/2013/06/04/visiting-nyu-lecturer-makes-waves-with-offensive-tweet-about-fat-people/.

25. Richard Van Noorden, "Twitter Buzz About Papers Does Not Mean Citations Later," *Nature*, December 12, 2013 DOI:10.1038/nature.2013.14354. http://www.nature.com/news/twitter-buzz-about-papers-does-not-mean-citations-later-1.14354.

26. *Ibid.*

27. Maryellen Weimer, "The Age of Distraction: Getting Students to Put Away Their Phones and Focus on Learning," *Faculty Focus*,

January 8, 2014. http://www.facultyfocus.com/articles/teaching-professor-blog/the-age-of-distraction-getting-students-to-put-away-their-phones-and-focus-on-learning/.

28. *Ibid.*

29. Nancy K. Napier, "The Myth of Multitasking," *Psychology Today*, May 12, 2014. http://www.psychologytoday.com/blog/creativity-without-borders/201405/the-myth-multitasking.

30. Marc Parry, "Online Professors Pose as Students to Encourage Real Learning," *Chronicle of Higher Education*, May 26, 2009. http://chronicle.com/blogs/wiredcampus/online-professors-pose-as-students-to-encourage-real-learning/7177.

31. Richard N. Landers, "Online Plagiarism and Cybercheating Still Strong—61.9%." *Neoacademic* February 4, 2011. http://neoacademic.com/2011/02/04/online-plagiarism-and-cybercheating-still-strong/.

32. Gerry Smith, "Why Study? College Hackers Are Changing F's to A's," *Huffington Post*, March 8, 2014. http://www.huffingtonpost.com/2014/03/05/student-hacking_n_4907344.html.

33. Carl Straumsheim, "Adjunct v. Student," *Inside Higher Ed*, July 3, 2014. http://www.insidehighered.com/news/2014/07/03/former-central-michigan-u-adjunct-instructor-sues-student-over-fake-twitter-account#sthash.i8XrRBm9.dpbs.

Chapter Five

1. World Health Organization and The World Bank, *World Report on Disability*, WHO, 2011. http://whqlibdoc.who.int/hq/2011/WHO_NMH_VIP_11.01_eng.pdf?ua=1.

2. Quoted in Katie Ellis and Mike Kent, *Disability and New Media* (Florence, KY: Routledge, 2010), 1–2.

3. Vannvar Bush, "As We May Think," *The Atlantic*, July 1, 1945. http://www.theatlantic.com/magazine/archive/1945/07/as-we-may-think/303881/.

4. Katrina M. Holmes and Nessa O'Loughlin, "The Experiences of People with Learning Disabilities on Social Networking Sites," *British Journal of Learning Disabilities*, September 7, 2012, 42, 3–7. http://onlinelibrary.wiley.com/doi/10.1111/bld.12001/pdf. See also Debra Ruh, "Accessibility in Social Media," *SSB Bart Group*, August 1, 2013. https://www.ssbbartgroup.com/blog/2013/01/08/accessible-social-media/.

5. Ellis and Kent, 4.

6. Ellis and Kent, 16–17. The Rehabilitation Act of 1973 was amended in 1998 to include web accessibility through section 508.

7. Tracy Mitrano, "Accessibility Standards, Cloud Computing and Innovation," *Inside Higher Ed*, July 14, 2014. http://www.insidehighered.com/blogs/law-policy-and-it/accessibility-standards-cloud-computing-and-innovation#ixzz37XdcK9Az.

8. Léonie Watson, "Design Like We Give a Damn!" http://vimeo.com/album/3108947/video/110965713.

9. See Ellis and Kent for a longer discussion of this important case, 74–75.

10. *National Federation of the Blind, the National Federation of the Blind of California Versus Target Corporation. September 5, 2006.* http://writ.news.findlaw.com/ramasastry/nfbvtarget90606ord.pdf. Accessed July 2014.

11. Quoted in Ellis and Kent, 22.

12. "Social Networking Sites Lock Out Disabled Users," 18 January 2008. http://www.abilitynet.org.uk/advice-information/enation/social-networking-sites-lock-out-disabled-users.

13. American Foundation for the Blind, "Facts and Figures on Adults with Vision Loss," May 2014. http://www.afb.org/info/living-with-vision-loss/blindness-statistics/adults/facts-and-figures/1235.

14. Mark Zuckerberg. "Mark Zuckerberg on a Future Where the Internet Is Available to All," *Wall Street Journal*, July 7, 2014. http://online.wsj.com/articles/mark-zuckerberg-on-a-future-where-the-internet-is-available-to-all-1404762276.

15. Sally Whittle, "Social Networks: Not as Inclusive as You Might Think," *Zdnet*, November 5, 2007. http://www.zdnet.com/social-networking-not-as-inclusive-as-you-might-think-3039290559/.

16. Ellen Perlman, "Social Media Sites' Handicap Hurdle," *Governing.com*, October 2009. http://www.governing.com/columns/tech-talk/Social-Media-Sites-Handicap.html.

17. Parimala Raghavendra, Denise Wood, Lareen Newman and Jan Lawry, "Why Aren't You on Facebook? Patterns and Experiences of Using the Internet Among Young People with Disabilities," *Technology and Disability* 24 (2012): 149–162. DOI: 10.3233/TAD-2012–0343. http://0-eds.a.ebscohost.com.library.winthrop.edu/ehost/pdfviewer/pdfviewer?sid=b3ec4533-a1a4-48b7-9248-61e2d94f4c0d%40sessionmgr4001&vid=8&hid=4205. Registration required.

18. I am indebted to Professor Jennifer Cease-Cook for pointing out these aids. See

also disabledcommunity.net, livewithdisability.com and disibilinet.com.

19. A. Jahoda and J. Pownall, "Sexual Understanding, Sources of Information and Social Networks: The Reports of Young People with Intellectual Disabilities and Their Non-Disabled Peers," *Journal of Intellectual Disability Research* Vol. 58 (5), April 19, 2013.

20. Holmes and O'Loughlin. Both stories are recounted in this article.

21. A good summary is found here: Yong Zhao and Wei Qiu, "The Potential of Social Media for Students with Disabilities," in *Breakthrough Teaching and Learning: How Educational and Assistive Technologies Are Driving Innovation*, edited by T. Gray and H. Silver-Pacuilla. tp://link.springer.com/chapter/10.1007%2F978-1-4419-7768-7_5#page-1. DOI 10.1007/978-1-4419-7768-7_5. Subscription required. Accessed November 2014. I am indebted to Professor Jennifer Cease-Cook for this reference.

22. Jane Seale, E.A. Draffan, and Mike Wald. "Digital Agility and Digital Decision-making: Conceputalising [sic] Digital Inclusion in the Context of Disabled Learners in Higher Education," *Studies in Higher Education*, Vol. 35 (4), June 2010, 445–461. See also Jane K. Seale, *E-Learning and Disability in Higher Education: Accessibility and Practice*, 2nd Edition (New York: Routledge, 2013).

23. Seale, *E-Learning and Disability*, 202–204.

24. Paul Schroeder, "Kindle Sparks a Flame War but Fails to Light a Fire for Accessibility," February 27, 2009. http://www.afb.org/blog/blog_comments.asp?TopicID=4426.

25. Theodore Tsaousides, Yuka Matsuzawa, and Matthew Lebowitz, "Familiarity and Prevalence of Facebook Use for Social Networking Among Individuals with Traumatic Brain Injury," *Brain Injury*, Vol. 25 (12), November 2011, 1155–1162. http://0-eds.a.ebscohost.com.library.winthrop.edu/ehost/pdfviewer/pdfviewer?sid=b3ec4533-a1a4-48b7-9248-61e2d94f4c0d%40sessionmgr4001&vid=13&hid=4205. Subscription required.

26. Chris Crum, "YouTube Launching Automatic Video Captions," *Webpronews*, November 19, 2009. http://www.webpronews.com/youtube-launching-automatic-video-captions-2009-11. A similar quote is also found in Ellis and Kent, 57, but with a different source.

27. Let me add that more work is needed. The point I am making here is that these groups, once fiercely marginalized, are less likely to be so now. Persons with disabilities,

however, tend to be forgotten until someone reminds us they are still here.

28. Ellis and Kent, whose book I have relied on more often than not in this chapter, favor this approach.

29. For more on this and how to meet the standards, see "Web Content Accessibility Guidelines (WACG) Overview," *Wc# Web Accessibility Initiative*. http://www.w3.org/WAI/intro/wcag.

Chapter Six

1. Audrey Williams June, "Google-Stalking Job Candidates: Tempting but Risky," *Chronicle of Higher Education*, October 3, 2014. http://chronicle.com/article/Google-Stalking-Job/149193/.

2. National Conference of State Legislatures, "Employer Access to Social Media Usernames and Passwords," *NCSL*, May 30, 2014. http://www.ncsl.org/research/telecommunications-and-information-technology/employer-access-to-social-media-passwords-2013.aspx.

3. Yuki Noguchi, "Can't Ask That? Some Job Interviewers Go to Social Media Instead," National Public Radio: "All Things Considered," April 11, 2014. http://www.npr.org/blogs/alltechconsidered/2014/04/11/301791749/cant-ask-that-some-job-interviewers-go-to-social-media-instead.

4. "H.R. 537: Social Networking Online Protection Act," February 6, 2013. https://www.govtrack.us/congress/bills/113/hr537.

5. Galen Moore, "Hiring Strategies Shift toward Social Media," *MIT: Journal of New England Technology*, August 14, 2009. http://www.masshightech.com/stories/2009/08/10/weekly14-Hiring-strategies-shift-toward-social-media.html.

6. Mike Isaac, "For Millennials, There Is No One True Social Network," *Re/Code*, February 5, 2014. http://recode.net/2014/02/05/for-millennials-there-is-no-one-true-social-network/.

7. Heather A. Morgan and Felicia A. Davis, *Social Media and Employment Law: Summary of Key Cases and Legal Issues*. Paul Hastings, 2013. http://www.americanbar.org/content/dam/aba/events/labor_law/2013/04/aba_national_symposiumontechnologyinlaboremploymentlaw/10_socialmedia.authcheckdam.pdf.

8. Jennifer Grasz, "Forty-five Percent of Employers Use Facebook-Twitter to Screen Job Candidates," *Business Report*, August 24,

2009. http://oregonbusinessreport.com/2009/08/45-employers-use-facebook-twitter-to-screen-job-candidates/.

9. Yuki Noguchi, National Public Radio: "All Things Considered," April 11, 2014. http://www.npr.org/blogs/alltechconsidered/2014/04/11/301791749/cant-ask-that-some-job-interviewers-go-to-social-media-instead.

10. Audrey Williams June, "Google-Stalking Job Candidates: Tempting but Risky," *Chronicle of Higher Education*, October 3, 2014. http://chronicle.com/article/Google-Stalking-Job/149193/.

11. Although several years old, a good discussion about this is Carly Brandenburg, "The Newest Way to Screen Job Applicants: A Social Networker's Nightmare," *Federal Communications Law Journal*, Vol. 60 (3) (2008). http://www.repository.law.indiana.edu/fclj/vol60/iss3/6.

12. James Nye and Victoria Woollaston, "Celeb Hacker 'on the Run': FBI Investigates as Mystery Man Who Calls Himself 'Original Guy' Claims Responsibility for Stealing Hundreds of Stars' Nude Photos," *Mailonine*, September 1, 2014. http://www.dailymail.co.uk/news/article-2740003/Celeb-hacker-run-Mystery-man-stole-celeb-nude-pics-admits-running-authorities-deep-web-hackers-congratulate-him.html.

13. "Social Media Posts Are Scuttling More Job Applicants," *Central Valley Business Times*, June 25, 2014. http://centralvalleybusinesstimes.com/templates/print.cfm?ID=26147.

14. "Employers Rejecting Candidates Who Bad Mouth Previous Jobs on Social Media," *HR Review*, September 19, 2014. http://www.hrreview.co.uk/hr-news/recruitment/employers-rejecting-candidates-who-bad-mouth-previous-jobs-on-social-media/53717.

15. "Social Media Posts Are Scuttling More Job Applicants," *Central Valley Business Times*, June 25, 2014. http://centralvalleybusinesstimes.com/templates/print.cfm?ID=26147.

16. A good discussion may be found here: Richard McMunn, "Avoiding Legal Issues When Posting on Social Networks," *Guidestar Blog*, March 7, 2014. http://trust.guidestar.org/2014/03/07/avoiding-legal-issues-when-posting-on-social-networks/.

17. Jason Del Rey, "Social Media's Cold, Hard Reality: It Still Doesn't Drive E-Commerce Sale, IBM Says," *All Things D*, November 29, 2013. http://allthingsd.com/20131129/social-medias-cold-hard-reality-it-still-doesnt-drive-e-commerce-sales-ibm-says/.

18. Cooper Smith, "One-Third of Marketers Generate a Return on their Social Media Efforts," Business Insider.com, January 13, 2014. http://www.businessinsider.com/one-third-of-marketers-generate-a-return-on-their-social-media-efforts-2014-1#xzz2qOPRUrWS.

19. Mike Melanson, "Forrester: If You Think Social Media Marketing Is Worthless, You're Doing It Wrong," *Read Write Web*. http://readwrite.com/2010/07/19/forrester_if_you_think_social_media_marketing_is_w.

20. Lon Safko, *Social Media Bible: Tactics Tools, and Strategies for Business Success* (Hoboken: NJ: John Wiley and Sons, 2012), 3rd Edition.

21. Phillip L. Gordon, "Verdict Against Houston's Restaurant Demonstrates Risks of Accessing Employee's Restricted Social Networking Sites," *Asap*, July 2009. http://www.littler.com/files/press/pdf/2009_07_ASAP_VerdictHoustonsRestaurant_RiskAccessing_EmployeeRestrictedSites.pdf.

22. This case (and the one that follows it) may be found many places. I have used Lexis-Nexis Legal Newsroom Staff, "Social Media Blunders in Employment Law-How a Facebook Post Can Turn a Case Upside Down," *Lexis-Nexis*, March 11, 2014. http://www.lexisnexis.com/legalnewsroom/litigation/b/litigation-blog/archive/2014/03/11/social-media-blunders-in-employment-law-how-a-facebook-post-can-turn-a-case-upside-down.aspx.

23. A good summary is here: Mark Oppenheimer, "Astronomer Sues the University of Kentucky, Claiming His Faith Cost Him a Job," *New York Times*, December 18. 2010. http://www.nytimes.com/2010/12/19/us/19kentucky.html?_r=0. The case is here: United States District Court Eastern District of Kentucky, Lexington Division, *C. Martin Gaskell V. University of Kentucky*, July 10, 2009. http://graphics8.nytimes.com/packages/pdf/national/wazaimg/Kentucky2.pdf.

24. Steven D. Zansberg and Janna K. Fischer, "Privacy Expectations in Online Social Media—An Emerging Generational Divide?" Isklaw.com, n.d. http://www.lskslaw.com/documents/evolvingprivacyexpectations(00458267).pdf.

25. Heather A. Morgan and Felicia A. Davis, "Social Media and Employment Law: Summary of Key Cases and Legal Issues." Paul Hasting, March 2013. http://www.americanbar.org/content/dam/aba/events/labor_law/2013/04/aba_national_symposiumontechnologyinlaboremploymentlaw/10_socialmedia.authcheckdam.pdf.

26. Marshall Kilpatrick, "Shocking News:

Scientists Say Workplace Social Networking Increases Productivity," ReadWriteWeb, April 2, 2009. http://www.readwriteweb.com/ar chives/shocking_news_scientists_say_ workplace_social_netw.php.

27. Jacob Silverman, "How Much Time Do We Spend on MySpace at Work?" Howstuff works.com, September 17, 2007. http://com puter.howstuffworks.com/internet/social-net working/information/myspace-work.htm.

28. Jennifer Van Grove, "Study: 20% Increase in Companies Blocking Social Media Sites," August 21, 2009. http://mashable.com/ 2009/08/21/social-networks-blocked/.

29. Jon Browning, "Employers Face Pros, Cons with Monitoring Social Networking," Houston Business Journal, February 27, 2009. http://houston.bizjournals.com/houston/ stories/2009/03/02/smallb3.html

30. Alan Farnham, "Personal Tweets at Work: Here's One Answer to this Billion Dollar Problem," ABC News, January 30, 2013. http://abcnews.go.com/Business/personal-tweets-costing-employers-650b/story?id=18339518.

31. Jeanie Meister, "To Do: Update Company's Social Media Policy ASAP," Forbes, February 7, 2013. http://www.forbes.com/sites/ jeannemeister/2013/02/07/to-do-update-companys-social-media-policy-asap/.

32. Jeanie Meister, "Social Media Training Is Now Mandatory: Five Ways to Make Sure Your Company Does It Right," Forbes, October 31, 2012. http://www.forbes.com/sites/ jeannemeister/2012/10/31/social-media-training-is-now-mandatory/.

33. Alexis Williams, "The Agony of Instagram," The New York Times, December 13, 2013. http://www.nytimes.com/2013/12/15/fashion/ instagram.html?pagewanted=2&_r=0.

34. Ibid.

35. Matt McFarland, "Social Media Desperately Needs an Antidote for Bragging," Washington Post, December 18, 2013. http:// www.washingtonpost.com/blogs/innovations/ wp/2013/12/18/social-media-desperately-needs-an-antidote-for-bragging/.

Chapter Seven

1. The web has many places where one may follow Mr. Snowden and his travails. I cite one here that collects them in one place. "Edward Snowden," The Guardian, http://www. theguardian.com/world/edward-snowden.

2. Sydney Lupkin, "You Consented to Facebook's Social Experiment," ABC News, June 30, 2014. http://abcnews.go.com/Health/ consented-facebooks-social-experiment/ story?id=24368579. But see also Kamakshi Sivaramakrishnan, "We Shouldn't Have to Give Away Our Identity to Use the Internet," <Re/Code>, November 24, 2014. http://recode. net/2014/11/24/we-shouldnt-have-to-give-away-our-identity-to-use-the-internet/.

3. Reed Albergotti, "Furor Erupts Over Facebook's Experiment on Users," Wall Street Journal, June 30, 2014. http://online.wsj.com/ articles/furor-erupts-over-facebook-experi ment-on-users-1404085840.

4. James Grimmelmann, "Saving Facebook," Iowa Law Review 94 (2009): 1151. http: //works.bepress.com/james_grimmelmann/ 20. This may be the best summary of legal problems now available.

5. Nate Hoffelder, "Adobe Is Spying on Users, Collecting Data on Their eBook Libraries," The Digital Reader, October 6, 2014. http://the-digital-reader.com/2014/10/06/ adobe-spying-users-collecting-data-ebook-libraries/#.VDv4bfldWSo.

6. Arik Hesseldahl, "Americans Say They've Lost Control of Their Privacy—Again." Recode.Net, November 12, 2014. http://recode. net/2014/11/12/americans-say-theyve-lost-control-of-their-privacy-again/.

7. Thomas Halleck, "Snapchat Hack Could See 200,000 Users' Nude Photos Leaked Online in 'The Snappening,'" International Business Times, October 10, 2014. http:// www.ibtimes.com/snapchat-hack-could-see-200000-users-nude-photos-leaked-online-snappening-1703017. Pitched as a safe place that teens have been known to use, this could prove to be an even bigger scandal than the Apple hack of celebrity nude photos.

8. Peter Mika, Social Networks and the Semantic Web (New York: Springer, 2007), 220.

9. Michael Zimmer, "Mark Zuckerberg's Theory of Privacy," Washington Post, February 3, 2014. http://www.washingtonpost.com/life style/style/mark-zuckerbergs-theory-of-privacy/2014/02/03/2c1d780a-8cea-11e3-95dd-36ff657a4dae_story.html.

10. Evelyn Rusli, "Unvarnished: A Clean, Well-Lighted Place for Defamation," Techcrunch, March 30, 2010. http://techcrunch. com/2010/03/30/unvarnished-a-clean-well-lighted-place-for-defamation/.

11. Jean Twenge, "Social Media Is a Narcissism Enabler," New York Times, September 24, 2013. http://www.nytimes.com/roomford ebate/2013/09/23/facebook-and-narcissism/ social-media-is-a-narcissism-enabler.

12. danah m. boyd, "Social Networking Sites: Public, Private or What?" *Knowledge Tree*, Vol. 13, May 2007. http://www.danah.org/papers/KnowledgeTree.pdf.

13. Mimi Mudd, "Craigslist Murder Making Headlines Again," *Liberty Voice*, February 16, 2014. http://guardianlv.com/2014/02/craigslist-murder-making-headlines-again/.

14. Greg Brosnan, "#BBC Trending: Murdered for Tweeting in Mexico?" *BBC News Magazine*, October 27, 2014. http://www.bbc.com/news/magazine-29746651.

15. Matthew Lysiak, "Exclusive: Craigslist Killer Miranda Barbour Tells How and Why She Killed," *Newsweek*, April 28, 2014. http://www.newsweek.com/2014/05/09/exclusive-craigslist-killer-miranda-barbour-tells-how-and-why-she-killed-248670.html.

16. "En Banc 9th Circuit Panel Rejects Section 230 Immunity in Roommates.com Case," April 3, 2008. http://www.techlawjournal.com/topstories/2008/20080403.asp.

17. The power of pornography never ceases to amaze. A pornographer in the Czech Republic honed his skills enough to get a shot at the intelligence market. See Mark Mazetti. *The Way of the Knife: The CIA, a Secret Army, and a War at the Ends of the Earth* (New York: Penguin Press, 2013), 181–183.

18. James Fletcher, "The Revenge Porn Avengers," *BBC News Magazine*, December 11, 2013. http://www.bbc.com/news/magazine-25321301.

19. BBC News, "'Revenge Porn' Illegal Under New UK Law," *BBC News*, October 13, 2014. http://www.bbc.com/news/29596583.

20. Mary Adkins, "The Revenge Porn of #Twitterpurge," *Slate*, July 21, 2014. http://www.slate.com/articles/double_x/doublex/2014/07/_twitterpurge_is_revenge_porn_we_need_laws_to_stop_the_non_consensual_posting.html.

21. Mika, *Social Networks and the Semantic Web* (New York: Springer, 2007), 216.

22. Amar Toor, "'Gaydar' Facebook Experiment Reveals Sexual Orientation," *Switched*, September 21, 2009, http://www.switched.com/2009/09/21/gaydar-experiment-uses-facebook-to-find-your-sexual-orientation/.

23. Latoicha Givens, "Social Networking and Terms of Service Agreements. Read the Intellectual Property Clause Before Clicking Yes!" *Blackweb 2: A Different Perspective*, December 10, 2009. http://www.blackweb20.com/2009/12/10/social-networks-and-terms-of-service-agreements-read-the-intellectual-property-clause-before-clicking-yes/.

24. Ed Bayley, "Terms of (Ab)use: Are Terms of Service Enforceable?" http://www.eff.org/deeplinks/2009/11/white-paper-clicks-bind-ways-users-agree-online-te.

25. Kelly Jackson Higgins, "Report: Social Networking Phishing Attacks Up More Than 240%," *Dark Reading*, June 29, 2009, http://www.darkreading.com/security/attacks/showArticle.jhtml?articleID=218101868.

26. Glenn Fleishman, "Cartoon Captures Spirit of the Internet." *The New York Times*, December 14, 2000, http://www.nytimes.com/2000/12/14/technology/cartoon-captures-spirit-of-the-internet.html.

27. Ralph Gross, Ralph and Alessandro Acquisti, "Information Revelation and Privacy in Online Social Networks," in *Proceedings of the 2005 ACM Workshop on Privacy in the Electronic Society* (New York: ACM, 2005). http://0-delivery.acm.org.library.winthrop.edu/10.1145/1110000/1102214/p71-gross.pdf?ip=199.79.254.152&id=1102214&acc=ACTIVE%20SERVICE&key=A79D83B43E50B5B8%2E31FABCF69E054C32%2E4D4702B0C3E38B35%2E4D4702B0C3E38B35&CFID=457044687&CFTOKEN=20070346&&__acm__=1416334814_8fcb9dcefee5fcfbdb42c61c2cd2f283. (Subscription required).

28. Derek Williams, "What the Internet Can See from Your Cat Pictures," *New York Times*, July 22, 2014. http://www.nytimes.com/2014/07/23/upshot/what-the-internet-can-see-from-your-cat-pictures.html?_r=0. See also David Meyer, "An Explosion in Slow Motion: How 2013 Blew Apart Our Notions of Privacy," *Gigaom*, December 19, 2013. http://gigaom.com/2013/12/19/an-explosion-in-slow-motion-how-2013-blew-apart-our-notions-of-privacy/.

29. Charles Riley, "Facebook Faces Suit Over Private Messages," *CNN Money*, January 3, 2014. http://money.cnn.com/2014/01/03/technology/facebook-privacy-lawsuit/.

30. Grimmelmann, "Saving Facebook," 1164–1170.

31. Bobbie Johnson and Afua Hirsch, "Facebook Backtracks After Online Privacy Protest," *The Guardian*, February 19, 2009. http://www.guardian.co.uk/technology/2009/feb/19/facebook-personal-data.

32. Marshall Kirkpatrick, "Facebook's Zuckerberg Says the Era of Privacy Is Over," Readwrite.com, January 9, 2010. http://readwrite.com/2010/01/09/facebooks_zuckerberg_says_the_age_of_privacy_is_ov.

33. Betsy Issacson, "Documentary 'Terms and Conditions May Apply' Airs Confrontation with Mark Zuckerberg," *The Huffington Post*, July 22, 2013. http://www.huffingtonpost.

com/2013/07/22/terms-and-conditions-zuckerberg_n_3635504.html.

34. David Meyer, "MoreThan 20,000 People Are Now Suing Facebook in Europe Over Privacy," *Gigaom*, August 6, 2014. http://gigaom.com/2014/08/06/more-than-20000-people-are-now-suing-facebook-in-europe-over-privacy/.

35. Brian Feldman, "Facebook Reaches Settlement in Sponsored Stories Lawsuit," *The Wire*, August 27, 2013. http://www.thewire.com/technology/2013/08/facebook-reaches-settlement-sponsored-stories/68752/.

36. Vindu Goel, "Facebook Deal on Privacy Is Under Attack," *New York Times*, February 13, 2014. http://www.nytimes.com/2014/02/13/technology/facebook-deal-on-privacy-is-under-attack.html.

37. Will Oremus, "Facebook's Privacy Pivot," *Slate*, July 25, 2014. http://www.slate.com/articles/technology/future_tense/2014/07/facebook_s_privacy_pivot_mark_zuckerberg_s_plan_to_win_back_trust.single.html.

38. David Meyer, "Facebook Has Only "Pivoted" on One Kind of Privacy—In Other Ways, It's Becoming More Dangerous," *Gigaom*, July 28, 2014. http://gigaom.com/2014/07/28/facebook-has-only-pivoted-on-one-kind-of-privacy-in-other-ways-its-becoming-more-dangerous/.

39. Tracy Mitrano, "Facebook and the New World Order," *Inside Higher Ed*, July 24, 2014. https://www.insidehighered.com/blogs/law-policy-and-it/facebook-and-new-world-order.

40. Ruben Rodrigues, "Privacy on Social Networks: Norms, Markets, and Natural Monopoly," in Saul Levmore and Martha C. Nussbaum, *Offensive Internet: Speech, Privacy and Reputation* (Cambridge, MA: Harvard University Press, 2011), 241.

41. Mark Hefflinger, "Privacy Group Files FTC Complaint Over Changes to Facebook," *Digital Media Wire*, December 18, 2009. http://www.dmwmedia.com/news/2009/12/18/privacy-groups-file-ftc-complaint-over-changes-facebook.

42. Jonathan Stempel, "Google Must Face Privacy Suit Over Commingled User Data," *Re/Code*, July 22, 2014, http://recode.net/2014/07/22/google-must-face-privacy-suit-over-commingled-user-data/.

43. Tracy Mitrano, "Internet Ironies," *Inside Higher Ed*, March 16, 2014. http://www.insidehighered.com/blogs/law-policy-and-it/internet-ironies#sthash.vUwBQSTS.dpbs.

44. Ralph Gross and Alessandro Acquisti, "Information Revelation and Privacy in On-line Social Networks (The Facebook Case)." http://www.heinz.cmu.edu/~acquisti/papers/privacy-facebook-gross-acquisti.pdf.

45. Marc Langheinrich, "Privacy Invasions in Ubiquitous Computing," *Swiss Federal Institute of Technology*, 2002. http://citeseerx.ist.psu.edu/viewdoc/download?doi=10.1.1.6.6743&rep=rep1&type=pdf.

46. Mary Madden, Susannah Fox, and Aaron Smith, *Digital Footprints, Pew Internet. Pew Internet & American Life Project*, December 17, 2007. http://www.pewinternet.org/Reports/2007/Digital-Footprints.aspx.

47. M.G. Siegler, "Please Rob Me Makes Foursquare Super Useful for Burglars," *Techcrunch*, February 17, 2010. http://techcrunch.com/2010/02/17/please-rob-me-makes-foursquare-super-useful-for-burglars/.

Chapter Eight

1. Sara E. Berg, "Identity Theft," in *Encyclopedia of Cybercrime*, edited by Samuel C. McQuade (Westport, CT: Greenwood Press, 2008), 114. "Identify theft, also referred to as identity fraud."

2. Carl Timm and Richard Perez, *Seven Deadliest Social Network Attacks* (Burlington, MA: Elsevier, 2010), 84.

3. Erin Fuchs, "Identity Theft Now Costs Far More Than All Other Property Crimes COMBINED," *Business Insider*, December 12, 2013. http://www.businessinsider.com/bureau-of-justice-statistics-identity-theft-report-2013-12.

4. Berg, "Identity Theft," 114–115.

5. Ben Horowitz, "Belleville Woman Accused of Creating Fake Facebook Page to Mock Ex-Boyfriend Gets Probation," *The Star Ledger*, March 19, 2012. http://www.nj.com/news/index.ssf/2012/03/belleville_woman_accused_of_cr_1.html.

6. Maksim Reznik, "Identity Theft on Social Networking Sites: Developing Issues of Internet Impersonation," *Touro Law Review*, Vol. 29 (2), 2013. http://digitalcommons.touolaw.edu/cgi/viewcontent.cgi?article=1472&context=lawreview.

7. Robert Siciliano, "The Social Media Identity Theft of a School Director via Twitter," *Huffington Post*, January 28, 2013. http://www.huffingtonpost.com/robert-siciliano/highschooler-goes-social-media_b_2550541.html.

8. Erika Eicherlberger, "What I Learned Hanging Out with Nigerian Email Scammers," *Mother Jones*, March 20, 2014. http://www.

motherjones.com/politics/2014/03/what-i-learned-from-nigerian-scammers.

9. Timm and Perez, 20.

10. Timm and Perez, 85.

11. Tom Jagatic, Nathaniel A. Johnson, Markus Jakobsson, and Filippo Menczer, "Social Phishing," in *Communications of the ACM*, Vol. 50 no. 10, October 2007, 94–100.

12. "Chronology of Data Breaches," *Privacy Rights Clearinghouse*, April 20, 2005. http://www.privacyrights.org/data-breach. Updated December 31, 2013.

13. Owen Gibson, "Amir Khan and Frank Warren Threaten Facebook with Legal Action," *The Guardian*, September 10, 2009. http://www.guardian.co.uk/sport/2009/sep/10/amir-khan-frank-warren-facebook.

14. Brandon James Hoover, "The First Amendment Implications of Facebook, MySpace and Other Online Activity in Public High Schools," *Southern California Interdisciplinary Law Journal*, Winter 2009 (18 S. Cal. Interdis. L.J. 309).

15. Ryan Lex, "Can MySpace Turn into My Lawsuit: The Application of Defamation Law to Online Social Networks," *Loyola of Los Angeles Entertainment Law* Vol. 28 (1), January 1, 2008. http://digitalcommons.lmu.edu/elr/vol28/iss1/3.

16. "Passwords Will Be Obsolete if Google Has Its Way," *New York Post*, February 17, 2014. http://nypost.com/2014/02/17/passwords-will-be-obsolete-if-google-has-its-way/.

17. James Jardine, "What Do You Mean My Password Is Not Secure?" *Secure Ideas*, January 28, 2014. http://blog.secureideas.com/2014/01/what-do-you-mean-my-password-is-not.html.

Chapter Nine

1. James Surowiecki, *The Wisdom of Crowds* (New York: Anchor Books, 2005).

2. David Weinberger, *Everything Is Miscellaneous: The Power of the New Digital Disorder* (New York: Times Books, 2007).

3. Deborah Weinstein, "Researchers Give FDA Social Media Advice," *Medical Marketing and Media*, June 30, 2014. http://www.mmm-online.com/researchers-give-fda-social-media-advice/article/358550/.

4. American College of Physicians, "New Recommendations Offer Physicians Ethical Guidance for Preserving Trust in Patient-Physician Relationships and the Profession When Using Social Media," April 11, 2013.

http://www.acponline.org/pressroom/online_medical_professionalism.htm.

5. Jeanne M. Farnan, et al., "Online Medical Professionalism: Patient and Public Relationships: Policy Statement from the American College of Physicians and the Federation of State Medical Boards," *Annals of Internal Medicine* Vol. 158 (8), April 16, 2013. http://annals.org/article.aspx?articleid=1675927.

6. Stephen Fuzesi, "U.S. Targeting Fraudulent Medical Advice on the Net," *Los Angeles Times*, June 25, 1999. http://articles.latimes.com/1999/jun/25/news/mn-49998.

7. "Health Fraud Scams," http://www.fda.gov/ForConsumers/ProtectYourself/HealthFraud/default.htm.

8. "Health Quackery: Spotting Health Scams," *Webmd*, n.d. http://www.webmd.com/healthy-aging/guide/health-quackery-spotting-health-scams.

9. Erin McCann, "HIPAA Data Breaches Climb 138%," Healthcare News, February 6, 2014. http://www.healthcareitnews.com/news/hipaa-data-breaches-climb-138-percent. Lucas Mearian, "'Wall of Shame' Exposes 21M Medical Record Breaches," *Computerworld*, August 7, 2012. http://www.computerworld.com/s/article/9230028/_Wall_of_Shame_exposes_21M_medical_record_breaches.

10. See, for example, Indiana School of Medicine, "Guidelines for the Use of Online Social Networks for Medical Students and Physicians in Training," Indiana School of Medicine: Bloomington, n.d. http://msa.medicine.iu.edu/files/7113/2648/2858/OnlineProfessionalism.pdf.

11. In the interest of full disclosure, I have beaten up on it myself in two books, *Fool's Gold: Why the Internet Is No Substitute for a Library*, and *Are Libraries Obsolete: An Argument for Relevance in the Digital Age*, both by McFarland.

12. It isn't just me. Daniel J. Levitin feels much the same way. His story, told in *The Organized Mind: Thinking Straight in the Age of Information Overload* (New York: Dutton, 2014), 329–333, is a good case in point. I have written elsewhere on the dangers of overreliance on Wikipedia, much to the consternation of almost anyone not involved in information access.

13. E.J. Dickson, "I Accidentally Started a Wikipedia Hoax," *The Daily Beast*, July 29, 2014. http://www.dailydot.com/lol/amelia-bedelia-wikipedia-hoax/.

14. Robert T. Hasty, et al., "Wikipedia vs Peer-Reviewed Medical Literature for Information about the 10 Most Costly Medical

Conditions," *The Journal of the American Osteopathic Association*, Vol. 114 (5), May 1, 2014, 368–373.

15. "Wikipedia: Medical Disclaimer," http://en.wikipedia.org/wiki/Wikipedia:Medical_disclaimer. Emphases in the original.

16. Iltifat Husain, "Why You Shouldn't Give Medical Advice on Twitter," *Kevin Md*, May 21, 1013. http://www.kevinmd.com/blog/2013/05/give-medical-advice-twitter.html.

17. Elliot Rodger, "My Twisted World: The Story of Elliot Rodger," May 2014. http://www.documentcloud.org/documents/1173808-elliot-rodger-manifesto.html.

18. Asha Prakash, "When Social Networking Kills," *The Times of India*, February 24, 2014. http://timesofindia.indiatimes.com/lifestyle/relationships/man-woman/When-social-networking-kills/movie-review/29714977.cms.

19. Maureen O'Connor, "Addicted to Our Likes: How Social Media Feeds Our Neediness," *New York Times Magazine*, February 20, 2014. http://nymag.com/thecut/2014/02/addicted-to-likes-social-media-makes-us-needier.html.

20. Indeok Song, et al., "Internet Gratifications and Internet Addiction: On the Uses and Abuses of New Media," *Cyberpsychology & Behavior*, Vol. 7 (4) (2004). http://0-online.liebertpub.com.library.winthrop.edu/doi/pdfplus/10.1089/cpb.2004.7.384. Subscription required.

21. This occurred in a local school system where I live. Students were given the option of being suspended out of school for several days or turning their phones over for one week. They chose the former.

22. CBS News, "Study: Facebook Could Cause Obesity," December 23, 2012. http://atlanta.cbslocal.com/2012/12/23/study-facebook-could-cause-obesity/.

23. "Facebook Use Feeds Anxiety and Inadequacy, Says Small Study," *Mnt*, July 10, 2012. http://www.medicalnewstoday.com/articles/247616.php. "Could Facebook Be Making You Miserable?" *Mnt*, August 16, 2013. http://www.medicalnewstoday.com/articles/264902.php.

24. Mariah Bechman, "Social Media Is Addictive," *Guardian Liberty Voice*, June 21, 2014. http://guardianlv.com/2014/06/social-media-is-addictive/.

25. Chris Williams, "Nurse Charged with Aiding Suicides Over Web," *CBS News*, April 23, 2010. http://www.nbcnews.com/id/36739748/ns/us_news-crime_and_courts/t/nurse-charged-aiding-suicides-over-web/.

26. Eric C. Shore, "Giving Advice on Social Networking Sites," *Medical Economics*, Vol. 85 (March 7, 2008), 18.

27. Susannah Fox and Maeve Duggan, "Part One: Who Lives with Chronic Conditions?" *Pew Research Internet Project*, November 26, 2013. http://www.pewinternet.org/2013/11/26/part-one-who-lives-with-chronic-conditions/. Susannah Fox and Maeve Duggan. "Part Two: Sources of Health Information," November 26, 2013. http://www.pewinternet.org/2013/11/26/part-two-sources-of-health-information/.

Chapter Ten

1. The word has been spelled cyber-bullying, cyberbullying, cyber bullying and even CyberBullying. There appears to be no standard usage so far, but cyberbullying strikes me as the purest form of the word.

2. James P. Colt, "Cyber Bullying, Threats, Harassment, and Stalking," in *Encyclopedia of Cybercrime*, edited by Samuel C. McQuade (Westport, CT: Greenwood Publishing Group, 2009), 41.

3. "Cyber Bullying Statistics 2014," No bullying.com, n.d. http://nobullying.com/cyber-bullying-statistics-2014/.

4. "Policies and Laws," Stopbullying.Gov., March 24, 2014. http://www.stopbullying.gov/laws/#listing.

5. Suzanne Struglinski, "Schoolyard Bullying Has Gone High-Tech." *Desert News*, August 18, 2006. http://www.deseretnews.com/article/1,5143,645194065,00.html.

6. Nobullying.com, "Ryan Halligan Loses His Life to Taunts, Rumors, and Cyber Bullying," Nobullying.com. n.d. http://nobullying.com/ryan-halligan/.

7. "Cyber Bullying Statistics," Bullyingstatistics.org, 2013. http://www.bullyingstatistics.org/content/cyber-bullying-statistics.html.

8. Reid J. Epstein, "Oceanside Teen Sues Facebook, Ex-Classmates for $3 Million," *Newsday*, March 2, 2009. http://www.newsday.com/long-island/nassau/oceanside-teen-sues-facebook-ex-classmates-for-3m-1.896009?qr=1.

9. David Ardia, "Finkel vs. Facebook: Court Rejects Defamation Claim Against Facebook Premised on 'Ownership' of User Content," October 21, 2009. http://www.dmlp.org/blog/2009/finkel-v-facebook-court-rejects-defamation-claim-against-facebook-premised-ownership-user-.

10. *Ibid.*

11. Gregory Reynolds, *Ethics in Informa-*

tion Technology, Australia Cengage Learning, 2014, 208–209.

12. *Ibid.*

13. T.A. Bryer and B. Chen, "The Use of Social Media and Networks in Teaching Public Administration," in *Cutting-Edge Social Media Approaches to Business Education: Teaching with Linkedin, Facebook, Twitter, Second Life and Blogs*, edited by Charles Wankel (Greenwich, CT: Information Age Publishing, 2010), 261–261.

14. Patrick Arden, "Rate My Professors Has Some Academics Up in Arms," *The Village Voice*, October 26, 2011. http://www.villagevoice.com/2011–10-26/home/rate-my-professors-has-some-academics-up-in-arms/.

15. James Rhem, "Rate My Professor & Professors Strike Back," *The National Teaching and Learning Forum*, Vol. 18 (3) (2009). http://policy.rutgers.edu/faculty/popper/rateprofessor.pdf.

16. Vanessa Rogers, *Cyberbullying: Activities to Help Children and Teens Stay Safe in a Texting, Twittering, Social Networking World* (London: Jessica Kingsley Publishers, 2010), 17–18.

17. Douglas M. Malan, "YouTube Threat Draws Restraining Order," *The Connecticut Law Tribune*, January 6, 2009. http://www.law.com/jsp/legaltechnology/pubArticleLT.jsp?id=1202427221072.

18. Jenna Ross, "Student Banned from University After Facebook Posts," December 15, 2009. http://www.startribune.com/local/minneapolis/79361082.html. Login Required. For a more detailed discussion of this case, see chapter four.

19. Jenna Ross, "Student Banned from University After Facebook Posts."

20. Katherine Sellgren, "Cyberbullying 'on Rise'—ChildLine," *BBC News*, January 8, 2014. http://www.bbc.com/news/education-25639839.

21. "What Is a True Threat on Facebook?" *New York Times*, December 1, 2014. http://www.nytimes.com/2014/12/02/opinion/what-is-a-true-threat-on-facebook.html?hp&action=click&pgtype=Homepage&module=c-column-top-span-region&region=c-column-top-span-region&WT.nav=c-column-top-span-region&_r=0.

22. Amy Howe, "Court Difficult to Read on Facebook Threats: In Plain English," *Scotusblog*, December 1, 2014. http://www.scotusblog.com/2014/12/court-difficult-to-read-on-facebook-threats-in-plain-english/.

23. Carl Timm and Richard Perez, *Seven Deadliest Social Network Attacks* (Burlington, MA: Elsevier Science and Technology, 2010), 100–103.

24. Jennifer Steinhauer, "Woman Who Posed as Boy Testifies in Case That Ended in Suicide of 13-Year-Old," *New York Times*, November 20, 2008. http://www.nytimes.com/2008/11/21/us/21myspace.html.

25. William H. Freivogel, "Megan Meier MySpace Suicide Case in the News Again," *St. Louis Beacon*, September 29, 2009. https://www.stlbeacon.org/#!/content/20628/megan_meier_myspace_suicide_case_in_the_news_againhttp://www.stlbeacon.org/law_scoop/effort_to_appeal_myspace_suicide_case_.

26. Emily Brazelon, "What Really Happened to Phoebe Prince?" *Slate*, July 20, 2010. http://www.slate.com/articles/life/bulle/features/2010/what_really_happened_to_phoebe_prince/the_untold_story_of_her_suicide_and_the_role_of_the_kids_who_have_been_criminally_charged_for_it.html. Kayla Webley, "Teens Who Admitted to Bullying Phoebe Prince Sentenced," *Time*, May 5, 2011. http://newsfeed.time.com/2011/05/05/teens-who-admitted-to-bullying-phoebe-prince-sentenced/.

27. Sarah Perez, "In Wake of Teen Suicides, Ask.fm Faces a 'MySpace' Problem," *Techcrunch*, August 12, 2013. http://techcrunch.com/2013/08/12/in-wake-of-teen-suicides-ask-fm-faces-a-myspace-problem/.

28. Ben Makuch, "Want to Chat with a Western Jihadist? Try Ask.fm," *Motherboard*, May 8, 2014. http://motherboard.vice.com/en_uk/read/want-to-chat-with-a-western-jihadist-try-askfm.

29. Joe Miller, "Ask.fm Bought by Ask.com and Tinder Owner," August 14, 2014. http://www.bbc.com/news/technology-28776254#.

30. James Nye, "Family's Distress After Marine Documented His Suicide in a Series of Grisly Pictures on Facebook," *Daily Mail Online*, May 8, 2014, http://www.dailymail.co.uk/news/article-2623950/Familys-outrage-Marine-documented-suicide-series-grisly-pictures-Facebook-social-networking-site-refused-down.html.

31. Leo Kelion, "Facebook Lets Beheading Clips Return to Social Network," *BBC News*, October 21, 2013. http://www.bbc.com/news/technology-24608499.

32. Ryan Grenoble, "Amanda Todd: Bullied Canadian Teen Commits Suicide After Prolonged Battle Online and in School," *Huffington Post*, October 11, 2012. http://www.huffingtonpost.com/2012/10/11/amanda-todd-suicide-bullying_n_1959909.html.

33. Emily Freidman and Michele McPhee,

"'Craigslist Killer' Appears in Court, Shouts 'Not Guilty,'" *ABC News*, June 22, 2009. http://abcnews.go.com/US/story?id=7897975.

34. Mail Foreign Service, "Police Claim Clean-Cut Student Is 'Craigslist Killer' ... But His Fiancée Swears He Wouldn't Hurt a Fly," *Daily Mail*, April 21, 2009. http://www.daily mail.co.uk/news/article-1172372/Police-claim-clean-cut-student-Craigslist-killer-fianc-e-swears-wouldnt-hurt-fly.html.

35. Maria Cramer and Shelley Murphy, "Files Tell More About 'Craigslist Killer,'" Boston.com, April 1, 2011. http://www.boston.com/news/local/massachusetts/articles/2011/04/01/files_tell_more_about_craigslist_killer/.

36. Michelle McPhee, "'Craigslist Killer' Phillip Markoff Wrote Ex-Fiancée's Name in Blood as He killed Himself," *ABC News*, August 16, 2010. http://abcnews.go.com/US/TheLaw/craigslist-killer-philip-markoff-swallowed-toilet-paper-revived/story?id=11413302.

37. Doug Gross, "Twitter Reviewing Policies After Robin Williams' Daughter Harassed," *CNN Tech*, August 14, 2014. http://www.cnn.com/2014/08/13/tech/social-media/zelda-williams-twitter/.

Chapter Eleven

1. Irving Kristol, "Pornography, Obscenity and the Case for Censorship," Rense.com, n.d. http://www.rense.com/general87/obscenity.htm.

2. Igor Stravinsky, *Poetics of Music: In the Form of Six Lessons*, translated by Arthur Knodel and Ingolf Dahl (Cambridge: Harvard University Press, 1970), 194, 64–65, 63. Emphases mine.

3. Mark Bauerlein, *The Digital Divide: Arguments for and Against Facebook, Google, Texting, and the Age of Social Networking* (New York: Jeremy P. Tarcher/Penguin, 2011), x–xi.

4. Also quoted in Bauerlein, 2011.

5. Common Sense Media Research Study, *Social Media, Social Life: How Teens View Their Digital Lives*, June 26, 2012. https://www.commonsensemedia.org/research/social-media-social-life-how-teens-view-their-digital-lives/key-finding-1%3A-teens-are-avid%2C-daily-users-of-social-media.

6. Uversity [sic]. *Digital, Social, Mobile: The 2014 Social Admissions Report*, Zinch, 2014. http://www.uversity.com/downloads/presentations/2014-Social-Admissions-Report-Webinar.pdf.

7. Steven Dubner, "Is MySpace Good for Society? A Freakonomics Quorum," February 15, 2008. http://freakonomics.blogs.nytimes.com/2008/02/15/is-myspace-good-for-society-a-freakonomics-quorum/.

8. Carlee Adams, "Polls Show Confidence in College Preparation and Value of Degree Declining," *Education Week*, April 8, 2014. http://blogs.edweek.org/edweek/college_bound/2014/04/adults_view_of_their_own_preparation_for_college_is_more_favorable_than_for_their_children.html.

9. Gary Small and Gigi Vorgan, "Your Brain Is Evolving Right Now," in Mark Bauerlein, *The Digital Divide: Arguments for and Against Facebook, Google, Texting, and the Age of Social Networking*, 88–95.

10. Clive Thompson, *Smarter than You Think: How Technology Is Changing Our Lives for the Better* (New York: Jeremy P. Tarcher/Penguin, 2013), 29–35.

11. Ray Kurzweil, *The Singularity Is Near: When Humans Transcend Biology* (New York: Penguin, 2005).

12. Patrick Tucker, *The Naked Future: What Happens in a World That Anticipates Your Every Move?* (New York: Current, 2014), 37–39.

13. Steve Hamm, "Watson on Jeopardy! Day Two: The Confusion Over an Airport Clue," *Smart Planet*, February 15, 2011. http://asmarterplanet.com/blog/2011/02/watson-on-jeopardy-day-two-the-confusion-over-an-airport-clue.html.

14. N. Katherine Hayles, "What Does It Mean to Be Posthuman?" in *The New Media and Cybercultures Anthology*, edited by Pramod K. Nayar (Malden, MA: John Wiley and Sons, 2010), 22–25.

15. John Naughton, *From Gutenberg to Zuckerberg: Disruptive Innovation in the Age of the Internet*. (New York: Quercus, 2014), 14.

16. This is the point of Naughton's book, cited above.

17. Juliette Garside, "Facebook Will Lose 80% of Users by 2017, say Princeton Researchers," *The Guardian*, January 22, 2014. http://www.theguardian.com/technology/2014/jan/22/facebook-princeton-researchers-infectious-disease.

18. Larry Kim, "5 Things You Need to Know About Anti-Facebook Social Network Ello," *Inc.*, October 6, 2014. http://www.inc.com/larry-kim/5-things-you-need-to-know-about-anti-facebook-social-network-ello.html.

19. *NMC Horizon Report: 2013 Higher Education Edition*. http://www.nmc.org/pdf/2013-horizon-report-HE.pdf.

20. Brian Seltzer, "'Ashamed': Ex-PR Exec Justice Sacco Apologizes for AIDS in Africa Tweet," *CNN World*, December 22, 2013, http://www.cnn.com/2013/12/22/world/sacco-offensive-tweet/.

21. Adrienne LaFrance and Robinson Meyer, "A Eulogy for Twitter," *The Atlantic*, April 30, 2014. http://www.theatlantic.com/technology/archive/2014/04/a-eulogy-for-twitter/361339/.

22. Andrei Volgin, "The Demise of Social Networks," *Seeking Alpha*, February 25, 2014. Http://seekingalpha.com/article/2047923-thedemise-of-social-networks.

23. Selena Larson, "Time Out: Twitter Is Officially Mucking with Your Timeline," Read write.com, August 19, 2014. http://readwrite.com/2014/08/19/twitter-officially-changes-timeline.

24. Akshat Rathi, "WhatsApp Bought for $19 Billion, What Do Its Employees Get?" *Pandodaily*, February 24, 2014. http://pando.com/2014/02/24/whatsapp-bought-for-19-billion-what-do-its-employees-get/.

25. Bruce Upbin, "The Internet's Aswarm in Denial of Service Attacks and It's Getting Worse." *Forbes*, June 18 2014. http://www.forbes.com/sites/bruceupbin/2014/06/18/were-aswarm-in-denial-of-service-attacks-and-its-getting-worse/.

26. https://www.navdy.com/.

27. Phil LeBeau, "AAA Study: Hands-Free Connectivity Still Dangerous," *CNBC*, October 7, 2014. http://www.cnbc.com/id/102064045.

28. Jeff Elder, "Social Media Fail to Live Up to Early Marketing Hype," *Wall Street Journal*, June 23, 2014. http://online.wsj.com/articles/companies-alter-social-media-strategies-1403499658.

29. Iyad Rahwan, et al., "Analytical Reasoning Task Reveals Limits of Social Learning in Networks," *Journal of the Royal Society Interface*, Vol. 11 (93), April 2014. Doi: 10.1098/rsif.2013.1211.

30. Fariss Samarrai, "Doing Something Is Better Than Doing Nothing for Most People, Study Shows," *UVA Today*, July 3, 2014. http://news.virginia.edu/content/doing-something-better-doing-nothing-most-people-study-shows.

31. Neil Postman, *Amusing Ourselves to Death: Public Discourse in the Age of Show Business* (New York: Penguin Books), 2006.

32. Fox News, "Federal Workers Admit Watching Porn at Work Out of Boredom," Foxnews.com, August 3, 2104. http://www.foxnews.com/us/2014/08/03/federal-workers-admit-watching-porn-at-work-out-of-boredom/.

33. Dawn Chmielewski and Amy Schatz, "The Battle Over Net Neutrality Could Hit Wireless Carriers," *Re/Code*, September 16, 2014. http://recode.net/2014/09/16/the-battle-over-net-neutrality-could-hit-wireless-carriers/.

34. Brian Fung, "Obama on Net Neutrality: My Administration Is Against Internet Fast Lanes," *The Washington Post*, August 5, 2014. http://www.washingtonpost.com/blogs/the-switch/wp/2014/08/05/obama-strikes-a-populist-tone-on-net-neutrality/.

35. Brian Fung, "What to Make of Obama's Tepid Response on Net Neutrality," *The Washington Post*, May 17, 2014. http://www.washingtonpost.com/blogs/the-switch/wp/2014/05/17/what-to-make-of-obamas-tepid-response-on-net-neutrality/.

36. Amy Schatz, "President Obama Reaffirms Net Neutrality Support but Stays Out of Real Fight," *Recode*, October 10, 2014. http://recode.net/2014/10/10/president-obama-reaffirms-net-neutrality-support-but-stays-out-of-real-fight/.

37. Amy Schatz and Peter Kafka, "What President's Obama's Net Neutrality Proposal Means," *Recode.Net*, November 10, 2014. http://recode.net/2014/11/10/what-president-obamas-net-neutrality-proposal-means/.

38. Peter Lauria, President Obama's Net Neutrality Plan Crushes Cable Stocks," *Buzzfeed*, November 10, 2014. http://www.buzzfeed.com/peterlauria/president-obamas-net-neutrality-plan-crushes-cable-stocks.

39. "Internet Collapses Under Sheer Weight of Baby Pictures," *The Onion*, December 28, 2010. http://www.theonion.com/audio/internet-collapses-under-sheer-weight-of-baby-pict,18678/.

40. Vindu Goel, "Is Facebook Too Big to Care?" *New York Times*, March 30, 2104. http://bits.blogs.nytimes.com/2014/03/30/is-facebook-too-big-to-care/?_php=true&_type=blogs&_r=0.

41. Lev Grossman, "You—Yes, You—Are TIME's Person of the Year," *Time*, December 25, 2006. http://content.time.com/time/magazine/article/0,9171,1570810,00.html.

Bibliography

Aaker, Jennifer Lynn, Andy Smith, and Carlyle Adler. *The Dragonfly Effect: Quick, Effective, and Powerful Ways to Use Social Media to Drive Social Change*. San Francisco: Jossey-Bass, 2010.

Agranoff, Craig. "Social Media Mistakes Learned from Anthony Weiner." *The Huffington Post*, September 9, 2013. http://www.huffingtonpost.com/craig-agranoff/social-media-mistakes-lea>b>3852050.html.

Anorexia Blogs Nearly Killed Me." *Daily Mail*, August 21, 2013. http://www.daily.co.uk/health/article-2398749/Pro-ana-Anorexia-blogs-nearly-killed-Starving-girl-17-says-thinspiration-sites-encouraged-her.html.

Barabási, Albert-László. *Linked: How Everything Is Connected to Everything Else and What It Means*. New York: Plume, 2003.

Bauerlein, Mark. *The Digital Divide: Arguments For and Against Facebook, Google, Texting, and the Age of Social Networking*. New York: Jeremy P. Tarcher/Penguin, 2011.

Berners-Lee, Tim. *Weaving the Web: The Original Design and Ultimate Destiny of the World Wide Web*. New York: HarperCollins, 1999.

Bingham, Tony, and Marcia L. Conner. *The New Social Learning: A Guide to Transforming Organizations through Social Media*. Alexandria, VA: ASTD Press, 2010.

Blascovich, Jim, and Jeremy Bailenson. *Infinite Reality: Avatars, Eternal Life, New Worlds, and the Dawn of the Virtual Revolution*. New York: William Morrow, 2011.

Blass, Thomas. *The Man Who Shocked the World: The Life and Legacy of Stanley Milgram*. New York: Basic, 2004.

boyd, danah m. *It's Complicated: The Social Lives of Networked Teens*. New Haven: Yale University Press, 2014.

_____, and Nicole B. Ellison. "Social Networking Sites: Definition, History and Scholarship." *Journal of Computer-Mediated Communication*, Vol. 13 (1) (2007). http://onlinelibrary.wiley.com/doi/10.1111/j.1083–6101.2007.00393.x/full.

Bush, Vannevar. "As We May Think." *The Atlantic*, July 1, 1945. http://www.theatlantic.com/magazine/archive/1945/07/as-we-may-think/303881/.

Carafano, James Jay. *Wiki at War: Conflict in a Socially Networked World*. College Station: Texas A&M University Press, 2012.

Chapman, Roger. *Culture Wars: An Encyclopedia of Issues, Viewpoints, and Voices*. Armonk, NY: M.E. Sharpe, 2010.

Crompton, Diane, and Ellen Sautter. *Find a Job through Social Networking: Use LinkedIn, Twitter, Facebook, Blogs, and More to Advance Your Career*. Indianapolis: JIST Works, 2011.

Del Ray, Jason. "Social Media's Cold Hard Reality: It Still Doesn't Drive E-Commerce Sale, IBM Says." *All Things D*, November 29, 2013. http://althingsd.com/20131129/social-medias-cold-hard-reality-it-still-doesn't-drive-e-commerce-sales-ibm-says/.

Ellis, Katie, and Mike Kent. *Disability and Media*. Florence, KY: Routledge, 2010.

Espejo, Roman, ed. *Should Social Networking Web Sites Be Banned?* Farmington Hills, MI: Greenhaven Press, 2008.

Gelvin, James L. *The Arab Uprisings: What Everyone Needs to Know*. New York: Oxford University Press, 2012.

Ghonim, Wael. *Revolution 2.0: The Power of the People Is Greater Than the People in Power: A Memoir*. Boston: Houghton Mifflin Harcourt, 2012.

Goldman, Carrie. *Bullied: What Every Parent, Teacher, and Kid Needs to Know About Ending the Cycle of Fear*. New York: HarperOne, 2012.

Grimmelmann, James. "Saving Facebook." *Iowa Law Review* 94 (2009). http://works.bepress.com/james_grimmelmann/20.

Gross, Doug. "Twitter Reviewing Policies After Robin Williams' Daughter Harassed." *CNN Tech*, August 14, 2014. http://www.cnn.com/2014/08/13/tech/social-media/zelda-williams-twitter/.

Grossman, Lev. "You—Yes, You—Are TIME's Person of the Year." *Time*, December 25, 2006.

Hayles, N. Katherine. "What Does It Mean to Be Posthuman?" In *The New Media and Cybercultures Anthology*, ed. Pramod K. Nayar. Malden, MA: John Wiley and Sons, 2010.

Hoffman, Reid, and Ben Casnocha. *The Start-up of You*. New York: Crown Business, 2012.

"How Social Media Is Killing Student Success." *Online Courses*, May 22, 2013. http://www.onlinecollegecourses.com/2013/05/22/how-social-media-is-killing-student-success-2/.

Jaschik, Scott. "Fireable Tweets." *Inside Higher Ed*, December 19, 2013. http://www.insidehighered.com/news/2013/12/19/kansas-regents-adopt-policy-when-social-media-use-can-get-faculty-fired#sthash.fFG10OTX.dpbs.

Johnson, Derek. *Media Franchising: Creative License and Collaboration in the Culture Industries*. New York: New York University Press, 2013.

June, Audrey Williams. "Google-Stalking Job Candidates: Tempting but Risky." *Chronicle of Higher Education*, October 3, 2014. http://chronicle.com/article/Google-Stalking-Job/149193/.

Keen, Andrew. *The Cult of the Amateur: How Today's Internet Is Killing Our Culture*. New York: Doubleday, 2007.

Kelion, Leo. "Facebook Lets Beheading Clips Return to Social Network." *BBC News*, October 21, 2013. http://www.bbc.com/news/technolgoy-24608499.

Kirkpatrick, David. *The Facebook Effect: The Inside Story of the Company That Is Connecting the World*. New York: Simon & Schuster, 2010.

Kirkpatrick, Marshall. "Facebook's Zuckerberg Says the Era of Privacy Is Over." ReadWrite.com, January 9, 2010. http://readwrite.com/2010/01/09/facebooks_zuckerberg_says_the_age_of_privacy_is_ov.

Kosut, Mary. *Encyclopedia of Gender in Media*. Thousand Oaks, CA: SAGE, 2012.

Kristol, Irving. "Pornography, Obscenity and the Case for Censorship." Rense.com. n.d. http://www.rense.com/general87/obscenity.htm.

Kurzweil, Ray. *The Singularity Is Near: When Humans Transcend Biology*. New York: Penguin, 2005.

Lanier, Jaron. *Who Owns the Future?* New York: Simon & Schuster, 2013.

Leibelson, Dana. "Map: Here Are the Countries that Block Facebook, Twitter, and YouTube." *Mother Jones News*, March 28, 2014. http://www.motherjones.com/politics/2014/03/turkey-facebook-youtube-twitter-blocked.

Leiner, Barry M. "Internet Society." *Brief History of the Internet*. N.p., n.d. http://www.internetsociety.org/brief-history-internet.

Lepp, Andrew, Jacob E. Barkley, and Aryn C. Karpinski. "The Relationship Between Cell Phone Use, Academic Performance Anxiety, and Satisfaction with Life in College Students." *Computer in Behavior* Vol. 31, February 2014. DOI: 10.1016/j.chb.2013.10.049. http://www.sciencedirect.com/science/article/pii/S0747563213003993.

Levitin, Daniel J. *The Organized Mind: Thinking Straight in the Age of Information Overload*. New York: Dutton, 2014.

Levmore, Saul, and Martha Craven Nussbaum. *The Offensive Internet: Speech, Privacy, and Reputation*. Cambridge: Harvard University Press, 2010.

Levy, Steven. *In the Plex: How Google Thinks, Works, and Shapes Our Lives*. New York: Simon & Schuster, 2011.

Mandiberg, Michael. *The Social Media Reader*. New York: New York University Press, 2012.

Masum, Hassan, and Mark Tovey. *The Reputation Society: How Online Opinions Are Reshaping the Offline World*. Cambridge: MIT Press, 2011.

Mazetti, Mark. *The Way of the Knife: The CIA, a Secret Army, and a War at the Ends of the Earth*. New York: Penguin Press, 2013.

McFarland, Matt. "Social Media Desperately Needs an Antidote for Bragging." *Washington Post*, December 18, 2013. http://www.wwshingtonpost.com/blogs/innovations/wp/2013/12/18/social-media-desperately-needs-an-antidolte-for-bragging/.

McPhee, Michelle. "'Craigslist Killer' Philip Markoff Wrote Ex-Fiancee's Name in Blood as He Killed Himself." *ABC News*, August 16, 2010. http://abcnews.go.com/US/TheLaw/craigslist-killer-philip-markoff-swallowed-toilet-paper-revived/story?id=11413302.

McQuade, Samuel C., ed. "Internet." *Encyclopedia of Cybercrime*. Westport, CT: Greenwood Press, 2008.

Melanson, Forrester. "If You Think Social Media Marketing Is Worthless, You're Doing It Wrong." *Read Write Web*. http://readwrite.com/2010/07/19/forrester_if_you_think_social_media_marketing_is_w.

Mika, Peter. *Social Networks and the Semantic Web*. New York: Springer, 2007.

Mintz, Anne P. *Web of Deceit: Misinformation and Manipulation in the Age of Social Media*. Medford, NJ: CyberAge, 2012.

Morgan, Heather A., and Felicia A. Davis. *Social Media and Employment Law: Summary of Key Cases and Legal Issues*. Paul Hastings, 2013. http://www.americanbar.org/content/dam/aba/events/labor_law/2013/04/aba_national_symposiumontechnologyinlaboremploymentlaw/10_socialmedia.authcheckdam.pdf.

Morozov, Evgeny. *The Net Delusion: The Dark Side of Internet Freedom*. New York: Public Affairs, 2011.

_____. *To Save Everything Click Here: The Folly of Technological Solutionism*. New York: Public Affairs, 2013.

Naughton, John. *From Gutenberg to Zuckerberg: Disruptive Innovation in the Age of the Internet*. New York: Quercus, 2014.

Parks, Lisa, and James Schwoch. *Down to Earth Satellite Technologies, Industries and Cultures*. Piscataway: Rutgers University Press, 2012.

Partridge, Kenneth. *Social Networking*. New York: H.W. Wilson, 2011.

"Passwords Will Be Obsolete if Google Has Its Way." *New York Post*, February 17, 2014. http://nyppost.com/2014/02/17/passwordes-will-be-obsolete-if-google-has-its-way/.

Porter, Joshua. *Designing for the Social Web*. Berkeley, CA: New Riders, 2008.

Postman, Neil. *Amusing Ourselves to Death: Public Discourse in the Age of Show Business*. New York: Penguin, 2006.

Putnam, Robert. *Bowling Alone: The Collapse and Revival of American Community*. New York: Simon & Schuster, 2000.

Rainie, Harrison, and Barry Wellman. *Networked: The New Social Operation System*. Cambridge: MIT Press, 2012.

Reynolds, George. *Ethics in Information Technology*. Australia: Cengage Learning, 2014.

Rogers, Vanessa. *Cyberbullying: Activities to Help Children and Teens Stay Safe in a Texting, Twittering, Social Networking World*. London: Jessica Kingsley Publishers, 2010.

Rowan, Rachael. "Social Media Shocker: Twitter and Facebook Can Cost You a Scholarship or Admissions Offer." *Tuition.IO*. https://www.tuition.io.blog/2014/04/social-media-shocker-twitter-facebook-can-cost-scholarship-admissions-offer/.

Rudder, Christian. *Dataclysm: Who We Are When We Think No One's Looking*. New York: Crown Publishers, 2014.

Rushkoff, Douglas. *Present Shock: When Everything Happens Now*. New York: Current, 2013.

Sakawee, Saiyai. "Under Martial Law, Thailand Will Shut Down Some Websites and Monitor Social Media." *Techinasia*, May 22, 2014. http://www.techinasia.com/martial-law-sites-shutdown-social-media-watched/.

Salkin, Allen. *From Scratch: Inside the Food Network*. New York: G P. Putnam's Sons, 2013.

Schaflauser, John. "How Sexual Predators Are Targeting Children Using Google+:Part I—The Facts." *Prevent Child Abuse New Jersey*, February 2014. http://preventchildabuseenj.org/blog/2014/02/04/sexual-predators-targeting-children-google-part-facts-by-john-schafhausere-patty-mojita/.

Schepp, Brad, and Debra Schepp. *How to Find a Job on LinkedIn, Facebook, MySpace, Twitter and Other Social Networks.* New York: McGraw-Hill, 2010.

Schmidt, Eric, and Jared Cohen. *The New Digital Age: Reshaping the Future of People, Nations and Business.* New York: Vantage, 2013.

Schroeder, Jens. *"Killer Games" versus "We Will Fund Violence": The Perception of Digital Games and Mass Media in Germany and Australia.* New York: Peter Lang, 2011.

Silver-Pacuilla, Gray, and H. Silver-Pacuilla, eds. *Breakthrough Teaching and Learning: How Educational and Assistive Technologies Are Driving Innovation.* http://link.sprger.com/chapter/10.1007%2F978-1-4419-7768-7_5#page-1. DOI10.1007/978-1-4419-7768-7_5. November 2014.

Singer, Dorothy G., and Jerome L. Singer, eds. *Handbook of Children and the Media.* Thousand Oaks, CA: Sage, 2012.

Standage, Tom. *Writing on the Wall: Social Media, the First 2,000 Years.* New York: Bloomsbury, 2013.

Steiner-Adair, Catherine, and Teresa Barker. *The Big Disconnect: Protecting Childhood and Family Relationships in the Digital Age.* New York: Harper, 2013.

Steyer, James P. and Chelsea Clinton. *Talking Back to Facebook: A Common Sense Guide to Raising Kids in the Digital Age.* New York: Scribner, 2012.

Thierer, Adam. "Technopanics and the Great Social Networking Scare." *The Technology Liberation Front*, July 10, 2008. http://techliberation.com/2008/07/10/technopanics-and-the-great-social-networking-scare/.

Thompson, Clive. *Smarter Than You Think: How Technology Is Changing Our Minds for the Better.* New York: The Penguin Press, 2013.

Timm, Carl, and Richard Perez. *Seven Deadliest Social Network Attacks.* Burlington, MA: Elsevier, 2010.

Tucker, Patrick. *The Naked Future: What Happens in a World That Anticipates Your Every Move?* New York: Current, 2014.

Turkle, Sherry. *Alone Together: Why We Expect More from Technology and Less from Each Other.* New York: Basic, 2011.

Waldman, Joshua. *Job Searching with Social Media for Dummies.* Hoboken, NJ: John Wiley & Sons, 2011.

Weimer, Maryellen. "The Age of Distraction: Getting Students to Put Away Their Phones and Focus on Learning." *Faculty Focus*, January 8, 2014. http://www.facultyfocus.com/articles/teaching-professor-blog/the-age-of-distraction-getting-students-to-put-away-their-phones-and-focus-on-learning/.

Weinberger, David. *Everything Is Miscellaneous: The Power of the New Digital Disorder.* New York: Times, 2007.

Weinstein, Deborah. "Researchers Give FDA Social Media Advice." *Medical Marketing and Media.* June 30, 2014. http://mmm-online.com/researchers-give-fda-social-media-advice/article/358550/.

Whittle, Sally. "Social Networks: Not as Inclusive as You Might Think." ZDNet, November 5, 2007. http://www.zdnet.com/social-etworking-not-as-inclusive-as-you-might-think-3039290559/.

Williams, Alexis. "The Agony of Instagram." *The New York Times*, December 13, 2013. http://www.nytimes.com/2013/12/15/fashion/instagram/html?pagewanted=2&_r=0.

Index

www.ingramcontent.com/pod-product-compliance
Lightning Source LLC
Chambersburg PA
CBHW031219050326
40689CB00009B/1391